BOOK SELECTION POLICIES
IN
AMERICAN LIBRARIES

An anthology of policies from
COLLEGE, PUBLIC, and SCHOOL
Libraries

**Edited by
Calvin J. Boyer
and
Nancy L. Eaton**

**Armadillo Press
Austin, Texas**

APPLICATIONS OF LIBRARY SCIENCE

VOLUME 3

First Edition, 1971

○ Copyright 1971
by
Calvin J. Boyer

International Standard Book Number 0-912556-00-5
Library of Congress Catalog Card No. 77-161921

Armadillo Press
Box 8131
University of Texas Station
Austin, Texas   78712

Printed in the United States of America
By ATEX AUSTIN, INC.

$5.95

INTRODUCTION

PURPOSE OF THE BOOK

Whether it is a public library trying to present a wide spectrum of materials and viewpoints on basic issues or a college or school library trying to support the educational objectives of its parent institution, a library is always vulnerable to criticism from persons or groups who do not approve of material included in the library collection or who are unhappy because certain materials were excluded. Thus, each public, school, or college library should put in writing its selection policies and have them approved by the governing authority. This measure will put the library in a clearly defined position if its holdings or selection practices are challenged.

Furthermore, a selection policy should aid collection development in a library by establishing guidelines for selection. Merely the existence or presence of a policy does not guarantee a good collection. However, a collection of quality is more likely to occur when a well formulated selection policy exists and is followed by the selection staff. The staff must be aware constantly of the policy and must follow it consistently when making selection decisions for it to be an effective aid. The more detailed the policy is, the more helpful it is likely to be, both in selection for the library collection and in defense of the collection's contents.

It is hoped that this book, by providing in convenient form policies from various types of libraries, will aid librarians in creating, reviewing, or revising the selection policies for their own libraries. These materials are not readily accessible to the individual librarian who wants guidance. The editors hope that the librarian or administrator using this book will turn to policies for other types of libraries than his own, since there is much to be gained from reviewing the contents of policies from all types of libraries.

This compilation is intended also as a source book for teachers and students studying selection in library education agencies. For example, it might be used to aid students in evaluating policies, in the exercise of writing policies based upon some selected community characteristics, or in comparing how policy content differs for the various types of libraries. The number of ways a teacher might utilize the policies in this book is directly proportional to his ingenuity.

SCOPE OF THE BOOK

In choosing school, public, and college library selection policies for this volume, the editors interpreted "college" and "book" broadly. "College" library refers to a library for any institution of higher education. Whether the parent institution is a community college, four year college, or an institution which includes graduate studies, the "college" library selection policies are applicable.

"Book" selection is common terminology, even though library collections include non-book materials. "Materials" selection policy is the more accurate terminology. Within a materials selection policy, a librarian may want to include acceptable technical specifications for the various non-book materials, just as many policies specify the physical requirements for a good book in terms of binding, margins, paper, type faces, and illustrations. The general policies concerning intellectual freedom and subject coverage are applicable to all materials, regardless of form.

When determining the scope of this book, the editors excluded "acquisitions" policies from the volume. The distinction being made is the following:

A selection policy sets down general policies concerning (a) the intellectual framework within which decisions are made, such as intellectual freedom and the Library Bill of Rights; (b) final authority for selection decisions; (c) acceptable quality of materials, both physical and intellectual; (d) inclusion or exclusion of problem materials, such as gifts and controversial subjects; (e) maintenance of a high-quality collection by such means as weeding and discarding; and (f) the community served by the library.

An acquisitions policy is a detailed breakdown, subject by subject, of the depth in which a library expects to acquire materials in each subject area. The four levels of coverage often specified in acquisitions policies are (1) reference collection, (2) general collection, (3) comprehensive collection, and (4) research collection.

It is advisable that selection policies be accompanied by acquisitions policies for maximum effectiveness and consistency in building a good library collection.

A broad cross-section of policies was chosen for inclusion in this volume. In addition to presenting public, college, and school library selection policies, an effort was made to include policies from large and small institutions, religious and secular institutions, private and public institutions, as well as policies of varying lengths. Thus, many good policies were eliminated because another one already illustrated that particular type of institution or that point of view or because another policy said essentially the same thing in a more concise way.

Even though many of the materials presented in the appendices are available elsewhere, the editors included them in this volume for the convenience of the reader. The objective was a self-contained book. Also, editorial decisions required that some of them be included. The Library Bill of Rights, Freedom to Read, the Statement on Labeling, and the School Library Bill of Rights appeared as part of many selection policies received. Rather than printing them in full each time they were included as part of the text, the decision was made to print them once as appendices and to refer to them in brackets when they appear as part of a selection policy.

The Library Bill of Rights was revised at the June, 1971, American Library Association Conference in Dallas. This newly-approved version has not had time to be widely circulated or printed. The editors considered it a convenience to the reader to include the original and revised texts for comparison, particularly since most libraries have not had time to revise their policies in accordance with the new version.

The American Library Association has permitted the editors to include its interpretations of the Library Bill of Rights in this volume. Presently these interpretations are not readily available elsewhere.

CREATION AND UTILIZATION OF A SELECTION POLICY

A well-written, board-approved materials selection policy will: (1) provide a statement of philosophy and objectives for the guidance of those involved in the procedures for selection, such as the ALA Library Bill of Rights, the AASL School Library Bill of Rights, and the ALA Freedom to Read Statement; (2) define the role of those who share in the responsibility for the selection of materials, including who is legally responsible for selection and to whom responsibility has been delegated; (3) set forth criteria for selection and evaluation of materials; (4) outline the techniques for the applications of the criteria; (5) clarify for the community the philosophy and procedure used in evaluating and selecting materials; and (6) provide a procedure for the consideration of objections to the use of particular materials.[1]

The materials selection policy should be adopted officially by the governing board and communicated to library personnel and to the community.[2] Several libraries which submitted policies for consideration by the editors had produced an effective public relations tool by printing their policies in an attractive, well-designed format. The Tucson Public Library, Berkeley Public Library, and Finkelstein Memorial Library (Spring Valley, N.Y.) are three such libraries. The policy that the library adopts should be reviewed periodically and revised if the nature of the library collection has changed.[3]

The Council of the American Library Association, in its adopted censorship procedure for libraries, further suggests the following:[4] (1) A file recording the basis for decision should be kept for titles likely to be questioned or apt to be considered controversial; (2) There should be a clearly defined method for handling complaints. Any complaint should be required to be in writing, and the complainant should be identified properly before the complaint is considered. Action should be deferred until full consideration by appropriate administrative authority; (3) There should be continuing efforts to establish lines of communication to assure mutual understanding with civic, religious, educational, and political bodies; (4) Newspapers of the community should be informed of policies governing book selection and use. Purposes and services of the library should be interpreted through a continuing public relations program, as should the use of books in the school.

CONTENTS OF A MATERIALS SELECTION POLICY

The librarian or administrator creating, reviewing, or revising his selection policy should consider for inclusion the items in the following outline. This outline reflects what authorities say a policy should contain and what has appeared in the many policies reviewed by the editors. Two items appear only in very recent policies; they reflect recent events in society and are due careful consideration by librarians today. These two items deal with the selection of materials on drugs and drug usage and on explosives and their construction.

BIBLIOGRAPHY

The bibliography found at the end of this book cites materials treating the general concepts of selection policies, with one exception. The policy of the Enoch Pratt Free Library has been acknowledged as an extremely influential source document in many of the policies considered for inclusion in this book. That library has done a professional service to all librarians to whom it had made its policy available and should be commended. This selection policy is available from Enoch Pratt and is cited here as a basic reference source which should be consulted.[5]

ACKNOWLEDGEMENTS

The editors wish to thank all librarians who sent copies of their library's selection policy, with permission to publish, and all librarians who took the time to respond to our letters even though their library was without a current policy. The publication of this book was totally dependent upon the cooperation of these persons. The editors also wish to thank Dr. C. Glenn Sparks for reading their material and making many helpful suggestions.

Calvin J. Boyer, M.L.S.
Doctoral Student
Graduate School of Library Science
The University of Texas at Austin

Nancy L. Eaton, M.L.S.
Editor, SWLA Newsletter
Catalogue Librarian
The University of Texas at Austin

---

[1] California Association of School Librarians, Instructional Materials; Selection Policies and Procedures (Daly City, Calif., California Association of School Librarians, 1965), pp. 3, 5.

[2] Ibid., p. 5.

[3] Ibid.

[4] American Library Association, Intellectual Freedom Committee. ALA Bulletin, LVI (March, 1962), pp. 228-229.

[5] Evelyn Hart, et al., eds. How Baltimore Chooses: Selection Policies of the Enoch Pratt Free Library. 4th ed. Baltimore, 1968.

TABLE OF CONTENTS

COLLEGES

POLICY AND PROCEDURES FOR SELECTION
OF BOOK AND LIBRARY MATERIALS

POLICIES

I.* RESPONSIBILITY FOR BOOK SELECTION

Ultimate responsibility for book selection, as for all school activities, rests with the Board of Trustees. The President operates within the framework of policies determined by the Board. In turn, the administration delegates to the library staff and faculty the responsibility of book selection according to the policies of the Board and administrative directives.

II. GENERAL LIBRARY OBJECTIVES

The library accepts as its basic objectives the provision and servicing of expertly selected books and other materials which aid the individual in the pursuit of education, information, and in the creative use of leisure time.

The library is primarily an educational device. It is to the academic courses what laboratories and shops are to science and vocational courses, but it complements all classroom activity and is an integral part of the curriculum, paralleling it at all points in all departments. It offers resource and enrichment material for the students and for the faculty. Its materials are selected on the basis of the maturity and ability levels of all students.

The library attempts to foster reading as a habit through pleasurable exposure to printed materials during the formative years. Thus, it provides additional materials to attract students to reading as a source of pleasure and recreation over and above needed subject content.

The college library has certain reference responsibilities to its clientele, both school and community. Although not truly a "scholarly" library, it tends more to that goal than do usual small public libraries of similar or larger size. Its shelves contain classics in most fields of endeavor which are a part of our civilization. It possesses reference tools in greater number and of more scholarly significance than its neighboring libraries usually afford. These are needed and used by its college personnel, but they are also a regional resource. The determination of its purposes, content, and educational functions is a professional responsibility that requires the cooperative efforts of the faculty and the librarian.

No single library stands alone in its philosophy, its content, or its practice. Only applications and emphases differ, and the best thinking of the profession has applicability at the individual level. Therefore, the Chaffey Union Junior College District subscribes to the following viewpoints as principles in the selection of materials and the evaluation of any protests about library materials.

1.   As a responsibility of library service, books and other reading matter selected should be chosen for values of interest, information, and enlightenment of all people of the community. In no case should any book be excluded because of the race or nationality or the political or religious views of the writer.

2.   There should be the fullest practicable provision of material presenting all points of view concerning the problems and issues of our times, international, national, and local; and books or other reading matter of sound factual authority should not be proscribed or removal from library shelves because of partisan or doctrinal disapproval.

3.   Censorship of books, urged or practiced by volunteer arbiters of morals or political opinion or by organizations that should establish a coercive concept of Americanism, must be challenged by libraries in maintenance of their responsibility to provide public information and enlightenment through the printed word.

4.   The rights of an individual to the use of a library should not be denied or abridged because of his race, religion, national origins or political views.

5.   As an institution of education for democratic living, the library should welcome the use of its meeting rooms for socially useful and cultural activities and discussion of current public questions. Such meeting places should be available on equal terms to all groups in the community regardless of the beliefs and affiliations of their members as long as that usage is within the legal community service limitations of the Education Code.

III.   OBJECTIVES OF BOOK SELECTION

In the formulation of selection policies to implement these general objectives, the library places major emphasis on the educational and informational functions. According to the library's definition, a book has "educational" value if it contributes to the positive growth of the student, either as an individual or in the individual's relationship to society. Thus, the library recognizes the importance of both books of basic permanent value and timely materials of current value on public issues.

IV.   QUESTIONED OR CHALLENGED MATERIALS

Opinions may differ in a democracy, and the proper procedures (as outlined in PROCEDURES II) will be observed in recognizing those differences in an impartial and factual manner.

PROCEDURES

I.   TECHNIQUE OF BOOK SELECTION PRACTICE AT CHAFFEY COLLEGE

A.   Persons participating in book selection:

1.   Instructors:
a.   Request specific titles needed for reference material for their courses, both for students' use and as faculty resource material

      b.   Suggest titles for "general education" of undergraduate, as distinct from required reading for specific course work

2. Librarians:

      a.   Suggest specific titles applicable to specific courses

      b.   Suggest specific titles applicable to the administration or to special studies being undertaken

      c.   Accept responsibility for selection and purchase of noncirculating reference collection, except in highly specialized fields, based on felt need through daily contact with reference problems

      d.   Select and purchase, with or without specific faculty consultation, additional titles in areas of specialization, especially from clearance lists (university presses, remainder and review-copy dealers, etc.)

      e.   Assist in preparation of lists for use in courses added to the curriculum

      f.   Round out areas of repeated demand in all courses if neglected by instructors (term-paper topics, book reports, specific artists, composers and authors, historical figures, etc.)

3. Administrators:

      a.   Request specific titles in their fields

      b.   Suggest specific titles for general student use

      c.   Suggest titles of general interest valuable to a junior college collection

4. Students:

      a.   Suggest areas and subjects of special personal and/or student interest

      b.   Suggest specific titles of new books in an area of competency (music, drama, California history, etc.)

B. Generally recognized sources of information about available materials:

1. American Library Association
2. National Council of Teachers of English
3. National Education Association
4. The H. W. Wilson Company catalog series
5. Specialized-subject professional organizations
    a. American Chemical Society
    b. American Historical Society
    c. American Science Teachers Association
    d. American Home Economics Association
    e. Business Education Association
    f. National Recreation Association

g. Association for Health, Recreation and Physical Education
h. American Academy for Social and Political Science
i. American Economic Association
j. American Association of Physics Teachers
k. Others

C. Utilization of generally recognized and accepted selective list of library books:

1. Standard Catalog for Public Libraries and supplements. H. W. Wilson, 1958. Supplements 1959-1963
2. Bertalan, F. J. Books for Junior Colleges, ALA, 1954
3. Winchell, C. M. Guide to Reference Books, ALA, 1951. Supplements, 1952, 1958, 1962
4. Shores, L. Basic Reference Sources. ALA, 1954
5. McNiff, P. J. Catalogue of the Lamont Library. Harvard College, 1953
6. Jones, B. One Thousand Books for the Undergraduate College Library, 1960
7. Hoffman, H. R. The Reader's Adviser and Bookman's Manual. Bowker, 1964
8. Dickinson, A. D. The World's Best Books. H. W. Wilson, 1953
9. Haines, H. Living with Books. Columbia University, 1950
10. Carnegie Library of Pittsburgh. Basic Collection of Science and Technology Books. 1960
11. Florida State Dept. of Education. Basic Materials for Florida Junior College Libraries. 1960 and supplements
12. Others

D. Utilization of generally accepted current reviewing media:

1. Library Journal
2. ALA Booklist
3. Wilson Bulletin
4. Technical Book Review Index
5. Book Review Digest
6. Reviews in recognized literary magazines
7. Reviews in recognized special subject journals
8. Reviews in generally accepted current trade reviewing media
9. Others

E. Evaluation by faculty and librarians of possible available materials suggested by:
1. Publishers' and dealers' brochures, catalogs, review copies
2. Bibliographies included in adopted texts
3. Bibliographies consequent to in-service training of instructors
4. Bibliographies included in recognized specialized subjects, such as:
   a. Education Index
   b. Biography Index
   c. Bibliographic Index
   d. Essay and General Literature Index

5.   Examination of bookstore stock

6.   Examination of book exhibits and display

F. Criteria governing final consideration by librarian of all books added to the collection, either by purchase or gift:

1.   Does this book provide material needed for one or more courses in the curriculum?

2.   Does it offer faculty resource material for courses currently taught or anticipated?

3.   Is the subject content applicable to the undergraduate level?

4.   Is the content valid?

5.   Has it literary merit?

6.   Are additional titles needed in this particular section now?

7.   Is the format compatible to the service expected for the price?

8.   Is decision to purchase supported by its appearance on one or more of the generally approved lists or reviewing media?

9.   Does the new edition make the one presently owned obsolete; or does it merely include a new chapter, or has it merely revised the plates?

10. Has it dual or multi-purpose coverage for faculty, courses, or department?

11. Is this translation the best available?

12. Will the book contribute to "general education" at undergraduate level, even though not directly contributary to any specific course?

13. Does this book round out any special collection (music, art, literature, California history, etc.) even though not specifically requested by an instructor?

II.   PROCEDURE FOR HANDLING QUESTIONED OR CHALLENGED MATERIAL

A. Procedure:

1.   A study committee should be appointed by the Board of Trustees upon the recommendation of the College President. This committee would be composed of one Board member, two administrators, a professional librarian, and three faculty members.

2.   Criticisms may be registered with the school authorities and will be directed to the Board of Trustees. The criticism of a questioned item shall be presented by submitting a completed REQUEST FOR RECONSIDERATION form (see attached). The request must be signed and an address given which will allow proper reply.

3.   All complaints along with the questioned material, if available will be reported immediately to the Board of Trustees and to the study committee.

4. The written report and recommendation of the study committee will be sent to the Board of Trustees for action.

5. The President will inform the complainant and the study committee of any action taken by the Board of Trustees.

B. Guide lines for action:

1. The committee shall be guided in its recommendations by the statement of Objectives in Part II of this report.

2. All faculty should be thoroughly familiar with routines established for handling challenged materials.

3. No one is authorized to promise to remove a challenged book, regardless of source or degree of complaint; one may promise only to review it again through established channels in the light of the objections raised in writing.

4. All reviewers shall reconsider the book or materials with these specific objections in mind, regardless of original purpose for addition of the title.

5. Consideration should be given at the earliest possible time after a challenge arises.

6. The recommendation of the review body should be regarded as the result of the informed opinion of persons qualified to judge.

7. The Board of Trustees shall impound any challenged or questioned material pending the recommendation of the study committee if it is the Board's judgment that the situation warrants such impound.

*The content of each policy has been reproduced without alteration; the format of each policy has been reproduced as closely as possible. In some policies, outline tags (Roman and Arabic numerals) have been appended to aid the reader in identification of passages or sections within the policy.

Reprinted by Permission of Chaffey College, Mrs. Phyllis M. Smith, Public Services Librarian.

ACQUISITION POLICY

I. GOAL

The goal of Clatsop Community College Library shall be to have a working usable collection embracing as many fields as possible, but first the fields we teach. The goal shall not be a great number of books but books that are being used. Out-dated books will be discarded unless there is indication that the book will have historical significance.

II. GENERAL GUIDES TO SELECTION

A. Titles added to the collection shall be evaluated in terms of appropriateness for undergraduate use. Highly technical material is only to be acquired if a definite use is observable.

B. Recency of material is of major importance and once a basic collection is established, no title published more than two years previously shall be added to the collection unless it satisfies a very definite and specific need.

C. Generally speaking, no effort is to be made to censor the collection. We feel the faculty and students deserve all sides of questions.

D. The collection shall not be developed to serve the interest of any special student.

E. The collection shall include titles for the serious adult readers and rely on the public library for materials of a lighter nature.

F. Format shall be considered when more than one edition of a title is available, and preference shall be given to attractive and readable editions.

G. Paperbacks shall be used when available to meet the need for multiple copies or books of limited use.

H. Books for faculty research will only be purchased if they can be used by the undergraduate student body. Interlibrary loans will be used to satisfy faculty needs for research materials. However, books and journals that will help the whole faculty understand junior college problems will be added as needed.

I. In selection of books priority will be given in the following order:

    1. Class need. A new class will be given extra consideration in meeting its most pressing needs.

2. Material requested by the instructors to supplement their field.

3. General reference material.

4. Outstanding books in fields not covered by the present curriculum.

5. General reading material (purchased with money from fines).

6. Fiction is purchased if a class has a need for it. Note (1) above, otherwise our fiction collection is, for the most part, the result of gifts to the library.

III. REFERENCE COLLECTION

A reference book shall be defined as one used frequently to answer questions that do not involve extended study. If extended use of the book is necessary, it is better placed in the general collection where it may circulate.

A. Reference titles used regularly shall be shelved in this collection. Seldom used titles will be added to the regular collection to keep the reference collection small and more usable. If necessary the period of loan will be limited.

B. Only the latest edition of a reference title will be kept in Reference. Others will be transferred to the general collection.

C. The Reference collection shall not be a catch all for valuable books. If a book is too valuable for the open shelves, it will have to be housed in the workroom. These books are marked in the card catalog "for this book ask at the desk."

IV. CLASSICS

A. Reprints of germinal and landmark works shall be included freely in the collections.

B. Whenever possible, editions with notes or separately published commentaries about such works shall be included, keeping in mind that they are intended for the use of undergraduates and not for students engaged in graduate research.

V. WRITINGS OF LEADING FIGURES IN RESPECTIVE FIELDS

A. Preference will be given to acquiring good editions of the outstanding titles rather than complete works of an author.

B. The library will endeavor to secure representative selections of many authors in preference to complete works of a few.

C. Complete works of outstanding personalities will be accepted as gifts even though we do not make it a policy to purchase this material.

VI. FOREIGN LANGUAGE TITLES

A. Titles in a language not taught on this campus will not be purchased. However, gifts in other languages will be accepted if suitable for student use.

B. Good translations are preferred to the originals.

C. Language tools appropriate to the language being taught will be secured.

D. Since the public library has a Finnish collection all gifts in this field will be given to it.

VII. RESERVE BOOKS

A. All books from the regular collection may be placed on reserve at the instructor's option.

B. Additional copies will be purchased if the need is apparent. At least one copy for every ten students using it should be available. Instructors are encouraged to make reading assignments over a period of time rather than for the next day. One book can serve many more students this way.

VIII. PERIODICALS

A. Preference will be given to technical and professional journals. The public library has a good selection of popular magazines.

B. Popular magazines regularly used by the students will be purchased.

IX. BINDING

A. Books not available in hard covers that will be used extensively will be bound at once.

B. Magazines will not be bound but used as separate issues as long as they last. When worn out and a need is still apparent, the material will be replaced with films. The most heavily used periodicals will be acquired on film as issued.

X. FACULTY PARTICIPATION IN SELECTION

A. Each department shall have a portion of the library funds assigned to it for purchase of books appropriate to their discipline. At least half of the library book budget shall be so allotted.

B. The library will endeavor to secure for the staff announcements and reviews of books in as wide a field as possible so the individual instructors will not be short on materials to select.

C. The librarian fills in obvious gaps over-looked by instructors and maintains an up-to-date reference collection.

Reprinted by Permission of Clatsop Community College, Mrs. Lyle Anderson, Library Director.

Gloria Gaines Memorial Library
Marymount College
Tarrytown, New York
July 26, 1971

BOOK SELECTION POLICY

INTRODUCTION

The purpose of this document is to serve as a guide in the selection of books and other library materials for the Gloria Gaines Memorial Library at Marymount College, Tarrytown, New York. The policies stated herewith shall not be considered unalterable regulations or restrictions but may be amended when, in the judgment of the librarians, such amendments will permit the addition of valuable material to the general collection. Written amendments to this Policy must be approved by the Library Committee and the College President before becoming an official part of this document.

GENERAL

I.   THE LIBRARY SHALL USE ITS FUNDS FOR:

    A.   Current purchases

    B.   Rounding out the collection (scope)

    C.   Filling in gaps (retrospective)

II. BOOK COLLECTIONS

    A.   The book collection should contain the standard books of general reference

    B.   The book collection should contain the standard reference books useful in the specific fields covered by the curriculum of the college.

    C.   The book collection should further contain:

        1.   An adequate stock, for each curricular field, of books concerning

            a.   the field as a whole
            b.   those divisions of the field in which courses are offered and members of the teaching staff are interested
            c.   other significant divisions of the field

        2.   An adequate stock of books concerning such important specific fields of interest as may not be treated in the curriculum, and

        3.   An adequate stock of books appropriate for leisure reading.

    D.   The library should receive, bind, and preserve accessibly a selected number of general periodicals, and the standard scholarly periodicals in the fields covered by the curriculum. The continuity and completeness of the sets should be maintained.

SPECIFIC

I. BOOK COLLECTION

    A.   The library will not purchase multiple copies of textbooks. This will be considered a departmental function of the student's responsibility.

    B.   Single copies of textbooks will be purchased only when that title represents the best source of information in that field.

    C.   The purchase of rare books shall be discouraged. Although such examples of fine printing, binding, and illustration have an aesthetic and historical value, it is hoped that these books will reach the library through gifts of friends and alumnae.

    D.   The library will purchase popular fiction and non-fiction not related to any particular course of instruction. It is recommended that a definite, limited amount of money be set aside each year for the purchase of such material, and that these titles be carefully weeded after the demand no longer exists.

    E.   The purchase of research materials solely for individual faculty use should be subordinated to the adequate fulfillment of the primary book needs of students. Interlibrary loan should suffice for the occasional request for specialized materials.

II. PHONOGRAPH RECORDS

    A.   The library will purchase recordings of the spoken word, especially those items requested for use in connection with English and Social Studies.

    B.   The Library will rely on the Modern Language Department to purchase foreign language recordings, and on the Music Department to recommend purchases of musical recordings.

III. SCORES

    A.   The acquisition of scores shall be considered a function of the Music Library (Department). Scores are expensive and require special binding technique, thus increasing the initial expenditure.

IV. FILMS, FILMSTRIPS, SLIDES

    A.   The library will assist in the selection of films for departmental purchase or rental, but will not purchase films with library funds. The high cost of films and their relatively limited use makes rental far more satisfactory for a college of this size.

    B.   Filmstrips will be purchased by the library, but selection will depend, to a great extent, on their prolonged usefulness, as is often true with art, religion, and biology filmstrips. Financial affairs and current events, for example, will be purchased sparingly.

    C.   Slides will be purchased whenever the representation cannot be viewed equally well by using an opaque or overhead projector.

V.   PERIODICALS, NEWSPAPERS, MICROFILM

A.   Broken and incomplete sets of periodicals have little value to the College Library, therefore, the librarian may require that a particular title be in existence a minimum of one year before it is purchased by the library. Exceptions will be made whenever warranted.

B.   Selection of magazine titles may depend on whether or not they are indexed in at least one of the general or special periodical indexes.

C.   For economy in binding and storage, and for durability of content, microfilm may be purchased for periodicals and newspapers at the discretion of the librarian.

D.   Newspapers should be purchased to give local, metropolitan, national, and international news coverage. Their retention will depend on availability of storage space and/or microfilm.

VI.   MAPS

A.   Although many maps can be obtained at no cost, all maps should be updated or replaced regularly.

B.   Old or out-dated maps should be kept if they are of political or historical value, regardless of duplication in atlases.

VII.   MICROCARDS

A.   Microcards may be purchased by the library, remembering that the material must be read in the library and, therefore, the selection should include primarily those titles which need not be read in their entirety to be of value.

B.   The selection of microcards should, in general, be limited to books now out-of-print and likely to remain out-of-print, or those titles too costly to purchase in their original form.

C.   Titles should not be purchased on microcards if their primary value is in the maps, illustrations, or other visual material.

VIII.   EPHEMERAL MATERIAL (pictures, graphs, charts, photographs, postcards, pamphlets)

A.   Although much of this material reaches the library without expenditure of library funds, the librarian should purchase any of these written and visual forms necessary to strengthen the Vertical File and Pamphlet Collections. Often the only source of certain kinds of information is in this pamphlet or pictorial form.

IX.   GOVERNMENT PUBLICATIONS

A.   The Gloria Gaines Memorial Library is a non-depository library and, therefore, selections must be made and orders placed for each publication desired.

Reprinted by Permission of Marymount College, Sister Jeanne d'Arc, RSHM Librarian.

Monroe County Community College
Monroe, Michigan
Adopted March 13, 1967

LEARNING RESOURCES MATERIALS SELECTION POLICY

In the Monroe County Community College Bulletin for 1966-1968 President Ronald Campbell expressed the following philosophy:

> We believe that each student should have the privilege and opportunity of making himself a better citizen of the country, state, nation, and of the world through education, and hope that we are able to do our part in providing for the advancement and strengthening of the principles that make the United States of America a world leader.

In keeping with that philosophy Monroe County Community College Learning Resources Center recognizes its responsibility to serve as one instrument of the total instructional program. It endeavors to serve the academic community by stimulating the cultural development of students and faculty, by motivating students to acquire life-long interest in good reading, and by keeping the faculty abreast of the progress of scholarship. The Learning Resources Center further acknowledges its obligation to remove all artificial barriers between readers and books. As its guide in fulfilling these objectives, the College establishes the following criteria for selecting Learning Resources materials.

Materials are selected to support the college curricula and to provide recreational reading for the students and faculty. The Learning Resources Center's Library collection must include books on subjects of current interest and on all facets of controversial issues, as well as traditional literature in the subject and reference areas. Materials are selected to provide intellectual stimulation for students and faculty and to satisfy their intellectual curiosity.

In some areas specific statements concerning selection are made:

> Religion: Materials in a public community college library must be broad, tolerant, and without partisanship or propaganda. Selections are made with an attempt to maintain an impartial recognition of all religions while specializing in none. The choice among materials will be made on the basis of their authority, timeliness, and good literary quality.

> Controversial Issues: The Learning Resources Center asserts its duty to keep in its collection a representative selection of materials on all subjects of interest to its users (students and faculty) including materials on all sides of controversial questions. Materials on any subject, if published by reputable publishers, are properly admitted to the Learning Resources Center. The Learning Resources Center recognizes its respon-

sibility not to emphasize one subject at the expense of another nor to emphasize one side of a subject exclusively.

Recreational Reading: Recreational reading is defined as that which is done for pleasure in leisure time. The Learning Resources Center recognizes that pleasure reading is not the same for all. Some prefer fiction; others prefer travel, biography, and so forth. Therefore, the Learning Resources Center's collection of recreational reading materials will be well-rounded in order to satisfy the interests of all users (students and faculty).

Sex: The Learning Resources Center purchases materials about sex for use by students and faculty in the areas of sociology, psychology, philosophy, and biology and for use by our students and faculty in their own intellectual inquiry. The maturity of the readers, as community college students and faculty, is assumed.

Selection of materials is a primary duty of the Learning Resources Center's professional staff. Therefore, its members utilize such materials selection aids and tools as Library Journal, Choice, Times, Literary Supplement, Saturday Review, Publisher's Weekly, Wilson Library Bulletin, ALA Bulletin, and publishers' catalogs and materials lists. The Learning Resources Center recognizes the contribution of the college faculty and administration to request book and non-book materials. The responsibility for selection of materials rests in the Director of Learning Resources, who operates within the framework of the rules and regulations established by the College, and within the guidelines of the Faculty Learning Resources Committee, as outlined by this Learning Resources Materials Selection Policy statement.

General criteria for selecting Learning Resources materials will be followed by all (Learning Resources Center, counseling, and teaching faculty and College administrators): (1) the author's reputation and significance; (2) the importance of the subject matter to the collection; (3) scarcity of material on the subject; (4) timeliness or permanence of the book; (5) appearance of title in special bibliographies or indexes; (6) authoritativeness; (7) reputation and standing of the publisher; (8) price. It should be noted that material may be considered appropriate to a particular subject if the material meets one or more of the above stated criteria.

DEFINITIONS: Learning Resources materials: books, periodicals, including magazines, newspapers, annuals, etc., recordings, films, slides, filmstrips, etc.

ACKNOWLEDGMENTS

The following sources were used for suggestions of materials selection policy statements, statements of responsibility, and statements of philosophy:

Carter, Mary Duncan and Wallace J. Bonk. BUILDING LIBRARY COLLECTIONS. 2nd ed. New York: Scarecrow Press, 1964.
MONROE COUNTY COMMUNITY COLLEGE BULLETIN, 1966-68. Inaugural Ed.
Eyman, Eleanor G. and David L. Reich. LIBRARY FUNCTION STUDY, MIAMI-DADE JUNIOR COLLEGE. Miami, Florida. 1965.

(Adopted by the Board of Trustees, March 13, 1967).

Reprinted by Permission of Monroe County Community College, M. Joan Woodruff, Director of Learning Resources.

Nassau Community College
Garden City, New York
Approved October 8, 1968

LIBRARY ACQUISITIONS POLICY

I. INTRODUCTION

The planned development of the collection of a library requires the application of a stated acquisitions policy. No policy statement can be definitive for all time, since a library is not a static institution. Ideas about its nature and content are constantly evolving. Therefore, a policy to guide the development of a library's collection must be responsive to change.

The following represents a statement of acquisitions policy which can be applied in the selection of the various types of materials which Nassau Community College Library adds to and withdraws from its collection.

II. OBJECTIVES

Nassau Community College Library's objectives are parallel to the objectives of the college. They are concerned with the intellectual, emotional, and social growth and development of the students. Consideration is given to faculty and staff needs, too.

The major purpose of the library is to participate in the educational program of Nassau Community College by collecting, making readily available, and assisting in the use of books and other materials needed by students, faculty, and staff.

Although no library collection may be expected to meet all the demands which are placed upon it, students should not have to go to other libraries for materials used in their studies, except in the case of research for which rare, highly specialized, or very expensive items are required. Similarly, faculty members should not have to go off-campus for materials which are directly related to their teaching, as well as items for study and research, with the same exception noted in the preceding sentence. The library should also provide those materials needed by the Administration and staff in the conduct of college business.

Any material of sufficient importance to be mentioned in a course ought to be represented in the collection, so that no student will be prevented by the inadequacies of the library from following up an initial lead given him in class. Likewise, no innovation in the curriculum which is thought to be educationally sound, such as independent study, ought to be handicapped or obstructed by deficiencies in the library's collection.

It is of primary importance that the library should provide materials to support the curriculum in a systematic and comprehensive manner. The strength of the collection should lie in areas of evident faculty or student interest.

In addition to supplementing the curriculum, the collection should include selected material in all major subject fields, whether taught at the college or not. Moreover, books and other items in areas of cultural and recreational interest should be supplied for the use of students, faculty, and staff in a limited fashion because of the non-residential nature of the college and the great number of easily accessible public libraries in Nassau County.

Another objective of the library is to serve as the archive for all official records of Nassau Community College. Materials relating to the history, development and character of the college should be preserved.

Finally, in order to keep the collection alive and useful, an active and continuing program of selection for withdrawal, or weeding, should be maintained. It is important to prevent the shelves from becoming cluttered with materials of questionable historical value, even though they once had a temporary significance.

III. RESPONSIBILITY FOR ACQUISITIONS

The most important aspect of acquisitions work takes place before materials are actually ordered. This work involves the planned selection of items best qualified to strengthen the college's resources for instruction and research. The importance of wise selection has grown in proportion to the increase in the volume of available materials, the cost of those materials, and the costs of acquiring, cataloging, housing, and servicing.

Responsibility for the selection of library materials for the college lies with the entire college community. Faculty members are largely responsible for recommending the acquisition of materials in their subject fields. Any member of the faculty or staff may request that an item be added to the college collection by completing a request form and submitting it through the departmental representative to the Acquisitions Unit or the Periodicals Unit of the library. Students may also submit recommendations for purchases through the library's suggestion box.

The library staff should encourage the interest and activity of individual faculty members in selecting material for the Library to assure the building of a comprehensive collection. The librarians assume responsibility for systematically reviewing current and retrospective bibliographies and making selections from them in areas neglected by the faculty. Responsibility for coordinating the collection as a whole, for aiding the faculty with bibliographical assistance, and for making judgments as to the format, degree of completeness, and number of copies of materials to be acquired rests with the librarians. Final decisions regarding acquisitions are made by the Director of the Library, after consultation with appropriate members of the faculty and staff. The Faculty Senate Library Committee meets regularly with the Director of the Library to discuss the acquisitions policy and other matters.

IV. GUIDING PRINCIPLES

In striving to meet its objectives within the limits of its resources, the library should follow these general directives:

A. To meet the needs of students with differing levels of ability, the library shall acquire materials for students ranging in difficulty from those for high school juniors to those for college seniors. Students should be supplied with appropriate materials to supplement their textbooks.

B.   In the acquisition of new titles, the major emphasis should be on current publications, and among those, works which promise to fulfill future as well as current needs should receive preference. Both in-print and out-of-print materials should be purchased as required.

C.   Before materials that are rare, highly specialized, or very expensive are bought for students or faculty engaged in research, the holdings of neighboring academic and public libraries should be consulted to avoid unnecessary duplication. If the items desired are available within the New York area or from a research library elsewhere in the United States, there is no justification for the library buying them, unless they are required reading for a course or used regularly by a faculty member in preparing for his classes. Materials from other libraries can be obtained through the inter-library loan service.

D.   Multiple copies of titles may be purchased, as required, at the discretion of the library.

E.   Materials in foreign languages which can be used for teaching and exercises in language courses offered at the college are desirable purchases for the library. However, materials for non-language courses which are published in languages other than English, with the exception of dictionaries, encyclopedias, and other reference tools, shall be bought only in those instances when there is evidence of their immediate usefulness to students and faculty.

F.   No materials should be excluded from the collection because of the race or nationality of the authors, or the political, moral, or religious views expressed therein. All sides of a controversial issue should be represented in the collection.

G.   When there is a choice, hardbound books should be selected over paperbacks because of their greater durability in the library.

H.   It is the responsibility of students to buy their own copies of assigned textbooks. However, the library should provide copies of textbooks in its reserve section for limited use by students and others.

I.   Materials dealing with all geographical areas should be acquired. However, requests for items relating to the United States should be given priority over requests for materials about other individual countries. Similarly, items dealing with New York should be obtained ahead of materials relating to other individual states. Likewise, publications about Nassau County should be given priority over items dealing with other individual counties.

J.   For back files of serial publications, microforms should be selected over paper copies when both are available, except in the cases of indexes and art periodicals, when paper is preferred.

K. Recreational materials should be provided in a limited fashion because of the non-residential nature of the college and the great number of easily accessible public libraries in Nassau County.

L. The archives of Nassau Community College consist of (1) the publications and official records of the college, including catalogs, reports, periodicals, yearbooks, brochures, and minutes of meetings of the Board of Trustees, Department Chairmen, Faculty and Faculty Senate; (2) materials about the college.

M. Gifts of either library materials or money to purchase them will be accepted provided they fit into the above policies and provided there are no restrictions attached. The library must be free to dispose of any materials which are not needed; however, when considered desirable, the library may, at its discretion, maintain a gift collection as a separate entity.

N. Weeding, or the removal of obsolete materials for purposes of discarding, should be considered an integral part of the total organized effort to study and develop the collection. Excess duplicate copies of seldom used titles and badly damaged copies should be withdrawn from the collection. Similarly, items should be weeded if they contain outdated or inaccurate information. Weeding should be done with advisement by departmental representatives.

V. PERIODIC REVIEW

Since Nassau Community College is a dynamic institution, the library's acquisitions policy statement must be responsive to change. It is necessary that this statement be reviewed periodically by the Director of the library working with the Faculty Senate Library Committee, and revised accordingly.

Reprinted by Permission of Nassau Community College, Dr. Leonard Grundt, Director of Library.

Occidental College Library
Los Angeles, California
Approved January 21, 1958

LIBRARY ACQUISITIONS POLICY

The following acquisitions policy was approved by the Occidental College Faculty Library Committee on January 21, 1958.

I.   GENERAL

The primary objective of Occidental College is, through a balanced combination of general and specialized courses of study, to offer a superior liberal arts education.   Graduate instruction has been added to the problem in selected fields and only when it enhances rather than de-emphasizes the quality of the undergraduate curriculum.   Faculty members are expected to keep fully abreast of their fields of teaching, and are encouraged to devote themselves to original research insofar as such efforts do not divert them from their teaching responsibility.

The acquisitions program of the Occidental College Library is expected faithfully to reflect the educational objectives, and to support the approved programs, of the College.   The Library will acquire all of the most important books and periodicals in the fields of the undergraduate and graduate teaching programs which the College offers, appropriate to each level of instruction.   Special effort will also be made to acquire works which in scope are broader than any particular discipline or field of interest defined in the curriculum.   Support will be given to the development of a strong reference collection (with emphasis on bibliography, biography and research resources guides) because such a collection is the basic tool of scholarship and because it is comprised of books which cannot be borrowed from other libraries. The area of reference collecting also includes the classic and current monographs and journals which a superior teacher must have conveniently at hand to keep constantly oriented in his field and fully informed of new developments, though such specialized works may not be needed regularly for student use even at the graduate level.   The Library will not always be able to meet the needs of all faculty members for their published research, but no faculty member should have to depend upon another library for the preparation of his lectures and teaching.

The Library will not, through gift or purchase, seek to develop special research collections except: (1) to support special programs of graduate study defined in the College course offering, or (2) to complement or supplement, rather than duplicate, the research collections in other libraries of the Los Angeles area which are open to scholars and advanced students under responsible guidance. Special collections already held by the Library (see Occidental College Library Guide to Special Collections) will, insofar as funds permit, be further strengthened through additional acquisitions in proportion to their significance as research assets to the College and the region.

II. RESPONSIBILITY OF THE LIBRARY STAFF

The College Librarian, and the Library Staff, advised by the faculty, will be responsible for the development of collections of general works, i.e., books, periodicals, pamphlets, maps, microtexts, etc., which do not fall within the scope of any single teaching department's program, but which are of value to the programs of more than one teaching department or the program of the College as a whole. Again with the advice of the faculty, the College Librarian and the Library Staff will be responsible for developing established special collections of interdepartmental scope. In general, first attention will be given to most recent or definitive editions, works in English and other Roman alphabet languages, and to standard rather than ephemeral publications or manuscripts. It is recognized that this rule of collecting emphasis cannot be applied to special collections which are already supported fully by the general works necessary for their convenient use.

III. RESPONSIBILITY OF THE FACULTY

An adequate college library can be developed only through the active interest of faculty members in recommending acquisitions pertinent to the teaching fields in which they respectively specialize. To this end, each teaching department is allocated a share of the library budget each fiscal year to spend for library materials (i.e., library materials acquired upon the recommendation of a department will not be designated for the exclusive use of any person or group). Each department chairman, or his appointed representative, is expected to make an equitable distribution of the departmental library allocation in such a way as best to provide library support for the work of his entire department. Departments are expected to recommend library purchases which will develop the total library collection in accord with this general library acquisitions policy.

The specific library acquisitions policies, formulated by the several teaching departments of the campus, will be appended to this general library acquisitions policy in the order in which the departments are listed in the current Occidental College Bulletin.

IV. REGIONAL EMPHASIS AND SPECIAL CURRICULA

It is recognized that the Library can legitimately acquire highly specialized and ephemeral material pertinent to southern California, California, the West, and the Southwest including Baja, California, and northern Mexico. Except for bibliographical studies, works of recognized importance, and a sampling of inexpensive or free ephemera, however, the Library's regional collection will avoid duplication of the holdings of other research collections in the area (e.g., Southwest Museum, Huntington Library, USC, UCLA, and the Los Angeles Public Library).

Occidental cannot rely entirely upon the resources of neighboring libraries to support the special curricula (see Occidental College Bulletin) it offers; but neither can it hope to develop completely adequate research collections in these broad areas of study. It is expected that teaching departments (see above, III--Responsibility of the Faculty) will, in their recommendations, emphasize purchasing in support of the approved special curricula. Further, the Library must accept a measure of responsibility in enriching the total research resources of the area if the College expects to refer its faculty and students to neighboring libraries (see below).

V.   COOPERATION WITH OTHER LIBRARIES

Insofar as available funds permit, the Library will enter into cooperative acquisitions agreements with the research libraries of the Los Angeles area. Since Occidental faculty members and advanced graduate students are given liberal access to the area's research libraries, Occidental recognizes reciprocal responsibility: (1) to lend liberally to other college libraries in order to reduce total demands upon research libraries, (2) to purchase, if possible, the works regularly consulted in other libraries or repeatedly requested on interlibrary loan, when these works can be identified, and (3) to purchase, whenever funds are available, a reasonable amount of research material to enhance total regional resources.

VI.   PERIODICALS

Periodical subscriptions are recommended in the same manner as books. Purchase will be of the entire volume (from no. 1) of the current year with no back file. The current volume (i.e., one year's subscription) will be charged to the book allocation of the teaching department which recommends subscription. Thereafter the subscription will be carried on the periodicals fund and will be automatically renewed. The amount expended on periodical subscriptions for a teaching department (i.e., recommended by it) will be a factor considered in allocating book funds.

If it is essential to acquire a back file (up to five years), this should be recommended at the time of original subscription in order to secure an unbroken run. See below for extensive back files.

VII.   BACK FILES OF PERIODICALS

Back files of newspapers, journals, proceedings, etc., are the most expensive of library acquisitions (original cost, binding cost, space cost, handling cost, and maintenance cost are all higher than the corresponding costs of standard books). Necessarily, the acquisitions of back files will be highly selective and whenever possible such acquisitions as are made will be in microtext editions (microprint, microfilm, microcard, microlex, etc.). The Library will be selective in the binding of files of the periodicals to which it currently subscribes. Broken files acquired by gift will be offered to other libraries whenever a larger file in the area can thereby be made more complete. Short files and single issues of periodicals will not ordinarily be preserved as serials, but will be discarded or incorporated in pamphlet collections.

VIII.   DUPLICATE SUBSCRIPTIONS

Since all library materials are accessible to the entire campus, and in order to gain the widest possible periodical coverage on the funds available, second copy subscriptions will not be placed by the Library except under special circumstances. Any faculty member recommending a duplicate subscription will accompany such request by a letter of justification. The College Librarian will seek the advice of the Faculty Library Committee before he denies such a request. At the opening of each fiscal year the Faculty Library Committee will, at the College Librarian's request, review the duplicate subscriptions list with the object of reducing it.

IX. MULTIPLE COPIES

Library funds are not appropriated for the purpose of acquiring multiple copies in lieu of text-books for specific courses. On the other hand, the Library has a responsibility for having on hand sufficient copies of titles which are assigned reading in classes of average size. Therefore, the Library will not purchase additional copies in excess of a total of five per title. Under special circumstances (e.g., large, required undergraduate classes such as History of Civilization or Basic Speech), the Library will add unaccessioned copies in any number provided such copies (beyond five) are purchased on non-library funds.

X. TEXT-BOOKS

The Library will not acquire even single copies of text-books which students are expected to purchase, unless the instructor specifically recommends Library purchase.

XI. REPLACEMENT OF LOST BOOKS

Lost books are replaced after two years, or immediately as needed, if the College Librarian or a member of the faculty approves replacement; otherwise the lost books are de-cataloged and recorded in the withdrawn files. It is a responsibility of the College Librarian to notify the appropriate members of the faculty when losses are discovered.

XII. WITHDRAWING AND DISCARDING

In accordance with defined procedures, the College Librarian is expected to withdraw (for sale, discard, exchange, or storage) titles which are obsolete and no longer appropriate in the Library's collections. Preliminary decisions to withdraw books will be made in consultation with the faculty members most directly concerned with possible future use of the books. Two weeks before final action is taken on withdrawing or discarding any item, the College Librarian will announce such contemplated action as an official notice to the faculty as a whole in the Occidental Bibliogram. Faculty members will thus be given time to request further consideration before any volume or item is actually withdrawn or discarded.

Reprinted by Permission of Occidental College, Mr. Tyrus G. Harmsen, College Librarian.

Park College Library
Parkville, Missouri
January 1, 1968

SELECTION AND ACQUISITIONS OF LIBRARY MATERIALS

I. GENERAL STATEMENT

   A. In selecting and acquiring materials for the Library, the following factors shall serve as guidelines:

      1. Since this Library serves an undergraduate college student clientele, materials acquired will be within the comprehension range of undergraduate students. This does not mean that the Library will acquire no materials of a level of difficulty beyond general undergraduate level or of a research nature. But such materials will be added in limited number and for appropriate reasons. (Such reasons may be to provide students with a sampling of the kind of materials they will encounter in their profession or in graduate work, or to provide adequate material for a superior student.) In general, material useful primarily to the graduate student, researcher, or professional will not be acquired.

      2. In selecting materials to be added, major consideration shall be paid to the accuracy and authority of the material under consideration, the reputation of the author and publisher, and the social and/or artistic merit or importance of the material. Such evaluation shall be based both on reviews in the professional literature and on the professional judgment of the faculty and library staff.

      3. Although the Library should make available a representative collection of material in all areas of human knowledge, primary attention shall be given in acquisitions to supporting those subject areas taught at Park College. Materials outside these areas will be acquired in limited number even though they meet the requirements of criteria 1 and 2 above. This does not set aside the Library's obligation to make available, in limited numbers, materials unrelated to the curricula, of general cultural, religious, and recreational nature.

   B. Censorship

      Because of Park College's status as a private college related to the United Presbyterian Church in the U.S.A. and governed by its own Board of Trustees, criticisms of Library-owned materials or attempts at censorship which originate outside the corporate structure of the College and outside the church to which the College is related will not be considered.

      In order to evaluate the criticisms of persons or groups legitimately related to the College who might wish to suggest censoring materials in

24

the College Library, and to establish a guideline for the acquisition of materials of potentially controversial nature, the following shall be the policy of this Library:

1. In an effort to support the obligation of the College to be a forum for the free exchange of all ideas in its pursuit of knowledge and truth, the Library will make available to students and faculty, books and other materials offering the widest possible variety of viewpoints, regardless of the popularity of these viewpoints or of the popularity or unpopularity of their authors.

2. In areas where there is honest disagreement concerning the truth or wisdom of particular issues, ideas, or beliefs, the Library will make an effort to see that the printed, visual, or recorded points of view of the best spokesman of all sides of the issue, idea, or belief are represented in its holdings.

3. Selection of materials for the Library will be based only on the criteria stated in section A (above) regardless of the frankness of language or controversial manner an author may use in dealing with subjects of religion, politics, sex, or social, economic, scientific, or moral issues.

In handling criticisms of materials or attempts at censorship, the Librarian will reply verbally or in writing to the person or group, quoting or referring to the above policy. Persistent or repeated criticism from persons or groups legitimately related to the College will be referred to the Library Committee.

II.   RESPONSIBILITY FOR BOOK SELECTION

A. It shall be the responsibility of the faculty of each academic department to recommend to the Library purchase of materials in support of their subject areas and curriculum. Such purchases, with the exception of subscription materials, shall be charged to that portion of the book budget allocated to that department.

B. Because the Librarians are in the best position to observe the quality and balance of all subject areas and because the Librarian is ultimately responsible for the overall quality and balance of the total collection, the professional Library staff will select and purchase materials in all subject areas. Such purchases will be charged to the Library's portion of the book budget.

III.   GIFT BOOKS

The college library is frequently offered books and other library materials as gifts. Although many excellent and important materials have been added to the collection as gifts, much of what is offered is of no value to this Library. Because this can often involve public relations concerns, a clearly stated policy on the matter of gifts and donors is necessary. No commitment to accept gifts shall be made by anyone except the Librarian. All such offers made indirectly shall be referred to the Librarian. In respect to gift books, the policy below shall be followed:

A. The Librarian shall have the prerogative to refuse to accept gift books he feels do not contribute to the mission and purposes of the Library or which do not measure up to the criteria as stated in section I.A (above). Where necessary, the Librarian's decision will be subject to presidential review.

B. With regard to gifts accepted, it shall be made clear to the donor that:

1. The Library will determine the classification, housing, and circulation policies of all gift items just as with purchased items.

2. The Library retains the right to dispose of duplicates and unneeded material as it sees fit.

3. The Librarian of Park College will not be responsible for the monetary valuation statement of the donor for tax or other purposes.

IV. SPECIAL MATERIALS

A. Foreign language materials

With the exception of materials acquired primarily for use of students and faculty in the departments of modern and classical languages, books and other materials printed in languages other than English will not be acquired. Exceptions to this policy will be foreign language dictionaries for reference use and other foreign language material determined to be necessary by the Librarian in consultation with the Library Committee.

B. Textbooks

Elementary and secondary school textbooks will be acquired by gifts from the publisher whenever possible for display and use in the Curriculum Collection. Titles deemed necessary to the collection which are unavailable on a gift basis will be purchased. College level textbooks of a general survey nature published primarily for classroom use will generally be avoided as library material. Individual exceptions to this policy will be made by the Librarian in consultation with the department involved.

C. Non-book Materials

Auditory and visual non-printed materials will be acquired by the Library as needed to support the curricular needs of the College. All non-book materials will be subject to the same criteria of selection as apply to printed materials. Non-book materials created primarily for group use or laboratory use will not be acquired. Non-book materials which require the use of specialized auxiliary equipment not generally available to borrowers will not be acquired except as that material as equipment may be necessary for in-library utilization.

D. Paperback Books

The type of binding on a book will not be a consideration in the decision to purchase except that the Library will exercise judgments of economy when a book is available in paper or cloth binding.

E. Materials of Unusual Cost

Subscription sets or series and individual titles and sets (with the exception of general encyclopedias) costing more than $100 will be subject to review by the Librarian in consultation with the requesting faculty member before purchase.

F. Periodicals

Suggestions from faculty and students for new periodical subscriptions will be held until summer each year, at which time a general evaluation of all periodical holdings and subscriptions will be made. Additions to the holdings will be made on the basis of the following criteria:

1. Importance of the recommended title to the curricula of this College.

2. Ability of undergraduate students to read and understand the material presented.

3. Number of journals currently received in the subject area.

4. Availability of adequate access to the contents through the indexing media.

No periodical subscription shall be dropped without consultation with the chairman of the department or departments most directly concerned.

G. Rare Books and Manuscripts

No attempt will be made by this Library to acquire single titles or to build a collection of rare books, manuscripts, incunabula, or archival material. Offers of gifts of such items will be subject to the policy stated in section III (above).

H. Out of Print Books

Out of print books desired by faculty members will be acquired from University Microfilms or other vendors of out of print titles in xerographic reprinted format, if available. Orders for those not available from this source will be submitted to a single out of print book dealer asking that quotations of price be submitted. At the end of twelve months, out of print orders not filled by the dealer will be cancelled and submitted to another dealer if still desired by the faculty member who made the original request.

V. MULTIPLE COPIES

Faculty members are encouraged to suggest the number of copies of a single title they deem necessary, but the final decision on the number of copies of a single title to be added to the collection will be determined by the Library staff after consultation with the requesting faculty member.

VI. SELECTION OF VENDORS

The selection of sources for the purchase of library materials will be left to the discretion of the Librarian. Domestic in-print materials will be ordered from jobbers or publishers giving the best service and price discounts. Of primary importance will be quality of service: speed, accuracy, special services. Foreign in-print materials will be ordered through U.S. dealers with the exception of British and Canadian publications which will be ordered directly through British and Canadian dealers and publishers.

Reprinted by Permission of Park College, Mr. Harold F. Smith, Librarian.

Phillips University Graduate Seminary Library
Enid, Oklahoma
January, 1962

BOOK SELECTION POLICY

I.   RESPONSIBILITY FOR SELECTION

The Librarian is ultimately responsible for the selection of all books and other materials to be acquired for the Library with aid and advice of the faculty and within the limits set by the budget. The Seminary faculty has an unusual competence and awareness in the area of theological books, and their recommendations and advice are actively sought. Weekly lists of new books published are provided to each member of the faculty for checking. In addition a monthly list of new accessions is distributed.

The right of the Librarian to select books and other materials representing all sides of controversial issues and various viewpoints concerning Christian doctrine is safeguarded by the Seminary, and any attempts at censorship from whatever sources or for whatever reasons will be resisted. In no case is a book excluded because of the race, nationality, political, or denominational background of the writer.

II.   FACTORS INFLUENCING ACQUISITION

The following factors are taken into consideration in the purchase of books and other materials:

A.   The needs of the curriculum, including the long-range development of the Seminary with reference to its degree programs and research interests.

B.   The need to create a well-balanced and adequate coverage of the major disciplines of theology for faculty study, for extensive term papers and thesis work, and for graduate research and extension work.

C.   The number of students majoring in each area and the demand for books by students writing theses.

D.   The research needs and literary production of the various professors.

E.   The maintenance of the special collection focused around the history, theology, and life of the Christian Church.

F.   The accessibility of books in other libraries.

G.   The budget funds available.

H.   The book itself. Criteria that are considered here include the author's significance as a writer, the importance of the subject matter to the collection, the scarcity of material on the subject, the timeliness or permanence of the book, the appearance of the book in bibliographies or indexes, the authoritativeness of the work, the reputation of the publisher, the format, and the price.

III. GROUPS OF READERS TO BE SERVED

The Seminary Library seeks first of all to serve the needs of students. Not only the basic materials for all men and women entering church vocations must be acquired but specialized resources for those entering the hospital ministry, mission field, campus ministry, religious education, etc., must be provided as well.

The Library seeks to serve the faculty, either purchasing or securing through interlibrary loan those resources needed for their study and research.

The Library also recognizes its responsibility for the continuing theological education of its graduates and ministers in the surrounding area through library loans and directed study programs.

Undergraduate students and adult citizens of Enid are welcome to use library materials within the Library, and may obtain permission to borrow books at the discretion of the Circulation Librarian providing the material is not needed by Seminary students or faculty. Materials, however, are not selected to meet the needs or wishes of non-Seminary users.

IV. FORMS OF MATERIAL

A. Books

Priority for books and other materials to be purchased for the Library is given to those materials which meet the curricular needs of the students in the courses offered, including items needed for class assignments, collateral reading, references in textbooks, supplementary individual study, or for use in preparing term papers or theses, and including those reference bibliographical tools which will facilitate finding and using these materials.

After the primary needs have been met then consideration is given to other desirable materials which will give balance to the collection or meet special interests or needs of the students or faculty.

Fiction, except for representative titles needed for an understanding of contemporary literature and its relation to the Christian faith, is not purchased. Students are encouraged to use the facilities of the University Library in this area.

Textbooks for courses offered by the Seminary are not ordinarily purchased. Juvenile literature, except for that needed for the curriculum of religious education, is not purchased.

Paperback books may be bought for any one of several reasons. If a title is one which has never appeared in a bound edition, or is out-of-print and otherwise unobtainable in better format, the paperback edition will be purchased and then bound or reinforced so that it may become part of the permanent collection. If there is a heavy temporary demand for a particular work available in a paperback edition, for the sake of economy the additional copies may be purchased in paperback. A paperback edition may also be purchased if a title would be useful only for the occasional reader and the Library would not be justified in buying the more expensive edition.

B. Serials

Periodicals are purchased, or accepted as gifts, chiefly for one or more of the following reasons: (1) to keep the Library's collection up-to-date with current thinking in various fields, (2) to provide information not available in books, (3) to provide in some measure for the research needs of advanced students and faculty, (4) to keep the faculty informed of developments in their fields, and (5) to serve the staff as book selection aids, book reviewing media, and professional reading. Individual titles are chosen for the following reasons: (1) accuracy and objectivity, (2) accessibility of content through indexes, (3) ease of consultation, (4) demand, (5) need in reference work, (6) representation of a point of view or subject needed in the collection, and (7) cost of the subscription in relation to its possible use.

Because of previous weakness in the acquisition of periodicals the Library is engaged in a vigorous program to procure the back files of periodicals needed for theological study.

Newspaper subscriptions provide news coverage at the national, state, and local level and include the New York Times, the Christian Science Monitor, the Daily Oklahoman, the two Enid dailies, and the Oklahoma Christian. The other papers are kept in a permanent file at either the University or Carnegie Library.

C. Archival Materials and Manuscripts

Printed, manuscript, and other archival materials pertaining to the Graduate Seminary are collected and preserved. Because of the lack of facilities and processing costs general manuscripts are not actively sought, although some occasionally are accepted as gifts.

D. Pamphlets and Documents

An active pamphlet file is maintained and regularly weeded. Pamphlets of permanent value are bound and reinforced. Although most pamphlets are received free of charge, some are purchased, provided they meet the same high criteria as described for the purchase of books.

Since the Carnegie Library serves as a United States Documents Depository, government documents, except for rare items such as the publication of congressional prayers, are not purchased. Reports of the U.S. Bureau of the Census, however, are purchased so that Seminary students may study intensively the areas which they serve as student pastors and later as resident ministers.

E. Maps, Music, and Audio-Visual Material

The Library limits its purchase of maps and atlases to those that will be of use in studying mission fields or Biblical geography and archeology. The Library purchases chiefly from publishers whose work is known to be satisfactory in accuracy, completeness, and clarity.

Music and audio-visual materials are not now purchased by the Library. A careful study will be carried out by the Librarian and faculty before any program of acquisition is begun in these areas.

F.   Microforms

The Library owns a Recordak Microfilm Reader, a small portable machine, and a Microcard Reader. The Library acquires, for research use, microfilm or microcards of materials not in the collection when they are needed either for general use or to round out some special collection. Microfilm is usually obtained only when the material is not available in the original form, or when the microfilm reproduction is preferable because of lower costs, reduced bulk, or the fragile nature of the original. Microcards are acquired, as a rule, only for titles not available in book or periodical form. Since they do not circulate, microcard editions bought by the Library are ordinarily reference work, scholarly titles, theses, or items needed to fill broken periodical sets.

V.   SUBJECT AREAS

A survey of each of the subject fields of the Seminary Library should be made by the Librarian in cooperation with the faculty in the near future to discover the extent to which each field should be covered in acquisitions. A graded evaluation of each field based on the extent to which that field has been developed to meet the desired aim will then aid in determining future policy.

Four degrees of coverage, expressing the degree of concentration of any field, might well be used.

A.   The Supplementary Research Collection

This would refer to a collection that is out-of-scope as far as ever having enough material to support advanced research in that particular subject. For example, in the Library Latin and Greek authors are important as background material for the thought of the world in Biblical times and, therefore, they would form a supplementary research collection.

B.   A Research Collection

This would refer to a collection adequate for the needs of graduate study of the subject and would include the major proportion of materials required for independent research. The primary criterion for selection in this field would be that the information contained in the work be currently valid. It would include the principal monographs and periodicals in the field. The accent would be placed upon works in the English language, whether original or translated.

C.   A Comprehensive Collection

This would be a research collection having all the materials in the previous category, plus a wider selection of books and periodicals having value for current research and including the most important works for historical research in the field. It would aim to cover the best of thought in any of the principal European languages so long as it is germane to the scope of the subject.

D. An Exhaustive Collection

This would be a collection which endeavors to include everything written on the subject in all editions and translations and in all languages of all time. Exhaustive collections will be undertaken, naturally, only in limited areas (probably of selected fields such as Oklahoma Disciples history and literature).

VI. FORMAT AND VALUE

Because of limited funds, rare books are not to be bought and are accepted as gifts only if given without stipulation about special treatment. Very expensive, seldom used books are not bought. Second-hand books in poor condition are not bought and are not accepted as gifts unless in sound condition for binding and the cost of binding them is much less than the cost of a copy in good condition. The physical format of each book is considered in all purchases.

VII. SPECIAL PROBLEMS

A. Gifts, Duplicates, and Exchanges

Gifts of books and other materials are accepted only if the Library may dispose of them if they fail to prove desirable additions to the collection because of their physical condition, obsolescence of material contained, or failure to be of sufficient use to the patrons of the Library. The Librarian is to be the judge of what disposition is to be made of gifts.

No special collection will be set up and maintained as a unit within the Library, but gifts of books added to the collection, or books purchased with money given to the Library, are incorporated within the Library's general collection. A book plate to identify the donor is inserted in gift books or books bought with gift funds.

There is very little duplication of books except where the needs of students and the continued demand for the book make it apparent to the Librarian that additional copies should be secured. For most materials initially only one copy of a title is purchased.

A modest exchange program is carried on with other theological libraries and is particularly used to build up the Library's collection of the major periodicals of other denominations.

B. Foreign Language Materials

The provision of materials in foreign languages is a proper function of the Seminary Library. While the present student body may not be equipped to use foreign language publications effectively, such material will be required by the Library to provide for the needs of the faculty and for the occasional graduate student engaged in a serious theological pursuit requiring books not available in English. German remains the basic language for Old Testament study, and German scholarship and to a lesser degree French are important for other theological disciplines. The importance and the place of Greek, Hebrew, and Latin are well recognized in theological scholarship.

In addition to several foreign language periodicals, new works of outstanding importance by foreign scholars are purchased in the original on publication; the English translation is also bought if it later appears. The Library's policy with regard to the purchase of important works of less than outstanding value is based on the following considerations: (1) the availability of an English translation; (2) the availability of abstracts; (3) the familiarity of at least a few potential readers with the language concerned; and (4) the availability of material in nearby libraries.

C. Maintenance of Materials

It is not the Library's policy to replace automatically all books withdrawn because of loss, damage, or wear. Need for replacement in each case is weighed with regard to several factors: (1) the number of duplicate copies; (2) the existence of adequate coverage of a field; (3) other similar material in the collection, especially later and better material; and (4) demand for the particular title or subject. Every effort is made to replace important titles, including advertising or listing out-of-print items with special dealers.

In order to keep binding costs to a minimum, books are bought in good format, and in reinforced binding when possible. When a volume is worn out, the cost of replacement, either of the particular item, a later edition, or of a different title with more up-to-date content, is compared with the cost of binding.

All periodicals taken by the Library that are indexed in the indexes regularly received are bound; other periodicals are held in unbound form for a limited period of time, at the end of which period a decision, on a highly selective basis, may be made to bind some titles. The others are to be disposed of by sale or exchange.

D. Evaluation, Weeding, and Discarding

Periodic evaluation of holdings by checking against standard bibliographies and check lists in the different subject areas is undertaken by the Library staff. Results of such surveys may be referred to appropriate faculty members for their advice.

A systematic and periodic program of weeding is carried out by the Library in cooperation with the faculty. Obsolete materials, such as outmoded books, superceded editions, broken files of unindexed journals, superfluous duplicates, and worn-out or badly marked volumes are withdrawn from circulation and discarded. Because of adequate space at present, no volumes are weeded for storage in other areas of the building.

E. Relation to Other Libraries

Materials not basic to the curriculum and available in the University or Carnegie Library are not ordinarily duplicated in the Seminary Library. Careful planning and periodic discussions with the librarians of these two libraries avoid needless duplication of books and insures cooperation and mutual understanding.

Although no cooperative book selection program has been worked out with the other seminary libraries in the region, the Librarian should take an active role in encouraging the development of such a program.

Interlibrary loan relationships are maintained with other libraries in accordance with the Interlibrary Loan Code.

VIII. ANNUAL REVISION

In order to maintain a dynamic book selection program and keep up-to-date with current developments in the library and theological world, this Book Selection Policy shall be evaluated and revised annually by the Librarian in cooperation with the Library Committee.

Reprinted by Permission of Phillips University Library, John L. Sayre, Librarian.

United States Merchant Marine Academy
Kings Point, New York
Approved February 2, 1965

BOOK SELECTION POLICY FOR THE ACADEMY LIBRARY

INTRODUCTION

The planned development of the book collection of a library requires the application of definite book selection policies whether written or unwritten. The preparation of this written book selection policy has been inspired by a recommendation in the Report of the Evaluation Committee of the Middle States Association of Colleges and Secondary Schools which visited the Academy on November 18-21, 1962.

It has been prepared by the Librarian with the advice of the Faculty Library Committee and members of their departments. It presents general policies which can be applied in the selection of all the different types of books which the Academy Library adds to its collections.

In this statement of policy, the word "books" shall be used as a collective noun to encompass all classes of materials which a library collects in its efforts to maintain the records of civilization.

THE ACADEMY LIBRARY

The primary purpose of the Academy Library is to participate in the educational program of the Academy by collecting, making readily available, and assisting in the use of the necessary books for the education of Cadets. The librarians thereby join the faculty in their classrooms and laboratories in contributing to the preparation of officers for the U.S. Merchant Marine.

The Library will serve the Academy in these important ways:

A.   Make available those books which the students will need in their studies.

B.   Supply for faculty members those books which are directly related to their teaching, as well as books for study and research.

C.   Provide those books needed by the Administration and Staff in the conduct of Academy business.

D.   Provide books in areas of cultural and recreational interest.

E.   Provide books of basic information in all areas.

F.   Provide books for research in the Maritime area.

RESPONSIBILITY FOR SELECTION

The overall responsibility for the development of the book resources of the Academy is the Librarian's. This is one of his major professional activities and he will apply to it all of the knowledge, experience, bibliographic tools and time at his command.

He will be assisted in the systematic development of the collection by the active participation of members of his professional staff and members of the faculty who shall assume specific responsibility in their own subject fields. The faculty shall outline the boundary lines of their areas of instruction within which the Librarian shall operate in his selection of books for that particular area. (This has been done to some extent in departmental book selection statements on file in the Library). They shall thereupon make sure that the Librarian properly discharges his responsibility for the development of the collection in their subject areas. Faculty members shall make specific suggestions of titles for purchase and shall give opinions on titles referred to them by the Librarian.

Additionally, they shall periodically survey the titles already in the collection for their subject areas and suggest to the Librarian those titles which can be discarded as no longer useful.

Valuable assistance in all areas of selection can be offered by faculty, administration, staff, cadets and alumni whose suggestions for purchases will always receive a grateful welcome.

SOME GENERAL POLICIES FOR THE SELECTION OF TITLES

Books to be added to the Academy Library shall normally meet the following criteria:

A. "Worthwhile"--Titles selected shall, quite obviously, be "good" books. This does not mean that each one shall be a potential classic but that it shall have some degree of merit which shall justify its addition to the Library.

B. "Continued Usefulness"--Titles which are selected for the Academy Library shall be deemed to be of some enduring value to the collection. No title should be considered for purchase (unless possibly in the recreational area) which is obviously ephemeral in nature.

C. "College Level"--The content and quality of presentation in selected titles shall be appropriate for the users of a college library.

D. "General Interest"--Titles selected shall have some significance for any person who might be interested in the general subject of the book. No individual hobbies shall be ridden or highly specialized or very personal interests pursued.

E. "Academy Interest and Usefulness"--The interest and usefulness of titles selected shall be related to the mission of the Academy--that is, titles shall be selected in terms of their institutional value as well as their personal usefulness.

OUTLINE OF THE BOOK COLLECTION

I. THE GENERAL BOOK COLLECTION

    A. Working Collection in Curricular Areas

        1. Required reading materials such as reserve books

        2. Recommended reading materials

        3. Other books, as well as periodicals, needed to support the curriculum

        4. Books for faculty members

    B. Non-Curricular Collection

        1. Important general books

        2. Cultural books in subject areas outside the curriculum

        3. Recreational reading.

II. REFERENCE COLLECTION

    A. Standard books of general reference

    B. Standard reference books in the specific fields covered by the curriculum

    C. Standard reference books useful in areas outside the curriculum

III. RESEARCH COLLECTION

    A. General research collection adequate for the needs of under-class students in the preparation of subject themes

    B. Selective research collection adequate for the needs of upper-class students in the preparation of term papers and for the pursuit of other independent research in specialized areas

    C. Materials for faculty research and advanced study

    D. Nautical books

POLICIES OF SELECTION FOR THE VARIOUS DIVISIONS
OF THE BOOK COLLECTION

I. THE GENERAL BOOK COLLECTION

    A. 1 & 2. Required and Recommended Reading Materials

        The Academy Library will supply all books required or recommended by the faculty for reading by the students. While it does not strengthen the book collection to purchase multiple copies of a single title, the Library will obtain in adequate number, all reserve books which instructors wish to assign to their classes.

3. Books to Support the Curriculum

This is a standard collection of titles on subject areas in the curriculum. The collection will consist of two main divisions--a background collection of "classic" titles and an up-to-date collection of basic books. These are the books which should be in any library serving a college offering the indicated subjects. In other words, these are works which the Library can be expected to have simply because the subject is being taught at the Academy. They are the best editions of the major writers who have explored these subjects. These titles are over and above any immediate demonstrated requirement of Faculty or Cadets but because they are fundamental, these books will at some time be needed and used.

4. Books for Faculty Members

Materials needed by faculty members in their teaching shall be purchased by the Academy Library. Admittedly this is an area hard to define and in most cases, it will be left to the faculty member to do so. In general, these are books the supplying of which will be reflected in the quality of teaching.

B. Non-Curricular Collection

The responsibility of the Library for the purchase of recreational, cultural and general information materials has been mentioned. It shall be the aim of the Library to have available some books in all the non-curricular areas of interest of Academy personnel. As examples, books to read just for fun, books on sports and games, books on subjects not covered in the curriculum will be purchased as appropriate.

II. REFERENCE COLLECTION

This is a non-circulating collection of general and specialized books providing quick access to factual information on the entire range of human knowledge. Books will be selected, therefore, not only on matters of curricular interest but in all areas in which factual information may be desired.

III. RESEARCH COLLECTION

A. General Research Collection

It is believed that the normal selection process will serve to assemble the necessary books in this division

B. Selective Research Collection

These are books assembled in those areas in which research is part of the learning process. (The word "research" here means research in an under-graduate sense, not the research of a graduate student or faculty member). These titles will be of a more specialized nature covering in depth more limited areas of the subject. These areas will be designated by the faculty as areas of concentration and investigation and these specific subjects will receive priority in selection of titles.

C. Materials for Faculty Research and Study

Materials required by faculty members in outside study and research shall be supplied when the area is related to their teaching, when the books meet the general principles of selection, and when funds permit. It will be realized that faculty interests in study and research may be too highly specialized and beyond the scope of Academy interest to merit purchase of desired titles. When this occurs, the bibliographical resources of other libraries can be utilized, either by visits in person or by inter-library loan.

D. Nautical Books

In keeping with its location in an Academy devoted to the Merchant Marine, the Library will place particular attention on the sea as an area of concentration. It will endeavor to assemble a comprehensive research collection in the whole field of the Merchant Marine, past and present, as well as ancillary areas. This will be achieved in part through the Library's service to the curriculum. The Library will try to obtain at least one copy of every book in English relating to the Merchant Marine as well as key titles in foreign languages.

The Library maintains the Index to Maritime Periodicals and an accompanying reference collection of marine journals. It will engage in collecting titles in Maritime and Naval History but will probably find many of these titles both expensive and elusive and will need to encourage gifts in order to assemble a collection in this area.

In general, it should look toward a future as the National Library for the Merchant Marine.

Reprinted by Permission of United States Merchant Marine Academy, Everett H. Northrop, Commander, USMS, Librarian.

The Undergraduate Library
University of North Carolina
Chapel Hill, North Carolina
March 26, 1963

BOOK SELECTION POLICY

I.   STATEMENT OF PURPOSE OF THIS POLICY

This codification of a book selection policy for the Undergraduate Library will serve as a guide to those responsible for building the book collection of this library. It is hoped that this statement of policy will aid selectors in making judgments from a clearly recognized point of view so that the growth of the collection will be consistent with its stated objectives.

II. STATEMENT OF THE LIBRARY'S CLIENTELE

The Undergraduate Library is designed exclusively to serve the undergraduates of this University in the Division of Academic Affairs. The Undergraduate Library cannot undertake to supply the library needs of any graduate school or division, of the faculty, or of off-campus groups, this being the responsibility of the Main Library at this University.

The Undergraduate Library will meet the library needs of General College students (i.e., 1st and 2nd year undergraduates) completely. In addition this library will meet all except specialized requirements of 3rd or 4th year undergraduates. These upperclass students will be encouraged to make increasing use of the Main Library as they progress in their academic maturity and specialization.

III. STATEMENT OF LIBRARY OBJECTIVES

Because the functions of the library determine the character of the book collection it is essential to know precisely what these functions are. The conscious objectives of the Undergraduate Library, therefore, are:

A.   To support the undergraduate curriculum with adequate materials in those subjects taught by the College. This involves supplying (1) required reading for courses, often in multiple copies; (2) supplementary and ancillary reading for courses; and (3) a basic reference collection.

B.   To provide a basic collection aimed at the development of the "humane," the "liberally educated" person, apart from curriculum requirements. This involves (1) a collection of standard authors and works; (2) a representative collection of the best modern fiction and non-fiction, and (3) a small collection of outstanding current periodicals and back files.

C.   To encourage the habits of browsing and independent reading and to foster among undergraduates a love of books by providing an interesting collection of useful books in utmost accessibility.

IV. STATEMENT OF STANDARDS AND CRITERIA OF SELECTION

The following criteria should be observed in the selection of books for the Undergraduate Library.

A. Materials acquired should meet high standards of quality in content, expression, and format.

B. Books selected must be of _value_ to the undergraduate at this University either as required or supplementary reading for courses or as fulfilling the general aims of a liberal education.

C. Only those works will be acquired whose level of maturity and specialization is such as to make them serviceable to the needs of the undergraduate student. This criterion is intended to exclude the more abstruse and specialized books whose level of treatment is beyond the academic maturity of the undergraduate.

D. Only those books will be retained in the Undergraduate Library collection which are actively _used_ by undergraduates and the factor of _potentiality of use_ must be a criterion in the selection of books for this library. The Undergraduate Library will in no way be a storage or research collection, but will be a working collection from which books infrequently used will be eliminated.

E. Out of date works will also be eliminated from the collection. Thus books selected for the Undergraduate Library should be the _latest and the best works_ available in each field, the word "best" always being interpreted as best for the undergraduate level and not necessarily the most scholarly or definitive.

F. The most reliable editions of standard works should be selected against the criteria of completeness, quality of editing and readability (modern spelling, size of type, quality of paper)--again, not necessarily the most scholarly. For most undergraduate purposes a well edited reprint of the _Canterbury Tales_ would be of more value than would the eight volume variorum edition.

G. Books selected should be in the English language except for basic collections of recognized and representative literary classics of foreign literatures taught on the undergraduate level at this University. French, Spanish, and German literatures should be emphasized. Italian, Russian, Portuguese, Greek and Latin literatures should be represented only by the literary classics of each language.

V. STATEMENT OF LIMITING FACTORS AND SPECIALIZED CATEGORIES

The following specialized categories will be dealt with according to the policies noted:

A. _Maps:_ Maps are not acquired except those in standard atlases and gazetteers for reference purposes.

B. _Pictures:_ are not acquired.

C. <u>Federal, state, city and local documents</u>: are not acquired except for a very few that are valuable for basic reference purposes (e.g., <u>The Congressional Directory</u>).

D. <u>Microfilm, microcards, etc.</u>: are not acquired.

E. <u>Disk and tape recordings</u>: Musical recordings are not acquired. Literary, dramatic, and documentary spoken-word recordings are acquired if they meet the basic criterion of value to the undergraduate.

F. <u>Rare books</u>: are not acquired.

G. <u>Textbooks</u>: are not normally acquired unless they cover an area of interest to undergraduates for which there is no other general material available.

H. <u>Newspapers</u>: For the present no newspapers will be acquired except for the <u>New York Times</u> and <u>Raleigh News and Observer</u>.

I. <u>Periodicals and serials</u>: Only those periodicals and serials are subscribed to which meet the primary criterion of value to the undergraduate and the ancillary criterion of active use by the undergraduate. A smaller, highly selected number of periodicals are bound and retained by the Undergraduate Library, these being determined by their outstanding nature and coverage by indexes often used by undergraduates.

J. <u>Musical scores</u>: are not acquired.

K. <u>Gifts</u>: the selection of materials from books received as gifts by the library will be governed by the same criteria that govern the selection of new purchases.

The Undergraduate Library book collection should be developed in size roughly along the lines outlined in the "Projected Profile" in the Appendix since this configuration of the size of the various collections best meets and supports the University's emphases in its undergraduate curriculum program at the present time. As the emphases change, so should the strengths of the book collection change to conform to those of the undergraduate curriculum.

The collection will be well-rounded only in the sense that it adequately meets and supports these curriculum emphases. It will not be well-rounded in the sense that the collection will have material on all subjects in equal intensity of coverage whether or not there are groups in the library's clientele interested in the various subjects. That is, the library collection does <u>not</u> have any needs of its own apart from the needs of the clientele which it serves.

In the concept of the distinction of several levels of intensity or coverage applicable to building a library collection, the following levels should be observed:

A. At the levels of <u>total coverage</u>, <u>advanced research coverage</u>, and <u>wide coverage</u>, no subject shall be so represented in the collection.

B. At the level of <u>survey coverage</u>, recognized standard works in English (or exceptionally in French, German, Spanish) are collected which summarize the state of knowledge for some broader subject area. However, no attempt at completeness shall be made, and survey coverage will vary in intensity concurrent with the intensity of curriculum coverage of these areas. Thus, History and Literature will comprise half the collection, and works in the Social Sciences will be the third largest segment of the collection (62 per cent of the undergraduates major in one of the 3 fields). At 8,000 volumes the category of biography is the 4th largest because it cuts across all other fields. The pure sciences (500's in the classification) will be represented by a collection of 6,000 volumes to provide a good, elementary science collection for the use of science concentrators as well as others.

Below this level the collections will include only the most standard and useful works in any given area because these areas are not of major curriculum interest at the undergraduate level in this university or because most undergraduate needs are met by the departmental libraries in these areas. They include Journalism, Religion, philosophy, and linguistics (respectively, 4 per cent, 1 per cent, 3 per cent, and 3 per cent of undergraduate majors), the applied sciences (4 per cent), and art (5 per cent of undergraduate majors).

C. At the level of <u>recreational reading</u>, a small number of items will be added to the collection (practically all of them in English), preferably those which have some literary merit or otherwise transcend the merely ephemeral. In this category may be classed: books on sports and hobbies, modern fiction other than recognized standard authors, recreational material, non-fiction of current interest, etc. This reading material should be the best of its kind that can be selected.

Reprinted by Permission of the University of North Carolina Library, D. W. Schneider, Undergraduate Librarian.

PUBLIC LIBRARIES

Akron Public Library
Akron, Ohio
Second Edition, 1964

MATERIALS SELECTION POLICY

I.   OBJECTIVES OF THE LIBRARY

The primary objective of the Library is to provide and organize significant books and other printed or recorded materials, and to give guidance in their use; to help people in their search for greater understanding, in their quest for reliable information, in their exploration of a more secure and creative pattern for living.

The Akron Public Library, as a multi-purpose organization, serves the whole man. To develop his many interests the library provides for his cultural, informational, and recreational needs.

Work with children shares the major objectives of the Library. Its aim is to extend, cultivate, and encourage life-long education, and to promote voluntary, individual enjoyment of reading by children through use of public library resources.

The Library has a special responsibility in serving the educational needs of individuals and groups in the community. As part of this program the Library provides:

A.   Expertly selected books and other materials for use in development and enrichment of the human spirit.

B.   Advice and guidance in the use of these materials.

C.   Information and research services to aid in the search for knowledge and learning.

D.   Cooperation with groups and agencies in the community in stimulating education and cultural activities.

E.   Sponsorship of discussion groups, institutes, and film forums to encourage continuing learning through use of books and other materials.

Its task is to provide the means by which men and women can get a clearer conception and keener grasp of the problems that confront them.

II.   BASIC STANDARDS OF SELECTION

In developing the standards for selecting materials, the library follows those set by Public Library Service: guide to evaluation with minimum standards:*

"Within standards of purpose and quality, collections should be built to meet the needs and interests of people. Public libraries exist to serve their constituents. Materials are added because they

---

*American Library Association, 1956.

serve agreed purposes, meet quality standards, and are of interest to local readers and to local organizations. Selection follows from the conscious study of the needs of various groups--children, businessmen, gardeners, music-lovers, to name only a few. Sensitivity to interests, early recognition of needs before they are clearly expressed, and catholicity of contact and viewpoint mark the librarian who keeps the collection in tune with its owners. Selection must go beyond the requests of particular groups who have come to use the library regularly, and reach out to segments in the population which do not as readily turn to this facility."

In order to build this kind of a collection "continuous and periodic study of its community . . . to know people, groups, and institutions thoroughly, and to keep up with developments and changes" is very important in the job of selecting materials. Each agency of the library should participate in community activities in its area in order to keep in close and continuous touch with its needs. This gives vitality, purpose, and relevancy to the selection of materials.

III. CRITERIA FOR SELECTION OF MATERIALS

    A. Materials should meet high standards of quality in content, expression and format.

    B. The content should be timely, timeless, authoritative, and significant in subject matter.

    C. It should be of immediate or anticipated interest to individuals or to the community.

    D. It should include the widest possible subject coverage consistent with the needs in the community.

    E. It should meet the standards of acceptability as to accuracy, effective expression, significance of subject, sincerity, and responsibility of opinion.

    F. It should meet standards of physical and technical excellence.

IV. ADULT MATERIALS SELECTION POLICY

Since the Library's primary function is to contribute to the growth and maturity of people, the art of selection is designed to obtain books and other materials to further the Library's program of providing inspiration, recreation, and information. The Library provides fundamental, significant, and standard items in a wide variety of fields, including the sciences, the arts and the humanities.

In carrying out these objectives these factors are of importance:
(1) Interests existing in the community, either organized or individual.
(2) Needs of age groups such as young people, the aged and/or others.
(3) Flexibility to meet and satisfy new and changing community interests and needs.
(4) Coverage needed in the light of the limitations in the budget.
(5) Availability of materials in other libraries in this and nearby communities.
(6) The need to preserve publications of local authors and material on local history.

A. Books--General

In books for general reading, selection depends upon the ability and authority of the author, importance of the subject matter, needs, price, and availability of material in the region. The Library considers readability, popular appeal, quality of writing, and soundness of author's attitude and approach.

B. Fiction

In selecting fiction, the primary factors are honesty and sincerity of approach, literary quality, and good taste. The book is judged by the author's purpose and his ability to accomplish it. The Library buys distinguished and important fiction titles; it also selects those which are competent, popular, and experimental. Where opinions of reviewers differ, the book is given special study.

C. Subject Fields

In subject fields selection is based upon authority, accuracy, up-to-dateness, and the honesty and integrity of the author. Scholarly and highly specialized materials are purchased as needs and budget justify.

Books on issues of current interest, which may be of temporary value, are purchased if timeliness gives them relevance and importance.

Books having potential future value, for which immediate demand is small, are often purchased.

The Library rarely buys courses of study and textbooks adopted in the community and only if the material is not available in any other form. The Library does provide simple and introductory materials for adults who wish to pursue independent study.

D. Student Use

In providing materials for student use the Library's function is to serve a wide variety of interests and a diversified clientele. It does not provide multiple copies of individual books for student assignments, nor can it duplicate subject materials extensively (either in circulating or reference books) as a result of class assignment demands.

E. Reference Materials

In technical and reference books, subject value is stressed. In special fields such as rubber and plastics almost all materials are purchased even if mediocre in quality of writing. In other subject fields the outstanding and significant contributions are purchased. Practical books, as well as scientific, are included in the collection. The interests and needs of the community, anticipated when possible, are the basis for much of the selection.

The purchase of expensive books, trade directories, and financial services is determined by the cost of the materials, their availability in the area, and their relative importance in the collection.

F. Books in Foreign Languages

The Library's book collection includes over thirty foreign languages with major emphasis on French, German, Italian, Spanish and Russian. With the exception of certain subjects, particularly in art and science, the books are shelved together under the language. Books for the foreign languages collection are selected to provide the following types of materials:

1. Classics in the original language.

2. Works of significant authors, past and present.

3. Beginning reading books for those learning the language.

4. Standard and special books, such as cookbooks and Bibles.

5. American classics and books concerning American culture, literature and history translated into foreign languages.

Gift books in a foreign language are accepted after careful investigation of the source, authority, point of view and need.

One of the chief sources used for selection of books "in foreign" languages is the A.L.A. Booklist.

G. Pamphlet Material

Selection of pamphlets follows the general policy outlined for other materials. Since this material is inexpensive and frequently free, useful pamphlets are duplicated at small cost. These serve as supplements to the book materials.

Since many pamphlets are issued for propaganda or advertising purposes, it is important that they be selected with great care. A balance of viewpoints on controversial subjects is the aim; inflammatory and emotional treatment is avoided. Pamphlets which contain advertising that distorts facts, intrudes commercial messages unduly or contains misleading statements, are not added to the collection. Pamphlet material to be acceptable should always have the issuing agency, be it publisher and/or organization, clearly identified.

H. Paperbacks

The same standards for selection are applied to paperbacks as to other materials. The original copy of a book is usually bought in hard cover, if available. Paperbacks, however, are purchased if:

1. There is great demand for a title.

2. No other edition is available.

3. If it is a title which has only occasional or temporary interest.

4. If original titles appear only in this form.

Branch libraries buy paper-bound titles that are in Main Library Collection. Paperbacks are carefully examined to make sure the text is complete and unabridged, that translations and illustrations are of acceptable quality.

The paperback collections (uncataloged) in Main and the Branches are primarily duplicate collections.

I. Periodicals

Periodicals are purchased to keep the Library collection up-to-date on current issues, to provide material not yet in book form, for reference work, and general reading. Principles governing selection are: community interests, accuracy and objectivity, accessibility of content through indexes, need in reference work, representation of variety of points of view, and price.

The selection of periodicals is reviewed annually in preparing the list for next year's subscriptions.

The Library evaluates all new magazines, especially those listed in Readers' Guide . . . with the purpose of adding to the periodical list. A file of rejected periodicals is kept which includes a sample of the magazine and the reason for the rejection.

A duplicate collection of magazines is available for circulation. Selection is based upon: balance of points of view and frequency of request.

J. Newspapers

The Library selects representative newspapers of leading cities, and those which contain outstanding or significant contributions to national thinking. Cities are chosen according to size, area represented, and geographical location. Microfilm editions of a few newspapers are maintained because of their importance as permanent reference material. All newspapers published in Summit County are purchased as sources of local information.

Newspapers for branches are bought or accepted as gifts in accordance with the needs of the patrons in the individual agency. Branches select newspapers from those approved at Main, depending on space and budget.

K. Picture Files

The Picture Files consist of prints, post cards, reproductions and magazine illustrations. The selection is based upon the significance and importance of the material, known present and possible future needs, authority of printmaker, clarity of reproduction, level of quality, fidelity of color, and historical accuracy.

The obvious and prettified are avoided. The scope is wide to cover the variety of uses.

A special file on the fine arts and local historical material includes reproductions of original drawings, post cards and photographs.

V.   CONTROVERSIAL MATERIALS

The overall purpose of a book is the chief criterion of selection. Books which are strictly pornographic, the dominant purpose of which is to appeal to the prurient interest, are eliminated. Books which contain coarse language or frank treatments of certain situations which may be objectionable to some people are often included, if, in the opinion of the librarians, the author is sincere in what he is trying to portray. The Library has a responsibility to protect the rights of mature or sophisticated readers.

The Library recognizes its responsibility in having available a representative selection of books on subjects of interest to its readers, including materials on various sides of controversial questions. In an endeavor to provide material which will enable the citizen to make up his own mind about controversial subjects, the Library will provide frankly argumentative works representing a variety of conflicting viewpoints toward a subject of this nature. Titles are selected on the basis of the content as a whole and without regard to the personal history of the author. In the case of controversial questions, variety and balance of opinion are sought whenever available. The Library provides a resource where individuals can examine issues freely and make their own decision.

It should be clearly understood and emphasized that the Library does not endorse all the opinions expressed in the materials which are stocked. Indeed, since books often hold diametrically opposite views, this would be impossible.

NOTE: Occasionally, for special reasons, books with extreme points of view or language, which do not meet our standards for objectivity or good taste, may be acquired but not assigned to the public shelves. Books which are extremely liable to theft or mutilation are also kept from the open shelves for that reason.

A.   Policy Statement Regarding United Nations

The Board of Trustees of the Library set the policy relative to the United Nations by the following statement adopted at a meeting on November 16, 1953.

"The Public Library is an educational institution whose major responsibility is to collect, organize and lend printed material on all subjects. Where different opinions occur on any topic, it is the duty of the library, within the limits of its resources, to represent all points of view. In controversial questions the staff in their official capacities should maintain an impartial position.

"There are certain questions, however, which are not controversial such as the inalienable rights to freedom and to the franchise and the responsibility of loyal citizens to be informed on the problems of the day.

"The right of free citizens to strive for world peace through negotiation and association has likewise been widely accepted by our people. Since membership in the U.N. has been approved by an overwhelming majority in Congress and since, as a result, our own government has become a very important member of the United Nations, the Library regards it as a duty to encourage its patrons to read, study, and discuss all phases of its structure and activities."

51

VI. SEX EDUCATION

It is part of the function of the Library to provide, in adequate quantity for lay readers, general books on sex which are well balanced, authoritative, sound, up-to-date, and scientific in treatment. Scientific and technical works written for specialists usually do not come within the scope of the Library's collection. Materials are provided which are adapted to several levels of educational background and reading ability as well as to differing social and religious beliefs.

VII. SEMI- AND PSEUDO-SCIENTIFIC MATERIAL

Special care is taken in the selection of books in those borderline areas in which subject matter or treatment is not recognized by reputable scientific authority. Careful examination of such books rules out those which are presented as scientifically accurate but are not. In doubtful cases, it is necessary to wait for authoritative reviews or to consult experts in the field.

Books catering to morbid interests, the esoteric, sensational, the rabidly reformist, are rarely added. Material on such subjects as alcohol, tobacco, and food fads are scrutinized for reliability and objective presentation.

Books by well-established authors and scientists who hold ideas which may be extreme in concept may be bought when the author's prominence makes his ideas of general intellectual interest. The reputation of the author, the tone of his work, and the method of handling his subject are deciding factors.

VIII. PHONOGRAPH RECORDS

A. Purpose of the Record Section

The purpose of the Record Section is to provide significant materials in recorded form for the use of individuals and groups in the community.

B. Scope of Materials

Musical records constitute the bulk of the collection. They are selected to cover a wide variety of music, excluding the ephemeral.

Significant speeches, plays, poetry, and short stories are purchased. Recordings of various sounds, records to be used as bases for group discussion, for learning a language, and those suitable for individual study in a variety of subjects are included.

C. Record Speeds

Most records bought are 33-1/3 rpm's, although a 78 rpm is added if that is the only speed on which the material needed is available. Other record speeds are not added to the collection.

D. Record Selection Policy

Certain works are bought because they are performed by a particular musical artist, conductor, or literary personage. In musical selections, several different records of a particular work are purchased in order to have different interpretations. In literary recordings there is little duplication of titles by different readers or speakers.

Records are selected with these points in mind:

1. Excellence of interpretation and technique.

2. Importance of artist.

3. Technical quality of the recording.

4. Need for material based on public request and present holdings.

5. Price.

E. Duplication

Eight to ten reserves for a record indicates that a duplicate record should be ordered, although, as in books, quality of the recording, timeliness or permanence of the requests, and cost are factors in the decision.

Most records are bought initially in duplicate, because many important records are available for only a brief time.

F. Discarding

Discarding of records is a necessity because of wear or damage to the disc. The decision is then made whether to replace with the same recording, or to buy the same work by a different artist.

IX. EDUCATIONAL FILMS

A. Films and Filmstrips

The Library collection consists of educational and documentary films (16 mm sound) and 35 mm filmstrips. Entertainment films such as animated comic cartoons, westerns, and Hollywood feature films are not ordinarily added to the collection. The films are usually bought in black and white; films are purchased in color when color is important in the presentation of the material or is not available otherwise.

B. Purpose of the Film Collection

The purpose of the Library's film collection is to provide significant materials in audio-visual form. Since films are primarily used in groups, the Library selects films that will fill the educational, cultural and aesthetic needs of groups in the community.

C. Scope of Selection

The Library buys films for use in informal adult education, for children's programs, for young people's discussion groups. It does not buy films especially designed for school curriculum purposes, or highly specialized or technical films.

D. Film Selection Policy

Selection policy for films follows the principles set up for other materials in the Library. Since audio-visual presentation has such a strong emotional impact in imparting ideas and attitudes, it needs special care in evaluation.

All films and filmstrips are previewed before they are purchased or accepted as a gift or on long loan. Factors important in the selection of films are:

1. Content of the film should have validity and significance; be accurate as to facts, reliable in presentation.

2. Method of presentation should interpret and illuminate the material.

3. Aesthetic quality of the film should be high, with imaginative photography and meaningful music.

4. Technical quality should include clear sound, effective photography and, if in color, good quality of color.

E. Children's Films

The same criteria will be applied to children's films but with special emphasis on simple, sensitive and imaginative presentation; narration that holds the interest of the child by adding fun and fancy without patronizing. Children's films should avoid cuteness, adult humor, and talking down to the child. The same principles apply to the selection of filmstrips.

F. Religious Films

The film collection includes films and filmstrips on comparative religion, those explaining various religious practices, art films that depict the life of Christ and historical films about the Holy Land. The Library does not purchase Bible stories or missionary films, since these are usually denominational in nature.

G. Sponsored Films

Sponsored films are those produced by or for a company, organization, society or individual to promote directly or indirectly activities or philosophy of such groups.

The inclusion of a sponsored film can be justified in terms of bringing the group a valuable experience that would otherwise be denied them.

These additional points are considered in evaluating sponsored films:

1. The sponsoring agency be clearly identified.

2. The content be factual--not distorted or simplified to prove a point.

3. The sponsor's aims must be sufficiently in accord with the objectives of the Library to justify inclusion of the film.

4. The advertising, hidden or direct, or any special pleading or point of view is fully evaluated before the film is accepted for deposit.

H. Film Duplication, Replacement and Discard

Films are rarely duplicated due to their cost, the limited loan period, and limitations of budget. But in case of special and legitimate need the Library will purchase or accept a gift of duplicate prints.

When the condition of a film makes it necessary to replace, careful consideration is given to its continuing value in relation to new material, revised edition and cost.

The film collection is constantly previewed for obsolete and dated material.

X.   MICROFILM

Microfilm editions of newspapers and periodicals are purchased to provide permanent reference materials. The quality of the paper, bulk of material when bound, and frequency of use are the considerations. Since it is necessary to subscribe to regular editions to be eligible to purchase microfilm editions, the choice is between binding and purchasing a microfilm edition. Valuable but infrequently used periodicals, bulky newspapers of permanent value (indexed or of local importance) and periodicals whose paper will disintegrate rapidly are purchased on microfilm as funds permit. Indexed periodicals of permanent value because of content and local interest illustrations are bound. Occasionally important books or other materials not available in original form (such as old census reports) are purchased on microfilm.

XI.   MAPS

The Library maintains a representative collection of maps of all countries in atlas form. Criteria for selection are accuracy, completeness, and timeliness. Free and inexpensive sheet maps, including street maps of major cities, are acquired to supplement those in books and atlases.

Historical maps of Ohio and Summit County are purchased, depending upon availability and cost.

The Library is a depository for the topographic maps of the Geological Survey of U.S. Government.

XII.   GOVERNMENT PUBLICATIONS

The Library is a selective depository for U.S. Government publications. Items offered to the Library (both original and new items) are evaluated by the division head in whose subject field they fall. Selections are reviewed at intervals so that little used items may be cancelled and those found to be needed may be added. In addition, non-depository material is selected on the same basis as books and pamphlets, and purchased or obtained gratis.

The Library is a depository for all publications of the Ohio Geological Survey and a selective depository for Ohio publications. Special attention is given to maintaining annual reports, statistical material, directories, and material of local importance. Publications of other states are purchased or requested as gifts on a very limited basis, usually as pamphlets and by the application of the usual standards for these items. The same policy applies to Canadian, United Nations and foreign documents.

XIII. GIFTS

    A.   The Library accepts gifts of books, pamphlets, periodicals, films, phonograph records, etc., with the understanding that they will be added to the library collections only when needed. The same principles of selection applied to purchases are applied to gifts.

    B.   Some items are accepted as gifts although they ordinarily would not be purchased. These include denominational literature, privately printed verse and poetry, highly technical or literary material, or very expensive items of limited interest. Older items are sometimes accepted as replacements, although another copy might not be purchased.

    C.   Gifts are added to branch collections only if Main Library has a copy. Gifts of titles not in the library system are placed in Main Library, so that all agencies have ready access to them. If requirement of the gift is that it be located in a specific agency, it may be borrowed from Main on indefinite loan.

XIV. DISCARDING

The Library maintains an active policy of withdrawal based on the elimination of unnecessary items, outdated material, books no longer of interest or in demand, duplicates, worn or mutilated copies. Frequency of circulation, community interest, and availability of newer and more valid materials are of prime consideration. Local history and material on local industry are an exception. Fiction, once popular but no longer in demand, is discarded, as are nonfiction books which were purchased to meet demands no longer existing.

In general, last copies of important books are retained at Main Library. Branches discard more freely and transfer to Main volumes of permanent value no longer in active use.

XV. DUPLICATION

Duplication of titles is determined by popularity, importance of the book and by budget. In general, Main Library duplicates on a basis of one copy for every five to eight reserves, while branches rarely duplicate unless eight to ten reserves are made. Material of special local interest or reference value is duplicated freely and immediately. Besides the mechanical rule of number of reserves, the following factors are considered:

    A.   The importance of the author or subject.

    B.   Continuing need for the material.

    C.   Budgetary limitations.

For filling reserves, paperback editions of highly popular material are bought. Pamphlets are duplicated if needed, because of their low cost and timeliness.

XVI. REPLACEMENT POLICY

Titles withdrawn by reason of condition, loss, or damage are considered for replacement. (Classics are replaced whenever possible in better format.) The same considerations applied in original selection apply to replacement. In addition, other factors must be considered:

A. The authority and importance of the author.

B. The value of the individual title, whether for literary quality, subject appeal, etc.

C. Availability of newer and better material in the field.

D. Timeliness of the material.

E. Requests for the title or subject.

F. Comparison with other books still in the Library.

XVII. BINDING AND REBINDING

The Library endeavors to bind, within budget limitations, any periodicals received which are of permanent or frequent reference value. Bound sets are usually available only at Main.

The choice of books for rebinding is made in accordance with the established policies of original selection, discard, and replacement. Factors for special consideration are:

A. Title is out of print and still useful.

B. Value of the title and possibility of replacement.

C. Physical condition.

D. Cost of rebinding versus cost of replacement.

E. Number of copies available.

Titles are ordinarily not rebound if:

A. Physical makeup, such as quality of paper, margins, illustrations, weight of paper, make binding expensive or destroy usefulness of the volume.

B. Condition is so poor, i.e., dirty, worn, cut or missing pages, crayon marks, mutilation, that rebinding will not be economically advisable.

C. The book has not been used or in demand. Usually ten years of non-use indicates discard rather than rebinding. For technical material five years may be sufficient unless of permanent or historical value.

D. Replacement costs are less than rebinding cost.

E. Better or newer material is currently available.

XVIII. YOUNG ADULTS MATERIALS SELECTION POLICY

The selection policy for Young Adults in the Akron Public Library shares the major objectives of the Library. The specific aims of this collection are to recognize the needs and interest of Young Adults; to promote books as a media of interpreting these needs and interest on both informational and recreational levels.

The purpose of this special collection is to provide books for individual reading that will stimulate, delight and encourage an interest in and curiosity about themselves and the world they live in. It should help increase their knowledge and broaden their vision; it should help them understand and accept the responsibility of becoming mature individuals.

A. Characteristics of the Young Adult

Young Adults in the Akron Public Library are the age group from approximately 14 to 18 years of age, or high school levels approximately 9th through the 12th grades.

Since this is a period of rapid physical, mental and emotional growth, it is also a period of changing ideas and attitudes. These Young Adults possess certain dominant characteristics which the Library recognizes and keeps foremost in selecting books and materials for them. Some of these are: awareness of self, uncertainty, hero worship, clannishness, and conformity, worry about the future, and evaluating of beliefs.

B. Criteria for Selection of Young Adult Materials

1. Materials should meet high standards of quality in content, expression, and format.

2. The content should be timely, authoritative, and significant in subject matter.

3. It should include the widest possible subject coverage to meet the needs and interest of Young Adults, and to encourage a catholicity of taste.

4. It should meet the highest possible standards of accuracy, effective expression, significance of subject, sincerity, and responsibility of opinion.

5. It should meet the standards of physical and technical excellence.

6. It should provide books for the actual and the potential reader, recognizing the wide range of reading levels and the variety of interests.

C. Selection of Materials for Young Adults

The wide differences of needs and interests as well as differences in the reading ability of Young Adults are of primary importance in the selection of materials. In books for general reading, selection depends upon the ability and authority of the author, importance of the subject matter, needs of the collection, and the price. The Library considers readability, popular appeal, quality of writing, and soundness of author's attitude and approach.

D. Selection of Fiction

Fiction titles in the Young Adult Collection are selected from both the adult and the young peoples fields. Occasionally books from the

Juvenile field are selected if the format is suitable and makes a significant contribution to their understanding.

Adult titles are selected for their readability and interest; in these are titles which present new ideas and develop awareness of new fields.

Classics in attractive binding and typography are an important part of this collection.

E. Standards to Be Met for All Fiction:

1. That they give an honest picture of the world, both teenage and adult.

2. That the characters are real and respond to life situations.

3. That the literary quality be acceptable with the language appropriate to the story.

4. That the codes of conduct and morals be valid, understandable and without sentimentality or preaching.

F. Standards of Selection of Nonfiction

Selection of nonfiction is based upon authority, accuracy, timeliness and the honesty and integrity of the author.

Nonfiction titles in subjects of specific interest to the Young Adult are purchased.

This collection provides materials on opposing sides of controversial questions to develop critical reading and thinking.

It provides poetry, drama and music to encourage an interest in the humanities. To broaden reading interests, simple but accurate, books in such areas as the sciences and the social sciences are included.

G. Periodicals and Pamphlets

Periodicals and pamphlets dealing specifically with the Young Adult's interest and problems are included in the Young Adult Collection. The standards for these follows the general policy outlined for other materials.

H. Reference Materials

In general, the reference needs of the Young Adults are to be met by the Adult Collection.

I. Other Materials

The film collection in the Group Service Department includes films on young people's problems. These are selected with a view to the interests and needs of Young Adults.

The Record Department, with music and spoken words records, is open to Young Adults.

J. Student Use

   The Library provides materials for student use in the general collection. The Young Adult Collection is primarily for recreational reading and makes no attempt to provide material for class assignments.

SELECTION POLICIES FOR CHILDREN'S MATERIALS

1963

I. GENERAL OBJECTIVE

   The Library's primary objective is to inculcate in children an enjoyment and appreciation of reading for pleasure and information by selecting materials which will appeal to their sense of wonder, develop an awareness of the world around them, widen their mental horizons, aid in the growth of their literary and esthetic tastes and contribute to their growth as intelligent world citizens.

II. TYPES OF READERS SERVED

   Books covering a wide range in age and mental development are selected for children from pre-school age through eighth grade. Books of interest to parents and other adults working with children are also included.

III. TYPES OF COLLECTIONS

   A. Main Children's Room

      1. General Collection

         At least one copy of each title approved for juvenile purchase is included in this collection. Books whose value is permanent in standard children's collections, but whose current use is slight, are retained in this collection and may be bought by other agencies if the need arises.

         Titles, ordinarily considered adult, but suitable for children, are purchased by the Main Children's Room to help relieve the demand for special subject materials in the adult subject departments, and to make the juvenile collection largely self-sufficient in meeting the needs of children in the subject fields. The extent to which this policy can be carried out is determined by the juvenile book budget.

      2. Resource--Non-circulating Collection

         a. Historical
         b. Eastman
         c. Fine Editions
         d. Book Fair
         e. Award Books

B.   Branch Collections

Branch collections consist of approved books selected according to the interests of the communities served. Effort is made to maintain a balanced and representative collection in all agencies.

IV.   GENERAL PRINCIPLES OF SELECTION

A.   Fiction

Each book of fiction is considered for its individual merit. Stories are selected which have well-knit plots, fresh approach, strong characterization and good literary style. They must be sincere in intent, wholesome in tone and stretch the imagination. Life should be portrayed in a plausible way, emphasizing positive attitudes of kindness, tolerance, honesty, love of one's fellowman and acceptance of responsibility. Over-emphasis of cruelty, violence, intolerance, racial prejudice and distortions of life must be avoided.

Children's classics are retained and current books purchased even though they may contain words or phrases that are usually unacceptable, provided they are needed to portray a period, character or incident with sincerity and truth and not for the purpose of derision or sensationalism.

Some books may be added which do not meet the highest literary standards if their good points over-shadow the weak ones. They are selected because they fulfill an emotional need or serve as stepping stones to better reading.

B.   Non-fiction

Non-fiction books selected must be accurate, up-to-date, unbiased and fulfill the need for maintaining a balanced collection.

The subject interest and vocabulary must be suitable to the knowledge level of those for whom it is intended. The facts must be presented in a straight-forward, understandable and precise manner.

C.   Format

In order to develop enjoyment in reading, consideration is given to the general physical make-up of the book. Illustrations, text, type, binding and paper should combine to produce an integrated and attractive format.

V.   REFERENCE COLLECTIONS

Encyclopedias, dictionaries, atlases and other general reference materials are included in all of the juvenile collections--Main Children's Room and the Branches. They are selected according to the basic selection policy for all non-fiction.

VI.   BOOKS FOR PARENTS AND ADULTS WORKING WITH CHILDREN

A limited collection of adult and juvenile books is maintained for use of parents, teachers and other adults working with children.

VII.   SERIES BOOKS

Series books are purchased with care. Each book is evaluated separately.
Books with hackneyed plots, wooden style and lifeless characters are rejected.
For these reasons, some series books do not appear on library shelves.

VIII.   CLASSICS

Effort is made to maintain a representative collection of the classics in all
agencies. The Main Children's Room endeavors to maintain a representative collection of the varied editions that meet literary standards.

IX.   ADAPTATIONS AND ABRIDGEMENTS

Adaptations and abridgements are carefully compared with the originals and
only those which retain the spirit of the originals are purchased.

X.   TEXTBOOKS

Textbooks are purchased only if the information fulfills needs not met by the
rest of the collection and is not available from any other source. Readers adopted
by the local school systems are not purchased. Other readers for the first three
grades are purchased sparingly as the library does not consider the teaching of reading skills its responsibility. The readers purchased are mainly to supplement the
school texts and create a delight in reading for children of limited reading ability.

XI.   EASY READING BOOKS

Picture books and other easy reading books are purchased extensively to create
satisfaction and delight in reading in the formative years. These are selected by the
same basic selection policy as other fiction.

XII.   FOREIGN LANGUAGE BOOKS

Books in foreign languages are purchased to meet the needs of the community.
A collection of books representing the best literature for children of foreign countries is maintained in Main Children's Room. Books for the purpose of learning a
foreign language are bought sparingly due to the constant change in demand.

XIII.   FOLK AND FAIRY TALES

In belief that the folk and fairy tales frequently form the basis of a child's
literary heritage in addition to advancing an understanding of the world's peoples,
the library makes an effort to maintain a representative collection in all branches
as well as the Main Children's Room. Effort is also made to maintain in the Main
Children's Room as many titles as possible to provide a complete coverage of the
Folk Literature of the world in a variety of approved editions. (Eastman Collection).

XIV.   RELIGION

Realizing that the spiritual development of children is important, the library
supplies certain books on religious subjects--Bible stories, lives of the Saints,
biographies of religious characters and books on the customs and traditions of the

great religious faiths. Books that promote specific doctrines are not purchased from library funds or approved for the public library collection.

XV. SEX

The library provides books which explain the processes of human physical development and reproduction in a simple, dignified and scientific manner.

XVI. PERIODICALS

A dearth of satisfactory periodicals for children limits the number of approved titles accepted. An annual list of approved periodicals is issued from the Co-ordinator's Office and only those on this list may be added to any agency.

XVII. PICTURE COLLECTIONS

The Main Children's Room maintains a limited collection of pictures on subjects of particular interest to children. They are selected for accurate, clear detail from free or inexpensive materials, discarded books and magazines. All advertising material used is carefully examined for bias and inaccuracies. In branches where picture collections are maintained, the same standards are applied.

XVIII. PAMPHLETS

Pamphlets are purchased to supply materials in fields in which few books are available and to supplement the book stock in other fields. Of ephemeral value, these may be easily discarded when better or more recent material becomes available. Pamphlets are selected which are within the reading abilities of the children. For other criteria in selecting pamphlets see Adult Materials Selection Policies-- Pamphlets.

XIX. LOCAL AUTHORS

Books by local authors are purchased only if they meet the standards of the basic book selection policy or fill a particular need not met by other available resources.

XX. DUPLICATION

Duplication is largely contingent upon the size of the book fund and the demand of the children for the material, always keeping in mind the state of the collection as a whole and the comparison of the particular book with other titles already in the collection. No effort is made to provide multiple duplication to fulfill the needs of mass assignments of the local schools.

Because of the overlapping of interests and reading abilities of some children some adult titles approved by the evaluation committee are duplicated in the juvenile collections. The decision for such duplication is left to the discretion of the branch and children's librarians with the advice, if necessary, of the Coordinator.

XXI. REPLACEMENTS

A committee of children's librarians are constantly reevaluating the collection so that only books worthy of continued use are replaced and duplicated in the agencies. A basic replacement list forms the basis from which books are ordered by all agencies. Before the last copy of any juvenile title is discarded from any agency and the agency does not intend to replace it, the title is approved for discard by the Coordinator.

Every effort is made to keep in the collection certain standard juvenile titles, although, in some cases, if the title is available in the Main Children's Room, it will not be replaced in a branch.

XXII. NEW TITLES

The library receives a number of copies of juvenile titles from publishers and others are ordered on approval because of the reliability of the publisher, author, illustrator or the favorable inclusion in book reviewing periodicals make them seem worthy of examination.

Staff members are required to read and write reviews for as many new titles as possible. Staff reviews, along with reviews from professional sources such as Horn Book, School Library Journal and Booklist are used by the Book Selection Committee to determine which will be available for purchase. Debatable books are read by more than one person.

The Coordinator of Children's Services is responsible to the Head Librarian for the final selection of all children's books.

Subject to budget limitations, every effort is made to maintain a balanced and well rounded collection.

Reprinted by Permission of Akron Public Library, John H. Rebenack, Librarian.

Bedford Free Public Library
Bedford, Massachusetts
Revised January, 1971

MATERIALS SELECTION POLICY STATEMENT

I.   OBJECTIVES OF THE LIBRARY

The Bedford Free Public Library provides free service to all individuals in the community, both children and adults. Its objectives include the provision of expertly selected books and other materials to aid the individual in the pursuit of education, information, pleasure, or research, and in the creative use of leisure time.

To achieve these ends, the Library provides educational service to adults, seeking thereby to assist the individual in a continuing learning process. It also provides special service to children and young people and seeks to direct and stimulate these readers by offering them a carefully selected collection of books and skilled personal guidance.

The Library provides service to all, within the context of library objectives, regardless of race, creed, color, occupation, or financial position.

II.   RESPONSIBILITY FOR MATERIALS SELECTION

Ultimate responsibility for materials selection policy lies with the Board of Trustees. The Board of Trustees delegates to the Librarian the selection of library materials and the development of the collection.

III.   CRITERIA FOR SELECTION

The objective of selection is to collect those books and other library materials that will inform, entertain, and contribute to enrichment of mind and spirit.

Library materials are selected by the Librarian and staff. Competent reviewing media and basic lists of standard works are consulted as an aid in selection. Recommendations from the public are welcomed.

The Library will review decisions regarding specific materials upon written request. A form for this purpose is available at the circulation desk.

Basic to the Library's Materials Selection Policy is the Library Bill of Rights and the Freedom to Read Statement adopted by the Council of the American Library Association, which are appended.

Within standards of purpose and quality, the library's collections will be built to meet the needs and interests of the community.

Every book (or other library material) must meet such of the following criteria as are applicable to its inclusion in the collection:

A. Current usefulness or permanent value.

B. Authority and competence in presentation.

C. Importance as a record of the times.

D. Relation to the existing collection.

E. Relative importance in comparison with other works on the subject.

F. High standards of quality in content, format and binding.

IV. MATERIAL SELECTION FOR CHILDREN

The principles stated in the adult materials selection policy are applicable to the selection of materials for children. The Library co-operates with the school libraries so that the services of the two agencies may complement each other. The major function of the school library is to furnish curriculum-related materials. The public library seeks to provide a more comprehensive collection.

The children's collection is carefully selected for children of all ages, with emphasis on books, periodicals, records, etc., which stimulate imagination and help in the development of taste.

Materials for young people are selected to provide sound information and understanding of the world they live in.

V. THE USE OF THE LIBRARY'S MATERIALS

Library materials are not marked or identified to show approval or disapproval of the contents, and no book or other item is sequestered, except for the purpose of protecting it from injury or theft.

The use of rare and scholarly items of great value is controlled to the extent required to preserve them from harm.

Responsibility for the reading of children rests with their parents and legal guardians. Selection of materials for the adult collection is not restricted by the possibility that children may obtain materials their parents consider inappropriate.

VI. THE SCOPE OF THE COLLECTION

The Library seeks to draw upon the collections and resources of neighboring libraries and of the Eastern Regional Library System so as not unnecessarily to duplicate services and materials. Inter-library loan is used to secure from other libraries those specialized materials which are beyond the scope of the Library's collection.

Textbooks are not ordinarily purchased by the Library except in subject areas where material in another form is not conveniently available.

The Library acknowledges a particular interest in local and state history, and in the works of local authors. The Library will, however, apply the same standards of selection to the works of local authors as it does to other library materials.

VII. GIFTS

The Library welcomes gifts of books and other materials with the understanding that it will evaluate them in accordance with the criteria applied to purchased materials.

When the Library receives a cash gift for the purchase of memorial books or collections, the selection will be made by the Librarian in consultation with the donor. The name of the donor or person memorialized will be entered on the bookplate.

VIII. MAINTAINING THE COLLECTION

The same criteria will be used in "weeding" materials from the collection as are used in their acquisition. In order to maintain the collection in its most attractive and useful condition, the Librarian will use his judgment in removing from the collection materials which are no longer useful, or are not in a condition suitable for circulation. He will refurbish by repair or rebinding books which are deteriorating, whenever appropriate. Materials no longer useful to the Library may be given to other libraries or sold for the benefit of the Library.

IX. REVISION OF POLICY

This statement of policy will be revised as times and circumstances require.

Reprinted by Permission of Bedford Free Public Library, Mrs. Eleanor Arthur, Director.

Berkeley Public Library
Berkeley, California
Adopted 1963

BOOK SELECTION POLICY

I.   GENERAL OBJECTIVE

The objective of the Berkeley Public Library is to select, organize, preserve, and to make freely and easily available to the people of the community printed and other materials, within the limitations of space and budget, which will aid them in the pursuit of education, information, research, recreation, and in the creative use of leisure time. The goal of the Library is the maximum use of its collection by the greatest number of persons.

The Library seeks to promote endeavors which will stimulate and expand the reading interests of both children and adults and to coordinate this work with that of other educational, social, and cultural groups in the community in cooperative effort.

It is the responsibility of the Library to satisfy the diverse reading needs and interests of the residents of the community through the selection, acquisition, and organization of library materials and to provide skilled guidance in their use. This can be done by making known the resources of the Library through various activities and media within and outside the Library, and through utilization of the collection of the State Library and other library collections at its disposal.

In its selection of books and other materials, the Berkeley Public Library subscribes fully to the principles adopted in 1948 by the American Library Association in its Library Bill of Rights and endorses its stand that the freedom to read is essential to our democracy. It is the function and duty of the public library to provide the means, whenever possible, through which all persons may have free access to the thinking on all sides of all ideas.

Censorship of books, urged or practiced by volunteer arbiters of morals or political opinion, or by organizations which would establish a coercive concept of Americanism, must be challenged by libraries in maintenance of their responsibility to provide public information and enlightenment through the printed word.

II.   RESPONSIBILITY FOR SELECTION

Final responsibility for book selection rests with the City Librarian, who operates within the framework of policies determined by the Board of Library Trustees. However, the responsibility for initial selection of books and other materials is shared by every professional member of the staff, since no one person is omniscient nor fully qualified to determine the reading needs of all persons in all sections of the community. Suggestions from readers are always welcomed and given serious consideration.

III. CRITERIA OF SELECTION

A. Adult Non-Fiction

Chief points considered are readability of material, authenticity of factual matter presented, quality of writing, cost, format, existing Library holdings, and suitability of material to the community.

Non-fiction may be excluded for inaccurate information, lack of integrity, sensationalism, intent to incite hatred and intolerance, and text material of too limited or specialized a nature.

Titles are selected on the basis of the content as a whole and without regard to the personal history of the author. Important books of all persuasions should be carried. In no case, is any book included or excluded merely because of the race or nationality, or the political or religious views, of the writer.

In the case of controversial questions, variety and balance of opinion are sought whenever available.

B. Adult Fiction

Selection of adult fiction is made with reference to one or more of these criteria:

1. It should contribute positively to the individual's awareness of self, community, and social heritage.

2. It should contribute to the value of the library's collection as a whole by representing all types and styles of literature.

3. It should provide pleasure reading for recreation and the creative use of leisure time.

Serious works which present an honest aspect of life are not necessarily excluded for frankness of expression.

C. Children's Materials

The first objective in selecting children's materials is to encourage the child's joy in reading and in being read to.

Books are selected which offer adventures of mind and spirit to the growing child, cultivating an appreciation of literature both oral and written and encouraging the creative use of leisure time by inquiring minds. Special attention is given books of use and value to parents, teachers, and other adults working with children.

The public library does not provide basic texts or materials needed in quantity for school work. It accepts as its responsibility the providing of supplementary materials of varied kinds to enrich the resources available to the individual student and teacher.

Each book, old or new, is judged on its own merits and in its relation to the collection as a whole. To these ends, books selected are read, reviewed, and discussed by the staff's children's librarians prior to purchase.

D. Reference Materials

Factors considered in the selection of reference materials are authority, reliability, scope, treatment, arrangement, format, cost, and existing holdings.

E. Documents

The Library collects and preserves documents primarily of local importance, with emphasis upon those published by the municipal government of Berkeley, the cities and counties of the Bay Area, the State of California, and quasi-governmental agencies of local interest. U.S. documents of general interest are evaluated by the general criteria for adult non-fiction.

F. Magazines and Newspapers

Basic popular, general informational, and scholarly magazines are selected to supplement the book collection, bring book information up to date, and fill in those areas where book resources are weak, inferior or non-existent.

Newspapers are selected to meet reference and research needs of patrons, to provide current information, and to satisfy casual interest in current events. Local, national, and foreign newspapers are supplied upon sufficient demand and within budget and space limitations.

G. Non-Book Materials

The Library recognizes the importance of non-book materials both as a supplement to its book collection and to its concept of service.

Phonograph records representing classical, semi-classical, jazz, folk and related fields of music, as well as such non-musical recordings as poetry, plays, and speeches, are provided. Art reproductions are also available. Additional non-book materials may be supplied upon demand and within budget and space limitations.

IV. GIFTS

Gifts accepted by the Berkeley Public Library are judged upon the same bases as purchased materials. They are considered with the explicit understanding that such factors as duplication, lack of community interest, processing costs or inadequate shelf space may prevent their addition to the collection or permanent retention on the shelves. Gifts are accepted with the understanding that the Library, if it cannot use them, may at any time discard them in any way it sees fit.

Reprinted by Permission of Berkeley Public Library, Mr. Frank J. Dempsey, Director.

Evansville Public Library
Evansville, Indiana
Revised April, 1971

GENERAL LIBRARY MATERIALS SELECTION POLICY

POLICIES OF LIBRARY MATERIALS SELECTION
Approved by the Board of Trustees in August 1957

In our democracy, libraries are concerned with the preservation of American freedom through the development of informed and responsible citizens. To this end public libraries have the responsibility, as is appropriate:

(1) To provide materials that will enrich and support the varied interests, abilities, and maturity levels of the children, youth, and adults for whom they are selected.

(2) To provide materials for children, youth and adults that will stimulate growth in literary appreciation, in aesthetic values, in ethical standards, and in factual knowledge.

(3) To provide a background of information which will enable children, youth, and adults, as citizens, to make intelligent choices. Librarians do not necessarily endorse every idea contained in the materials they make available.

(4) To provide objective materials in the areas of opposing viewpoints and controversy, representing all sides of these areas, that as citizens they may develop the practice of logical, critical thinking and evaluation. In the case of children and youth, these materials should be chosen with careful consideration for their maturity level.

(5) To provide materials which are representative of the many religious, ethnic and cultural groups and their contributions to our American heritage.

(6) To place principle above personal opinion, reason above prejudice, and judgment above censorship (such as is urged or practiced by volunteer arbiters of morals or political opinion) in this selection of materials of the highest quality in order to assure an objective collection appropriate for the users of the library. Materials should be selected without regard to the personal characteristics of the author except where relevant to the content.

GENERAL LIBRARY MATERIALS SELECTION POLICY
Approved by the Board of Trustees in June 1960

In general only those books shall be purchased by the Library which, it is expected, will be used by the general public. If a title suggested for purchase is thought to be of use only to persons who already have their own library facilities, the title shall be referred to that library (e.g., the University Libraries, a parochial high school library, the Mead Johnson Library for a medical book, and the Vanderburgh County Law Library). Gift copies of such books may be accepted for inclusion in the Public Library collection.

STATEMENT ABOUT REQUESTS FOR THE WITHDRAWAL
OF A SPECIFIC TITLE IN THE LIBRARY CATALOG

Once a publication has been accepted as qualifying under the selection policies and rules of Evansville Public Libraries, it will not be removed at the request of those who disagree with it unless it can be shown to be in violation of these policies and rules.

BOOK AND PERIODICAL POLICIES
APPLIED TO VARIOUS FIELDS

Contents

I.   CONTROVERSIAL POLITICAL QUESTIONS
    (Adopted by the Board of Trustees, October 1963)

    A.   The basic book selection policy of this Library is to seek out and secure those materials which would enable any citizen to learn for himself what is to be said for and against any public question, within limits specified below. The purchase or acceptance of a particular book, pamphlet, magazine, film, or other item does not necessarily put the Library's stamp of approval on it. As a government body, the Library takes no sides on public questions. A book or other item is selected or rejected for inclusion in the Library's collection without regard to whether it agrees or disagrees with the opinions of any or all members of the staff on the merits of the question at issue. Once accepted, a book is not labeled or otherwise marked so as to prejudice a reader in advance as to its merits.

    B.   Materials on controversial political questions are to be considered critically in the following regards. The book should be at least reasonably well-written, it should represent a net addition to what the Library already has on the question, it should be written by an author who is known or thought to have some competence to discuss the question, and it should be at least a reasonably dispassionate statement of opinions or a reasonably accurate statement of facts. No book which is scurrilous, libelous, or marked by distortion of facts, suppression of truth, or extreme emotional imbalance will be approved for purchase or accepted as a gift. No book or other item will be purchased or accepted which specifically advocates and incites violence whether against individuals, groups, or institutions.

C. In considering doubtful cases of materials dealing with politically controversial questions, the Book Selection Committee should secure and consider all possible relevant information. It should examine a copy of the book in question, and secure opinions of other staff members, and of published reviews. In any case each work is to be considered by itself, and not be accepted or rejected solely because other works by the same author have been so treated. In turn, an author's work is to be judged solely on its own merits and not by his former or present political beliefs or affiliations.

D. Certain exceptions to these guide-lines are likely to occur. Some titles, which might otherwise be objectionable, have become classic statements or are of historical importance and should be made available, e.g., The Communist Manifesto and Hitler's Mein Kampf.

II. FICTION

The Library's collection includes representative novels of the past and present notable for literary quality and cultural value as well as biographical and historical novels, psychological novels, mystery, western, science fiction and other adventure novels and short stories. In order to serve the people of Evansville with their varying backgrounds, educations and tastes, the material chosen varies greatly. Novels are judged by the author's purpose and his success in achieving it. Structure and style must be considered. Our intention is to acquire fiction which is well written and based upon authentic human experience and to exclude weak, incompetent or cheap sentimental writing and the intentionally sensational, morbid and erotic. If the author is seriously trying to give an honest picture and if the book meets other standards, the library may buy it even though the author has felt it necessary to include a certain amount of vulgar language and frankness of detail in order to accomplish his purpose. In the selection of fiction titles the BSC looks for favorable critical reviews in reliable tools as Kirkus and Saturday Review.

A. Mystery Fiction (Adopted by the Board, October 1963)

1. Since this Library cannot and, for various reasons, should not buy all mystery fiction titles published, the following guidelines will be used to choose those titles whose purchase or rental will be allowed. These criteria are listed in order from the most general to the most particular, and any one rule is to be applied in the light of all previous or earlier rules. Individual exceptions to these rules may be made at any time if the circumstances clearly warrant it. This statement may be amended at any time and should be reviewed in its entirety at least every two years.

2. No mystery fiction title shall be purchased which is characterized by or dwells in an offensive way on sex violence, or gore, or which for

any other reason is considered to be poorly written as to be unworthy of inclusion in the Library's collection.

3. No mystery fiction title shall be listed for purchase unless it is approved in at least one book selection tool, such as The Saturday Review, The NY Times Book Review section, Kirkus, or The Fiction Catalog.

4. Only those mystery fiction titles which are ingeniously constructed and well-written should be listed for purchase.

B. Science Fiction (Adopted by the Board, October 1963).

1. It is recognized that science fiction is not a new literary form, that in recent years it has become increasingly more popular, and that there is a considerable amount of good writing being done in this field. It is taken for granted that science fiction should be represented on the shelves of this library.

2. In general no work of science fiction shall be listed for purchase unless it meets one or the other (and desirably both) of the following tests: It should be reasonably well written with some attention to the development of the characters portrayed, and it should not emphasize violence.

3. In general, no science fiction titles shall be listed for purchase unless they receive a favorable review in at least one of the standard book selection tools, such as The Library Journal, Kirkus Bookshop Service, The New York Times Book Review, The Saturday Review, or The Fiction Catalog.

4. In general, no science fiction titles shall be listed for purchase unless the author is known to have technical competence or an established reputation for writing the type of story which meets these standards.

C. Western Stories (Adopted by the Board, October 1963).

1. Although we recognize the decline of the popularity of the novel form labeled western, we still buy some westerns emphasizing adventure and action. Preference is given to historical novels recreating the days of the pioneers, the cattlemen, and the homesteaders, and which show craftsmanship, historical research, and authentic background.

2. Although the emphasis may be on adventure and action, the novel should not be characterized by frequent or constant shootings, lynchings, and fist-fights.

3. The characters should be recognized as human beings instead of stereotypes of hero and villain.

III. FOREIGN LANGUAGE BOOKS

A. The use of the Library's collection of foreign language books is a determining factor in acquisition. The titles added in each language are roughly proportioned to the relative size of the nationality group locally, the potential demand and the availability of material in the language. Although the foreign-born population in Evansville is small, the library is experiencing an increasing demand for books in foreign languages. These requests come from students, teachers, the foreign-born, and from adults who read one or more foreign languages for pleasure or in connection with their profession or studies.

B. The Adult BSC and the JBSC are responsible for the listing of all foreign language printed materials. The foreign language specialist in AID shall act as consultant whenever needed. In listing titles in foreign languages, the same care will be followed as is followed in the selection of the regular collection. An attempt will be made to buy a dictionary of each major language of the world for the reference collection. Fiction, biography, and drama, including the classics, will be selected in addition to books on the study and teaching of languages.

Suggested review tools to be used for selection are: Books Abroad, Booklist, publishers' catalogs, and dealers' lists.

C. It is recommended that branches purchase only readers, study books and books of conversation, except in paper backs; and that the remainder of the foreign language collection be purchased by AID and be assigned to Central. If a branch feels the need for a particular book, a request may be made through the current AID member of BSC for consideration. If approved, AID will order the title when funds permit. All foreign language books except those named above for branch purchase will be permanently assigned to Central and available upon request to branches. Books in the Central collection will be loaned to branches for one circulation but may be renewed once if necessary.

D. An attempt should be made through inter-library loan to secure specialized books, or books in a foreign language for which there are few requests.

IV. LOCAL AUTHORS AND HISTORY

Books written by local authors will be considered as carefully as are all other books and will not automatically be added to the collection. Normally it would be expected that a review of the book be available to the Committee before the title is considered for listing. If after examination the BSC feels that the Library needs a book by a local author because of its local nature even though reviews are not available, the book may be considered.

By the term "local," we intend to include authors and incidents of history pertaining to our tri-state area.

V. MEDICAL BOOKS AND BOOKS IN RELATED FIELDS
(Approved by Board of Trustees, June 1960)

A. The Public Library does not have nor expect to develop a collection of technical or professional medical literature, especially since the Mead Johnson and the various hospital libraries are as well developed as they are. It follows that the Public Library's collection of materials in medicine should be such as may be open to all laymen without the likelihood that they would physically harm themselves or others by acting on what they read. No books or other materials will be accepted or purchased which attempt or claim to show laymen how to diagnose their own illnesses or to treat them. By the same reasoning, books which show how to hypnotize oneself or others will not be accepted.

B. On the other hand, textbooks will be acceptable in personal and public health, hygiene, anatomy, physiology, zoology, nursing, chemistry, bacteriology, nutrition, and related subjects of interest and value to others than practitioners of the healing arts. Histories of medicine, medical dictionaries, and directories may be purchased or otherwise acquired, as may books which deal with first aid and home care of the sick or which explain and describe for the benefit of laymen hospital management, modern surgical techniques, psychiatry, dentistry, optometry, and specific diseases (including care of the patient but not alleged complete treatment or cure). Books which relate the history of hypnotism and describe it in general terms or its applications are acceptable. Books which describe and explain the principles of osteopathy or chiropractic may be acquired, as may books which explain in detail how to use yoga or how to have natural childbirth.

C. It is theoretically possible that any book may be of harm to an individual reader, so the criterion for not accepting books in medicine and related fields has to be set at a level where it is judged that a large number of readers could be hurt physically and seriously. This turns in part on the intent and competence of the author. Books which advocate health foods or food fads are to be judged on this same basis. We want books which inform readers, but not those which might reasonably be expected to mislead a number of persons to the detriment of their health.

D. Some of the criteria for the consideration of books in this field include:

1. The author should be known to be qualified and competent.

2. The book should be published by a reputable firm.

3. A favorable critical review should be found, possibly in a medical journal (Mead Johnson Library has appropriate indexes); or a review copy should be secured and perhaps examined by one or two local physicians.

VI. PERIODICALS

Periodicals are selected for their actual or possible use by the individual patrons, businesses, and industries of the area. The interests of the community, the accuracy and objectivity of the periodicals, the accessibility of content through indexes, the representation of various points of view, price, and the availability of the title in other institutions in the area are considered carefully before periodicals are listed for purchase.

A. Gift Periodical Subscriptions
   (Adopted in substance by the Board of Trustees in September 1956)

1. The staff Book Selection Committee shall hereafter approve all adult periodicals given by patrons to any library agency or available without charge. No such periodical shall hereafter be circulated or displayed by any library agency, save in accordance with these rules; and no library staff member shall accept a gift periodical from any patron without making it clear to him that BSC approval shall have to be secured for it to be used. A file of gift periodicals is kept on cards in the Technical Services Department.

2. Though individual exceptions are always possible, it is to be assumed that the BSC will approve a gift subscription, for any agency, of a periodical which is currently received by (and approved for) some other library agency either on a paid, gift, or free-of-charge basis. In the case of all gift periodicals a copy of the periodical should be sent by the head of the agency in question to the chairman of the BSC with the request for the review and decision. Such decisions shall be recorded in the periodical file in the Technical Services Department. Library science periodicals received on an exchange or other free-of-charge basis, or gift periodicals distributed by the Library Office or Technical Services Department will not normally be reviewed by the BSC.

3. Normally any free periodical will be approved by the BSC if it expounds or presents the beliefs of a religious, political, or other group. No periodical will be accepted, however, which is devoted solely or mainly to attacking another religious, political or other group by name. No periodical will be accepted which advocates or preaches the violent overthrow of our form of government or violence toward any particular group of citizens, which is objectionable because of its treatment of sex, or which is written in a sensational and inflammatory manner and without regard to known facts. In approving or disapproving a gift periodical, the BSC shall consider the number of other periodicals in the same field or of the same organization which are already being received by the Library.

4. It shall not be the function of the BSC to decide how long an agency shall or may keep the issues of a gift periodical which is approved. But any decision by the BSC in regard to a gift periodical may be reversed at a later date, if the situation calls for it.

5. A record of all gift periodicals received and approved will be kept at each agency.

VII. POETRY

In general, the Book Selection Committee will list for purchase books of poetry which represent the standard works of nationally and internationally recognized poets. For a contemporary poet, volumes of collected poems will be preferred to individual works. Anthologies of contemporary poetry will be recommended as often as possible as well as anthologies of older poets. All reviews in the selection of poetry titles should, if feasible, come from sources that make use of subject specialties.

To insure the quality of our poetry collection in all agencies, periodic checks should be made to see that we have the basics represented in the system. Tools used for this purpose may include such titles as <u>Public Library Catalog</u>, <u>Senior High School Library Catalog</u>, <u>Junior High School Library Catalog</u>, <u>Children's Catalog</u>, <u>Granger's Index to Poetry</u> and <u>Brewton's Index to Poetry</u>.

Note: Previous Poetry section approved by Board, October 1963.

VIII. PSEUDO-SCIENCE, OCCULT SUBJECTS, AND OTHER BORDERLINE MATERIAL

Titles in the area of the pseudo-sciences such as astrology, numerology, phrenology, palmistry, etc., may be listed for purchase because of their timeliness or because of a great degree of current interest in them. As one librarian said, "These subjects are given credence by many people while their claims to authenticity are scornfully rejected by others."

It is suggested that the librarians serving on the Book Selection Committee and the librarians suggesting titles to the BSC in the field consider the following factors in dealing with questionable scientific, health, and borderline materials:

A. Author (reputation, professional or academic position, other publications, etc.)

B. Publisher (whether book is privately printed by author, a bookshop, a small unknown press, or whether notice gives only P.O. box)

C. Source (whether sent unsolicited by author, distributor, or propaganda organization)

D. Content and Purpose (whether authoritative, in accepted tradition of handling the subject matter, whether the book attempts to examine the subject objectively)

E. Literary Style and Vocabulary (whether nebulous, full of abstract or unusual jargon)

F. Typographic Format (quality of paper, presswork, binding, general impression of the book as a book)

Adapted from <u>Enoch Pratt Book Selection Policy</u>, 4th edition, 1968.

Since reviews of books in these fields are seldom found, the above mentioned criteria must be given careful consideration.

IX. RELIGIOUS BOOKS AND BOOKS IN RELATED FIELDS
(Approved by the Board of Trustees, June 1958)

A. The Public Library is neutral and impartial in all matters of religious controversy, both those of doctrine, those arising between religious sects or groups, and any others. The main consideration is, insofar as possible, to identify and secure copies of all those publications which are serious attempts to deal with important questions and which are reasonably well-written. Inclusion or non-inclusion in the Library's collection of any book or other item in the field of religion shall be based on the considerations described here and not on the personal religious conviction of any one staff member or group of staff members. The desire is to maintain a bal-anced collection which reflects all main points of view. Similarly, no book shall be removed from the collection solely because it is objected to by any religious or other group in the community, when it is in harmony with this policy statement.

B. The Library will strive always to have copies of all important editions of the Bible, and to include as many as possible of the other important sacred books of the world religions (such as, the Koran and the Talmud). Books which present the beliefs, practices, or point-of-view of a reli-gious group (including small or fringe groups) may be accepted for pur-chase or as a gift. All such materials must be approved as usual by the staff Book Selection Committee, and the desirability of more such litera-ture on any one sect may well diminish after the first few pieces. All such material is subject to withdrawal for the usual reasons of physical condition, being out-of-date, lack of use, presence of newer or better books on the same subject, etc.

C. A book which attacks religion in general or any one religion or religious group in particular may be included in the Library's collection if it is reasonably evident that the author is sincere, emotionally restrained, does not malign or insult individuals or groups, uses facts when appro-priate (and correctly), and is attempting to throw light on a situation and not solely to engender argument.

D. The Library will not itself distribute (or allow others to use library facili-ties to distribute) to the public free literature of controversial religious content. Materials of generally philosophical or factual nature may be so distributed if they pertain to events or topics of general interest and especially if they come from a group of churches.

X. SEX (Adopted by the Board of Trustees, October 1963)

A. In the field of factual books (such as those on anatomy, physiology, marriage, etc.) any title which deals seriously in part or in whole with sex will be selected for listing as acceptable for purchase on the basis of the same consideration as are other books (such as, the value of the contribution of the individual book, and the extent and adequacy of books already in the Library on the subject). The fact that the book deals with questions of sex does not in this case call for special con-sideration, other than that frankly erotic or pornographic literature will not be selected for purchase. Even books which explicitly describe and discuss sexual intercourse or sexual abnormalities will be considered for purchase, so long as their content is deemed to be accurate, the style of presentation restrained and serious, and their objective educa-tional and not titillation.

B. In the field of creative composition (especially novels), books listed for purchase are expected to be characterized by an integrity of purpose and of execution which clearly warrants the extent and detail of the treatment of matters of sex which are found in the book. Passages taken out of their context may deal frankly or even brutally with sex, so long as it seems to be true that the author is not using the story as a mere vehicle for repeated bedroom scenes. In making these decisions, we are guided by the opinions of literary critics and of our own staff members; as in the case of all books, novels that include reference to sex will be expected to be at least reasonably well-written to be considered for purchase. Because it is particularly hard to make accurate decisions on this point, we lean in the direction of listing only those titles which have literary merit or other values that would seem to indicate an honest attempt to use harsh language or reference to sex as necessary parts to a larger picture which the writer is trying to convey. In making these decisions, we ignore both the present popularity of a title or the extent of realism with which the author chooses to convey his ideas. Furthermore, the work of no author shall be automatically accepted or rejected because of the way his previous writings were considered, and any decision made once--either way--shall always be subject to review.

C. These considerations are based on the assumption that adult books selected for the Library's collections are to be chosen in the light of the needs and interests of mature, normal, and responsible adults and not of abnormal or immature persons. Undeniably there are some persons of the latter kind in every community and their use and abuse of these (and any others of the Library's) books is to be guarded against in other ways than by depriving the vast majority of citizens of those books. Thus, though books dealing with sex are not automatically or regularly to be placed on closed shelves or withheld from general adult use, it is the prerogative of any librarian in any agency to withhold any such adult title from use by a child or any other person for whom it will be clearly unfit and unwise.

Reprinted by Permission of Evansville Public Library, Edward Allen Howard, Director.

Fort Worth Public Library
Fort Worth, Texas
no date

BOOK SELECTION POLICY

I. PURPOSE OF POLICY

    A. To further the stated objectives of the Fort Worth Public Library

    B. To guide librarians in the selection of materials.

    C. To inform the public about the principles upon which selections are made.

II. DEFINITION OF BOOK SELECTION

"Selection" refers to the decision that must be made either to add material to the collection or to retain material already in the collection.

III. GOALS OF BOOK SELECTION

    A. To maintain a well-balanced and broad collection of materials for information, reference and research.

    B. To support the democratic process by providing materials for the education and enlightenment of the community.

    C. To provide recreational resources.

IV. RESPONSIBILITY FOR SELECTION

The responsibility for selection lies with the professional staff of the Library operating within the areas of service to children, young adults and adults. The general public and staff members may recommend materials for consideration. The ultimate responsibility for book selection rests with the Director of the Library who operates within the framework of policies determined by the Library Board of Trustees.

V. GENERAL PRINCIPLES

    A. Selection is based on the merits of a work in relation to the needs, interests and demands of the Fort Worth community. Basic to this policy is the Library Bill of Rights, as adopted by the American Library Association, to which this library subscribes, which states, in part, "In no case should any book be excluded because of the race or nationality or the political or religious views of the writer. There should be the fullest practicable provision of material presenting all points of view concerning the problems and issues of our times--international, national, and local; and books or other reading material of sound factual authority should not be proscribed or removed from library shelves because of partisan or doctrinal disapproval."

B. Responsibility for the reading of children rests with their parents or legal guardians. Selection should not be inhibited by the possibility that books may inadvertently come into the possession of children.

C. Materials with an emphasis on sex, or containing profane language, should not be automatically rejected. Selection should be made on the basis of whether the book presents life in its true proportions, whether characters and situations are realistically presented, and whether the book has literary value.

D. Based on the services it is expected to perform, it is the responsibility of the Library to provide circulating, reference, and research material for the general public and the student, to the graduate level. Special collections in depth (earth sciences, business, technology, local history, etc.) shall also be maintained when indicated by community interest.

E. Branch libraries shall be responsible for maintaining collections of basic reference works and circulating collections of standard and currently popular materials comparable in quality to those of the Central Library. Reference and research in depth shall remain the province of the Central Library.

VI. SPECIFIC PRINCIPLES FOR SELECTION

The following principles will condition selection:

A. Contemporary significance or permanent value

B. Accuracy

C. Authority of author

D. Relation of work to existing collection

E. Price, format and ease of use

F. Scarcity of information in subject area

G. Availability of material elsewhere in community--Holdings of other libraries within this community are considered in developing the Library's collections. Materials, particularly those of highly technical nature, may be borrowed from area libraries by inter-library loan.

H. Popular Demand--The Library should make available materials for enlightenment and recreation even if not enduring in value, interest or accuracy. A representative sampling of experimental or ephemeral material should be purchased but will not attempt to be exhaustive.

I. Duplication of materials already in collection--Purchase of additional copies of material should be governed by intrinsic or historical value and need. Paperbacks may be used to satisfy a temporary heavy demand.

VII.   TEXTBOOKS

Providing textbooks and curriculum materials is generally held to be the responsibility of the schools. Textbooks should be purchased for the collection when they supply information in areas in which they may be the best, or the only, source of information on the subject.

VIII.   NON-BOOK MATERIALS

Purchase of non-book materials should be governed by the same principles and criteria applied to book purchase.

IX.   GIFTS

Selection of gifts should be governed by the same principles and criteria applied to the selection of an item for purchase.

X.   MAINTENANCE OF COLLECTION

The collection should be periodically examined for the purpose of weeding, binding or repair of materials to maintain a balanced, attractive book stock.

XI.   PROVISION FOR REVIEW OF POLICY

This policy may be revised as time and circumstances require.

Reprinted by Permission of Fort Worth Public Library, Mrs. Mabel Fischer, Director.

Hawaii State Library System
Honolulu, Hawaii
Adopted May, 1967

ACQUISITIONS POLICY

GENERAL LIBRARY OBJECTIVES

By statute[1] the Hawaii State Library System provides general and special library services for all individuals and groups in the state. For this purpose, the Hawaii State Library System has formulated the following statement of its acquisition goals and functions.

THE HAWAII STATE LIBRARY SYSTEM

I. GENERAL

The Hawaii State Library System shall play the major role in developing the total subject, reference, and recreational resources which affect the economic, political, intellectual, and cultural life of the state.

In acquisitions, emphasis shall be on resources having both direct and indirect bearing on the total growth and development of our state. As administrator of public libraries, the State Librarian shall work towards the coordination of all state supported libraries and towards the cooperative building and use of all signiticant collections within the state.

II. BACKSTOP RESOURCES

The Hawaii State Library and other cooperating state supported libraries shall provide in-depth reference, bibliographic and interlibrary loan service to stand behind community and regional libraries.

Comprehensive, intensive, specialized bibliographic and reference needs of communities throughout the state shall be met through the backstop resources of the Hawaii State Library and cooperating special and scholarly libraries. Materials or information from materials, that are highly specialized, out of print, or expensive, shall be made available to community libraries from the backstop resources through the interloan system. The Hawaii State Library shall serve as a last copy depository, preserving and retaining at least one copy of each title needed for the permanent collection of the entire system. Sufficient book funds shall be allotted to the Hawaii State Library in order that it may provide such backstop resources while also meeting Honolulu's city needs.

---

[1] Article IX, State Constitution of Hawaii, and Act I, Section 18 of the First State Legislature, 2nd Special Session, and Executive Order 19, dated September 30, 1961.

As a general rule the Hawaii State Library System shall usually avoid duplicating collections in school libraries, academic institutions, and special libraries. It shall usually avoid stocking in its system: curriculum materials; textbooks per se; highly specialized and advanced works; scholarly journals and research materials in the field of the pure sciences; professional medical literature; art and literary criticism at the highly advanced level; detailed genealogical records; gifts that do not meet the same standards of quality, purpose, and need as are applied to materials purchased.

The Hawaii State Library System shall acquire and duplicate, as warranted, materials to supplement and enrich school materials; textbooks that are standard, leading works in their field. It shall acquire on a priority basis the history of its state, counties, and communities; materials dealing with and reflecting the ethnic cultures of Hawaii.

III. FREEDOM OF INFORMATION

The Hawaii State Library System shall, through its collections, maintain for the citizens of Hawaii, freedom to read and freedom of access to information and to materials of varying views.

The basic principles set forth in the American Library Association's publications, the Freedom to Read and the Library Bill of Rights, shall be maintained. To provide public information and enlightenment for all the people of the community, these principles shall be put into practice:

A. A publication shall not be excluded because of the race or nationality, or the political or religious views of the writer.

B. There should be the fullest practicable provision of material presenting all points of view concerning the problems and issues of our times, international, national, and local; and books or other reading matter of sound factual authority should not be proscribed or removed from library shelves because of partisan or doctrinal disapproval.

C. Censorship of books, urged or practiced by volunteer arbiters of morals or political opinion or by organizations that would establish a coercive concept of Americanism, shall be challenged to provide for the dissemination of public information through the printed word.

IV. DISTRIBUTION OF FREE MATERIAL

When in harmony with our acquisition policies and principles, distribution of free materials to the public may be provided through:

A. Addition to our book, pamphlet, serial, or audio-visual collections. Free materials offered would be accepted in accordance with principles and standards applied to purchased materials.

B. Coordination with displays arranged by the librarian in charge of public information and promotion activities. Selection or acceptance of free materials for distribution or posting at public libraries shall be at her discretion. She would apply standards of feasibility, quality, purpose, need, timeliness, and impartiality in presenting various views.

V. RESOURCES FOR STATE GOVERNMENT

The Hawaii State Library System shall play the major role in providing a rich supply of information and reference resources for government agencies and projects maintained by the state.

The Hawaii State Library shall provide resources needed by State government through its reference, subject, serial, Hawaiiana and documents collections, but will augment rather than duplicate professionally staffed and organized libraries now serving state government.

It is expected that special information and research service to the legislative branch will continue to be provided by the Legislative Reference Bureau and its library.

It is expected that the Supreme Court Law Library will continue to maintain a comprehensive collection of primary and secondary legal materials, to provide the best possible legal resources for the operation of state government and for the administration of justice. The Hawaii State Library System shall provide the necessary statutes, codes, regulations and texts needed by the business man, the professional man, the laborer, and the citizen, for an understanding of the legal system and laws governing his daily life.

It is expected that the Department of Planning and Economic Development Library will continue to provide economic and planning resources required by that Department. In contrast, the State Library System shall provide such major economic and planning publications as shall be needed to keep the layman, the specialist in related fields, and advisory board and commission members informed as to problems, issues, trends, and new developments in the field.

VI. RESOURCES FOR THE BLIND AND HANDICAPPED

The Hawaii State Library shall develop for the state a full range of reading and audio-visual materials for the blind and the handicapped. It shall maintain its rich collection of talking book records at its Library for the Blind. In addition a collection of specially selected visual and reading materials, including large print books, shall be developed for the handicapped.

VII. RESOURCES FOR STATE HEALTH AND CORRECTIONAL INSTITUTIONS

The Hawaii State Library shall participate actively in the development of libraries serving both the staff and the inmates at state institutions maintained for health and correctional programs. Such libraries shall be planned for purposes of bibliotherapy for inmates, to contribute to the educational, vocational, recreational, and cultural programs of these institutions and for the specialized, professional, and working needs of the staff.

HAWAII STATE LIBRARY

VIII. HAWAIIANA

The Hawaii State Library shall build and make accessible in one unit, a strong collection of state and local history.

The Hawaiiana collection of the Hawaii State Library shall be at the comprehensive level so that officials, research workers, and the public will have access to such materials in a single location. Although other Hawaiiana collections exist within the state, emphasis shall be given to the acquisition of Hawaiiana by the Hawaii State Library to insure public access to these materials.

Hawaiiana in audio-visual media shall be managed by the audio-visual unit with research and identification assistance from the Hawaii and Pacific Unit.

The collection, preservation, organization, and management of the state's archives shall remain the function of the Hawaii State Public Archives. The Hawaii State Library and regional libraries in the neighboring counties shall serve as depositories for the management of local, county publications.

IX. GOVERNMENT DOCUMENTS

A comprehensive collection of Hawaii's state and county documents shall be maintained and managed by the Hawaii and Pacific Unit. A regional depository collection of federal documents and a selective collection of the current documents of other states shall be developed and maintained at the Hawaii State Library.

The regional libraries in neighboring counties shall serve as regional depositories for Hawaii state and local documents and as limited depositories for selected documents of the federal government and other states.

X. SERIALS, REPORTS, MAPS

The subject resources of the Hawaii State Library shall include not only books but research and information reports; journals of trade, industrial and professional groups; files of state and major national newspapers; maps; and similar materials.

Extensive backfiles of these materials shall be held at the Hawaii State Library. Periodical holdings of small and medium sized community libraries in the system shall be based on titles in the Abridged Readers' Guide supplemented by other essential titles. Periodical backfiles for these smaller libraries shall be developed and retained as extensively as possible for selected, basic titles. For regional libraries periodical backfiles for a larger selection of titles shall be retained as extensively as space permits. Print copies of newspaper backfiles for all branches shall be limited to one year.

As efficient equipment is acquired in sufficient quantity, microform copy shall be acquired to supplement printed backfiles of periodicals and newspapers in bound volumes.

Hawaii state and local newspapers, old and current, in English and in foreign languages, shall be preserved in microform at the Hawaii State Library.

XI. AUDIO-VISUAL AND NEW MEDIA

The Hawaii State Library shall acquire rich collections of audio-visual and of other newer forms of communication to be made available to users throughout the state.

The emphasis in microform and in other forms of audio-visual materials shall be on adult materials for research, educational, informational, and cultural purposes.

A percentage of the total funds for audio-visual materials shall be for juvenile materials for the use of juvenile programs not directly related to school activities.

Community libraries shall maintain unified collections of pictures and recordings and add other audio-visual materials as funds permit. The full audio-visual resources of the Hawaii State Library shall be available to all community libraries through the interloan system.

The existing collection of pictures, sheet music, and scores at the Hawaii State Library shall be maintained to provide to the public free access to such materials.

XII. LIBRARY SCIENCE COLLECTION

The Hawaii State Library shall maintain a strong collection of library science materials with emphasis on public library service. The Library Science Collection shall serve as a separate, reference collection from which limited loans may be made to Hawaii State Library System staff to provide them with professional literature to meet their working needs. In addition, general, circulating material on library science shall be provided for public use from the general collection.

XIII. REGIONAL AND COMMUNITY LIBRARIES

The Hawaii State Library System shall include regional libraries to provide for every reader access to subject collections and staff in some depth in addition to the most used resources within his locality. Such higher level resources and services shall be at regional libraries at such locations that any serious reader may reach one such facility, use it, and return to his home all within one day.

Regional libraries shall provide resources related to the economic, social, and cultural development of the region.

Those regional libraries located in county seats shall provide resources and staff services to meet the major and recurring needs of county government agencies, commissions, and advisory boards. The Municipal Reference Library shall continue to provide for the needs of the agencies of the City and County of Honolulu with supplementary resources and services from the Hawaii State Library.

Regional libraries shall serve as intermediaries, augmenting the resources of smaller community libraries, where local educational, informational, and recreational interests and needs are emphasized.

Reprinted by Permission of The Division of Library Services, James R. Hunt, Librarian.

Madison Public Library
Madison, Wisconsin
June 9, 1970

BOOK SELECTION POLICY AND GUIDELINES*

I.   THE COMMUNITY

A knowledge of the community is a vital ingredient in the responsible selection of Library materials. There must be knowledge of residents' interests, capacities and problems, plus knowledge of the geographical and building patterns that affect the placement of materials to satisfy residents' needs.

Madison is a community with a generally prosperous, well-educated and younger than average population. It is the seat of government for Dane County and the State of Wisconsin, is the home of the University of Wisconsin and of several other major facilities in education, research and medicine. It is a center for manufacturing, finance, commercial trade and the home office for thirty-five insurance companies. The metropolitan Madison area has a stable economic base and was rated in 1969 one of the twenty-five most rapidly growing areas in the United States.

Madison has an unusual site. Its center is on an isthmus between Lakes Monona and Mendota, and its growth has mushroomed to the east and west, creating a city divided by many natural and man-made barriers. This difficult geography has had to be reckoned with in developing the branch library system: the absence of focal centers for large units has necessitated the use of many small branches.

II.   PURPOSE AND OBJECTIVES OF THE MADISON PUBLIC LIBRARY

The purpose of the Library, a public service agency, is to provide all residents of Madison and Dane County with a comprehensive collection of materials in a variety of media that record man's knowledge, ideas and culture, to organize these materials for ready access, and to offer guidance and encouragement in their use; to serve the community with reliable and easily available sources of information and reference.

Materials should be selected and services planned to satisfy residents both as individuals and as members of groups, with concern for all ages, backgrounds, interests, abilities, and levels of education. Materials and services should be in sufficient supply to make the Library a dependable resource for most of the people most of the time.

Furthermore the Library has an obligation to serve not only its current habitual users but to search for materials and methods that will meet the needs of members of

---

*Sections I through V are policy statements subject to Library Board action. The remaining sections are guidelines designed to implement the policy and may be further developed as required by the Library Administration.   The two elements are brought together in this document for the information of the Board and staff and other interested officials and citizens.

the community who have not traditionally been library users. Similarly, the Library must not freeze its program to present conditions and present service areas but must be alert to anticipating future needs of the city and county and of the region as well. Cooperation with the extensive governmental, academic and special resource centers in the area will be an increasingly important factor in meeting future needs.

The objectives of the Library are:

(1) To facilitate continuing education, both formal and informal;
(2) To supply sources of information from pre-history to the most recent developments in all fields of knowledge;
(3) To provide practical and vocational information that will improve occupational capabilities;
(4) To meet the basic informational needs of the community;
(5) To widen outlooks through reading experience in diverse culture patterns and in innovative thinking, past and present, so that discussion of contemporary problems may be informed with understanding both of traditional and experimental approaches;
(6) To stimulate thoughtful participation in the life of the family, the community, the country and the world;
(7) To support educational, civic and cultural activities of groups and organizations;
(8) To nourish intellectual, aesthetic, creative and spiritual growth;
(9) To promote the use of books and other library materials for recreation and enjoyment, i.e. the use of leisure time for personal and social well-being;
(10) To give every encouragement to individuals in the community who may be contributors to the increase of knowledge.

While formulating or revising the objectives, the Library is guided by professional standards: it consciously supports and is supported by the ALA Library Bill of Rights* and Freedom to Read Statements* which affirm that free and convenient access to the world of ideas, information, and the creative experience is of vital importance to every citizen today.

In conclusion, the Library strives to stimulate the development not only of learning, but of concern and understanding as well, and to provide materials and guidance in their use in order to enable as many people as possible to apply in their daily lives the record of what is known.

III. ORGANIZATION OF THE LIBRARY AS A FACTOR IN BUILDING THE COLLECTION

Madison Public Library is made up of interdependent agencies and collections that are designed to make its total resources readily available and widely accessible to the community it serves. These agencies range from the Main Library, with its special subject collections, large reference collections, and extensive materials for children and young adults, to the neighborhood branch libraries and the bookmobile, whose smaller collections of general reading and reference materials are planned to meet the particular needs of their neighborhoods. Because the needs of the users of the several agencies vary, so must the collections chosen for them, and it is in this respect that the structure of the Library affects the selection of materials.

---

*See appendix.

A. By Agency

1. Main Library

The Main Library is responsible for providing a well-rounded collection in considerable depth of reference and circulating materials for direct use by the public, as well as supplementary resources for the Library's branches, bookmobile, and Dane County Library Service. It provides audio-visual materials, special collections and services, and the major reference and bibliographic aids for the entire system. For requested materials not owned by the Library itself the Main Library relies upon the interlibrary loan system available through Dane County Library Service and upon the Wisconsin Reference and Loan Library, which provides access to the libraries of the University of Wisconsin and the Milwaukee Public Library in accordance with the Wisconsin Manual on Interlibrary Loan Service.

Selection is influenced by the existence in the community of other libraries and resources for materials. It is neither necessary nor desirable to duplicate highly specialized materials or multiple holdings that are available elsewhere. However, no matter how strong or how accessible these other specialized collections may be, the Main Library still has the responsibility of building adequate broad coverage of all subjects in which its public is interested.

2. Branches

Branch libraries make easily accessible to neighborhood communities small collections that will satisfy the most general and frequent needs of the residents. Selection usually emphasizes standard works in major fields of knowledge, basic reference materials, general periodicals, pamphlets, and a current browsing collection for all ages. Whenever the Branch is unable to supply an individual request it has access to the more comprehensive Main collection. As Branch selection is limited to titles purchased for the Main Library, all agencies cooperate in the selection of materials in order to best meet the needs of each.

In adapting Branch collections to the needs of a particular neighborhood, a careful balance is maintained among materials on current social issues, vocational and educational information, on home and family living, and recreational reading.

3. Bookmobile

The Bookmobile provides a current, popular browsing collection for adults and children in areas of the city not conveniently served by other library outlets. Although some basic titles in adult fiction, general nonfiction, and the standard titles in children's literature are stocked, the Bookmobile collection does not attempt to provide standard works in major fields of knowledge. The primary focus of the collection is on current social issues, up-to-date materials on home and family living, and recreational reading materials.

Files of periodicals and pamphlets are not maintained, although a few titles are selected to fill specific needs. Also, with the exception of a few reference tools, the Bookmobile collection is completely circulating. Finally, because it is necessarily a small collection, it must rely on the Main Library both for specific demands beyond its book stock, and for additional titles to keep the collection fresh and vital.

B. By Age Group

1. Adult

Adult collections are chosen for persons 14 years and older. Selection must be as broad in scope as the interests of the community. Besides aiming at variety and depth in content, it must recognize a wide range of reading ability. The adult services of the Main Library are divided into three subject areas: Art and Music, Literature and Social Sciences, and Business and Science. Although adult collections in the Branches include all subjects, they are not physically divided into separate areas.

2. Young Adult

Young adult services are organized as a separately identified section of the adult collection with the goal of providing a smooth transition from juvenile to adult literature. Through carefully chosen materials and through individual and group guidance, young adults are introduced to the Library's complete resources and encouraged to continue using them.

The Young Adult collections are chosen for patrons of about 14 to 18 years of age, with awareness of the variety of interests, backgrounds, reading skills and development levels within this age group. The collections are for browsing rather than for reference and are designed for the young adult not in his role as a student but to satisfy his special recreational, emotional and informational needs. They do not attempt to fill all YA needs for materials, since the resources of the adult collection are conveniently available.

The collections must be kept current and attractive, and should include not only hardcover books, but paperbacks, magazines, and pamphlets as well. The YA Librarian also represents the interests of young adults by recommending audio-visual materials for purchase. In addition, a selection of books for adults working with teens is maintained.

3. Children

In selecting materials for children, the objective is to make available a collection that satisfies the informational, recreational and cultural reading needs and potentials of children from preschool age to age 14. Books, magazines, records, pamphlets, and other materials are included which meet the general demands of the majority of children, along with those whose special qualities make them valuable to children with special problems or talents.

Materials are judged on: their own literary and artistic merits, their contribution to the balance of the total collection, and their suitability of content and vocabulary to the age of the readers. Children may use Young Adult or Adult collections also, even though these materials have not been specifically selected for them.

Adult books concerning children's literature which are helpful to parents and other people working with children are also purchased for Children's collections. These include historical perspectives of children's literature, information on children's authors and illustrators, bibliographies of materials for children, and appropriate professional materials.

IV. RESPONSIBILITY FOR SELECTION

The ultimate responsibility for selection of materials rests with the Library Director and Assistant Director, operating within the framework of policies and objectives determined by the Library Board.

Responsibility for initial selection rests with the Book Selection Committee, under the direction and supervision of the Assistant Director. The following staff members make up the Committee: subject division supervisors, the children's and young adult librarians, the branch and bookmobile librarians, and the supervisor of Technical Processes. The Assistant Director is chairman of book selection meetings, allocates materials funds, reviews all orders for book and non-book materials, approves gifts to be added, checks all withdrawals, and makes administrative decisions. Branch librarians, who have close contact with their respective publics, have the responsibility of reporting current trends and requests to the Committee. Main Library Committee members with their opportunity to specialize in a particular area of service, have the responsibility of bringing this knowledge and expertise to the Committee. The Technical Processes Division is responsible for recording orders at all book selection meetings, and for advising the Committee on matters concerning the acquisition and physical handling of materials.

Many other staff members participate in the selection process. It is the responsibility of everyone working with the public to record patron requests and needs so that they may be considered in selection. All librarians in Main Library subject divisions as well as many library assistants throughout the system are assigned areas in which they make recommendations to their supervisors on titles to be added and withdrawn. In addition, all staff members are encouraged to suggest areas or titles for consideration.

V. CRITERIA FOR SELECTION

To build collections of merit and significance, materials must be measured by objective guidelines. All acquisitions, whether purchased or donated, are considered in terms of the following standards. Clearly, however, an item need not meet all of the criteria in order to be acceptable. When judging the quality of materials several standards and combinations of standards may be used, as some materials may be judged primarily on artistic merit, while others are considered because of scholarship, value as human documents, or ability to satisfy the recreational and entertainment needs of the community.

GENERAL CRITERIA:

Suitability of physical form for library use
Insight into human and social conditions
Suitability of subject and style for intended audience
Present and potential relevance to community needs
Appropriateness and effectiveness of medium to content
Importance as a document of the times
Relation to existing collection and other materials on subject
Reputation and/or significance of author
Attention of critics, reviewers, and public.

SPECIFIC CRITERIA FOR THE EVALUATION OF WORKS OF
INFORMATION AND OPINION

Authority
Comprehensiveness and depth of treatment
Clarity, accuracy, and logic of presentation
Statement of challenging or original point of view.

SPECIFIC CRITERIA FOR THE EVALUATION OF WORKS OF
IMAGINATION

Representation of important movement (literary or social),
    genre, trend, or national culture
Vitality and originality
Artistic presentation and experimentation
Sustained interest
Effective characterization
Authenticity of historical, regional, or social setting.

Items having widespread demand may or may not meet the general and specific criteria contained in this policy. However, demand is a valid factor in book selection, and it shall be considered an important factor in cases such as books on best seller lists for which there is persistent local demand. Any such books that have had generally poor reviews shall be examined if purchased, and shall not be extensively duplicated.

As the social and intellectual climate of the community changes, materials which were not recommended for purchases may become of interest. Such materials will be re-evaluated on a continuing basis.

Because the Madison Public Library functions in a rapidly changing society, it must keep flexible attitudes toward changes in communicative materials, in relation to both new forms and new styles of expression. It must be, for example, responsive to the increased output and improved quality of such forms as recordings, films and paperbacks. Materials in these forms are selected when they are suitable in content and effective in treatment; they are judged in terms of their own kind of excellence and the audience for whom they are intended.

The collection must contain the various positions expressed on important, complicated, or controversial questions, including unpopular or unorthodox positions. The public library does not promote particular beliefs or views. It provides a resource where the individual can examine issues freely and make his own decisions.

The Library recognizes that many books are controversial and that any given item may offend some patrons. Selection will not be made on the basis of any anticipated approval or disapproval, but solely on the merits of the work in relation to the building of the collections and to serving the interests of readers.

Responsibility for the reading of minors rests with their parents and legal guardians. Selection of adult material will not be limited by the possibility that books may inadvertently come into the possession of minors. Upon request of parents, the Library will restrict the borrowing of children under 14 to materials in the juvenile collection.

VI. GUIDELINES FOR MAINTENANCE OF COLLECTION

A. Duplication

Every agency has the responsibility of evaluating demands and needs for the duplication of materials. While the problem differs in the various divisions and branches, the Library, in general, attempts to weigh a specific demand in relation to the total library program and policies. For example, no agency duplicates heavily at the expense of a first copy of important, less-called-for material needed in the permanent collection. A sound, readable book in heavy demand is duplicated if long use is anticipated. On the other hand, the Library believes that adequate stocks of significantly timely materials are necessary and, therefore, it may duplicate certain titles of short-time currency. The multiplicity of reserves is given weight as a guide for duplication, with a general rule of one copy for every five reserves. The Library has reciprocal borrowing privileges with other county libraries. It is, therefore, expected that the Main Library duplicate materials to fulfill its role in The County System.

Although students have primary resources for materials in their school libraries, the Library accepts responsibility for serving this large and important segment of its clientele with supplementary reading and reference materials. When demands are heavy, such materials are duplicated to a level that will ensure the general public access to the materials. Textbooks are purchased only when they provide the best coverage of a subject and are useful to the general public; they are not duplicated to satisfy the demands of a specific school course.

Duplication of the same title in two or more subject divisions of the Main Library is not considered desirable, the aim being inter-dependence among divisions. An exception is made in the case of a reference book needed in two or more places. A division which needs, as a reference tool, a book which is classified in another division may have a copy catalogued for its reference collection.

A certain amount of duplication is normal in the Main Library when titles are needed in a division and also in special collections. Examples of this type of duplication are the Family Living Collection and the Play Reading Collection.

B. Replacement

A replacement means an item purchased to take the place of an identical title previously in the collection of which the last copy has been withdrawn.

It is the Library's policy not to replace automatically all books withdrawn because of loss, damage, or wear. Need for replacement in each case is judged by two factors: (1) existence of adequate coverage in the item's field by similar material especially if this is later and better material; and (2) demand for the specific title. Efforts are made to replace important out-of-print titles by the maintenance of out-of-print files and by checking reprint lists. As a rule, the responsibility for keeping the collection complete in this manner is that of the Main Library divisions, although branches occasionally acquire important out-of-print items.

It is recommended that hardback editions be purchased if in print. Paperbacks bought as replacements when hardback editions are not available are reinforced or bound and catalogued before being added to any agency's collection.

C. Gifts

A gift for the Library collection may consist of materials or of funds for the purchase of materials. Funds may be given for acquiring materials recommended by the library staff or for the purchase of specific items suggested by the donor. The Library encourages gifts not earmarked for specific items in order to permit the most flexible use of the donation for the enrichment of the collection.

Gift additions must meet the same selection criteria as purchased materials. In some cases, titles are received or purchased which could not have been acquired from library funds because of budget limitations. If gifts of marginal value are offered, processing costs and use of shelf space are considered before the gift can be accepted.

Gifts are accepted subject to the following limitations:
(1) the Library retains unconditional ownership of the gift;
(2) the Library makes the final decision on its own use or other disposition of the gift;
(3) the Library reserves the right to decide the conditions of display, housing, and access to the materials.

An appropriate book plate will be included in each gift identifying the donor and purpose of the donation.

D. Binding, Mending and Withdrawal

Keeping materials in good physical condition is essential. Decisions must be made continuously on how to handle worn books—whether to mend, bind or withdraw them. Each decision is based on the actual condition of the book, current validity of its contents, availability for re-order and cost of binding vs. replacement. Replacement is preferable to binding if costs are comparable. Binding is preferable to mending if a title is expected to have long-term usefulness. Mending is done only when need is detected early except in special cases. In general, little attempt is made to mend non-accessioned materials, e.g. pamphlets, circulating duplicates of magazines and young adult paperbacks.

Since rebound books are generally less appealing than the original format, replacement is preferred in most cases, except when appearance is no factor in demand. Physical attractiveness is a special consideration in the children's, Young Adult, and branch collections.

Paperbound titles or trade editions of children's books may require pre-binding to withstand library use. Periodicals may be bound to preserve them.

In some special instances, an irreplaceable title of importance must be retained regardless of condition; special handling will be given such a title.

E. Theft and Mutilation

The liability of library material to theft or mutilation is not an influencing factor in original selection. However, because experience has shown that materials in certain subject fields are particularly susceptible to theft and/or mutilation, special care is taken in the processing of and the access to these materials. Stolen or mutilated materials will be replaced when they are deemed necessary for the maintenance of a well-rounded collection. Materials of marginal importance whose use cannot be adequately controlled may, at times, not be replaced.

VII. GUIDELINES FOR SELECTION IN SPECIFIC AREAS

The selection criteria outlined in Section V apply to all parts of the Library's collection. However, some areas of the collection have such unique characteristics that it is useful to define further guidelines for applying criteria to them.

A. According to Groups with Special Needs

1. Students

    a. Informal Study: Since independent self-education and informal education programs play a large role in the life of the Madison community, the Library attempts to provide material on various levels of complexity in the subject areas that the informal student may wish to pursue. The person who wishes to familiarize himself with a subject should be able to develop his interest from the elementary level to the advanced or specialized level within the resources of the Library.

    b. Formal Study: The Library recognizes that students make up a large segment of its clientele. School and college libraries and instructional media centers provide the primary resource for these students. The public library attempts to meet their needs with in-depth information that supplement their course texts and primary resource collections. The Library provides textbooks only when they offer the best available coverage of a subject.

2. Readers with Limitations

   a. Limited Reading Skill

   The Library attempts to meet the needs of adults who are functionally illiterate or unable to read well by providing a collection of special materials that is referred to as the "New Readers" collection. This collection provides materials aimed at improving reading skill, as well as practical information and recreational reading presented on a simple reading level. Care is exercised in obtaining material that is geared to adult interest and sensibility, despite its simplicity of language.

   b. Visually Handicapped

   For individuals who are limited by poor eyesight, the Library maintains a collection of large print books which contain material of general interest.

   The Library assists people who are unable to read conventional print materials to obtain talking books and other services from the Wisconsin Regional Library for the Blind and Physically Handicapped administered by the Milwaukee Public Library.

   c. Physically Handicapped

   The Library serves the physically handicapped reader with Projected Books, which have been received as a gift from the Madison Lions Club. Some physically handicapped readers also qualify for the talking book service mentioned above.

B. According to Form and Nature of Materials

   1. Paperbacks

   References have already been made to paperbacks: the paper formats (including spiral and ring bindings) are admissible to the collection and very desirable for some purposes. Some areas in which they are especially useful are: Young Adult and Children's collections, current issues, travel, duplicates of popular titles and subjects, duplicates of materials susceptible to theft or mutilation.

   General criteria on selection apply to the paperback's contents while the choise of the format pivots on the title's expected term of usefulness. If long use is anticipated, more substantial binding is preferred and, if a hardback edition is not available, the paper copy should be prebound, because mending is not feasible.

2. Periodicals

First consideration in the selection and retention of periodicals is given to those titles whose contents are analyzed in Library-owned indexes. The Library subscribes to all periodicals indexed in the Readers' Guide. Duplicate copies of many of the most popular indexed periodicals are purchased for circulation. Microfilm is purchased to replace some standard periodicals, particularly if the original magazines are worn or missing.

Periodicals for professional use by the Library staff are purchased for the Staff Library, and duplicate copies of some titles are purchased for use by the Divisions and the Branches.

In addition to the indexed periodicals, some titles are purchased, or accepted as gifts, to represent the diverse interests of the community, to meet the specialized needs of the Divisions within the Library, and to give representation to new publications on topics of current concern. Community and State publications of general interest are included. The non-indexed titles are selected by the same criteria as other library materials.

Branch libraries select a more limited list of periodicals and no titles which are not included in the Main Library. Branch selection favors periodicals of broad general interest, plus a few titles to reflect specific interest of a branch's clientele.

3. Newspapers

The Library maintains current files and microfilmed back files of the two daily Madison newspapers, and of a few indexed newspapers of national significance. Other Madison newspapers are also acquired when available. The Library does not acquire other Wisconsin community newspapers as they are available at the State Historical Society.

Current news coverage and a sampling of viewpoints are supplied through several daily papers from the Milwaukee, Chicago, and Minneapolis areas, and a limited selection of daily and Sunday papers of recognized journalistic standing published in various regions of the United States and a few foreign countries. These are kept for only short periods of time.

4. Pamphlets

Pamphlets are defined as unbound, inexpensive materials which are not catalogued and normally organized in a subject file. They are especially useful for providing information on how-to-do-it techniques, vocations, travel, subjects of local interest, current issues, and fields in which few books are available. They are also useful for readers of limited skill. Branches may add pamphlets not purchased by the Main Library.

General selection criteria apply to pamphlet selection. Because pamphlets are widely used for propaganda and/or advertising, it is necessary that they be carefully examined before being added to the collection. Pamphlets in some subject areas tend to be biased, but those whose propagandist intent is clearly indicated by publishers' name or statements of purpose are preferred to those which appear under imprints whose sponsorship is not clearly stated. Advertising pamphlets which distort facts, emphasize commercial messages unduly, or contain misleading statements are not added.

5. Government Documents

The Library has been a partial U.S. government depository since 1965, and is subject to government regulations regarding depository collections. Selection of items to be received includes information of a specialized nature to supplement other library materials. Duplicates and individual publications not received as depository items may be selected by divisions and branches on the basis of the general criteria. The Library actively solicits state and local documents as well. All documents are processed and organized according to their form and subject.

6. Maps

Individual maps are acquired in limited numbers to meet the general interests of the community in areas such as travel, history, and science. Files of Wisconsin topographical and county maps are maintained. Maps of states and cities are usually obtained through free distribution agencies. Foreign city maps are acquired whenever obtainable.

7. Picture File and Framed Reproductions

Pictures and posters on a variety of subjects and mounted art reproductions are selected to supplement and duplicate illustrations in books and magazines. Principal sources are discarded books and magazines and free or inexpensive materials.

Framed reproductions of works of art representing various styles and periods are selected for loan to individuals. Consideration is given to the quality of both reproduction and frame when adding a title to the collection.

8. Phono-records

The Main Library has a collection of musical and nonmusical phono-records. In the area of music, selection is guided by reviews in current periodicals and standard bibliographies and is based on composition, arrangement, performer, recording quality, and patron interest. The collection contains classical works of orchestral music, chamber ensembles, opera, choral works, vocal and instrumental solos, jazz, folk music of many countries, popular musical comedies, motion picture sound tracks, and examples of avant-garde music. No attempt is made to build a collection of current pop discs.

The nonmusical collection includes a wide variety of subjects. In the selection of poetry, drama, and literary prose, the importance of both authors and performers is considered; recordings of poets reading their own works are preferred to those by professional readers. In other subject areas, phono-records are selected by the same criteria applied to other library materials, plus consideration of the value of sound in conveying the subject matter.

Decisions on whether to withdraw or replace worn recordings are made on the same criteria that are used with printed materials.

9. Films

Films are an integral part of the Library collection and selection follows the general criteria for other materials. Consideration is given to films for all ages which stimulate discussion, provide information, entertainment, or an aesthetic experience. Films are selected for religious and civic groups, private organizations, city agencies, library program audiences, or individuals for home use. Films are not selected or loaned for classroom use since the local school administrators and the Bureau of Audio-Visual Instruction are responsible for the provision of basic classroom resources.

All films are sixteen millimeter sound, and are judged for content and technique. Titles are always previewed by a selection committee before being added to the collection. Content and treatment of subject matter are considered for validity, lasting value or timely importance, imagination and originality. Technical qualities of photographic and sound reproduction are examined.

Sponsored films on loan or deposit are added to the collection in accordance with the general selection and gift policies. Sponsored films which are primarily advertisements of commercial products or propaganda for special interest groups are not added.

Films may be withdrawn because of poor condition and obsolescence, and the same criteria are used for replacement and duplication of prints as for other library materials.

10. Microforms

The collection of microforms is generally limited to microfilm of older newspapers and periodicals. The purpose of this collection is to build back files which extend and sometimes replace badly worn sections of the periodical and newspaper collection. With the exception of local newspapers, it is limited to indexed materials. A very small number of nationally important newspapers and periodicals, plus the local newspapers, are currently subscribed to on microfilm, and do overlap with current issues in the original format.

C. According to Subject

1. The Sciences and Health

The Library attempts to provide for the general needs of its readers in the many branches of science; it checks scientific materials with emphasis on authority and lucid treatment. Since the needs of non-professionals embrace an increasing amount of technical information, selection of titles ranges from basic to somewhat specialized. For highly specialized materials, residents may turn to the special libraries in Madison.

The Library provides up-to-date, non-technical material on health, nutrition, hygiene and diseases; books in this area are chosen with very special concern for their reliability. When there is any uncertainty on the soundness of a book, the staff consults authorities in the titles' field, special bibliographies and reviews in professional journals. However, there can be differences among authorities, and if a title that has had mixed reviews is one that receives strong public demand, it may be purchased. Readers who seek technical information in medicine may turn to the William S. Middleton Library, University of Wisconsin.

2. Genealogy

The Library purchases some books of general information on methods of genealogical research. Patrons wishing to research individual family histories are referred to the State Historical Society.

3. Law

It is the policy of the Library to purchase standard and popular books in the field of law which are of interest to laymen. The State Law Library, The Legislative Reference Library, and the University Law Library are sources of specialized material.

4. Religion

In the area of religion, the Library attempts to maintain a well-balanced collection in which materials about all the major religions, including their sacred scriptures, are represented. Authoritative material which introduces and explains the basic concepts and practices of the various religions and beliefs is also included. The Library avoids including materials of a strictly proselytizing nature. In addition to material pertaining to individual beliefs, the collection contains basic authoritative studies in the areas of history of religion, theology, comparative religion, and mythology. The collection also encompasses popular studies on new trends, ideas, and movements which are taking place in the field of religion today.

5. Rare Books

Madison Public Library does not seek rare or valuable materials but does accept some as gifts and is particularly receptive to rare items of local interest. The Library usually refers other rare and valuable items to appropriate libraries and organizations in the community. The relatively few items of rarity in the collection are either gifts or have acquired their extra value through time and circumstance; they are maintained because their contents are useful, not for rarity's own sake.

6. Local History

Whenever possible the Library obtains and retains a reference copy of all printed materials which contribute to a knowledge of Madison and Dane County history, past and present. Duplicates of many items are available for circulation. The acquisition of governmental documents is a basic part of the policy. These include such items as the Proceedings of the Madison Common Council and of the Dane County Board of Supervisors, annual department reports, and special publications of the Madison Plan Department. Local studies made by the University of Wisconsin, and publications of local agencies comprise a part of the Library's holdings. We have a special interest in acquiring publications by local and regional authors.

Uncatalogued material which has outlived its usefulness in pamphlet files may, in some cases, be offered to the Dane County Historical Records Center. The unique local history items which are gradually being acquired by the Records Center supplements the Library's holdings. The Center's collection is housed in the Library, and is available for reference use by Library patrons.

While the Library does not have an active policy of acquiring pictures of historical interest, it does welcome offers of them as gifts. Phono-records and tape recordings of local interest are also acquired.

D. According to Special Collection

1. Bibliographic Center

The Bibliographic Center brings together indexes, directories, and bibliographies that are extensively used by more than one Division as well as by the public. The responsibility for selection rests with the Division to whose subject area the materials are classified.

Indexes for the Bibliographic Center are selected for their usefulness in locating information primarily in our own collection, secondarily in other library collections in the community.

2. Family Living Collection

This collection consists of books and pamphlets dealing with family life and family life education. Although materials from all subject divisions are included in this collection, the responsibility for selection lies with the Literature and Social Sciences Division. All materials in the Family Living Collection are duplicates of titles in the general collection. The Library attempts to provide materials in this collection which will be helpful to parents, students, discussion leaders, and professionals who work with family life situations. Some of the factors which enter into the selection of materials for this collection are significance of subject, factual accuracy, level of treatment, and effectiveness of presentation.

3. Foreign Language Collection

   The Foreign Language Collection attempts to provide a sampling of standard literary works and current writing of literary importance in each of the languages represented in the collection. In addition, many dictionaries and introductory language textbooks are provided. A limited collection of language instruction recordings are housed in the Art and Music Division.

   When available, the works of important and representative American writers are provided in translations. In the case of bi-lingual editions, copies are purchased for both the foreign language and general collections.

   The Collection is selected for Madison residents who read in a foreign language for pleasure and illumination, rather than for high school or university language students; therefore the languages chosen for representation are those for which there is demand or potential strong interest among city residents.

4. Play Reading Collection

   This collection of popular plays, purchased in sets of five, is selected and loaned only for the purpose of group reading. All titles included are available in the regular circulating collection as well. In selecting plays to be added to the collection, special consideration is given to an evaluation of how well a play "reads" and number of characters (a minimum of four).

5. Hathaway Collection

   The Hathaway Collection, originally named the Pinney Collection, was founded in 1911 with a fund of $2,000 presented to the Library in memory of Silas U. Pinney by his wife. Mr. Pinney was Mayor of Madison from 1874-1876 and was responsible for the ordinance establishing the Public Library in 1875. Since the depletion of the original fund, the collection has been maintained with other gift funds and endowments. When Pinney Branch opened in 1966, the collection was renamed the Hathaway Collection in honor of Charles Hathaway, whose substantial bequest has largely supported this collection since 1939.

   The collection consists of expensive books in the Fine Arts, often unusual in format, and is housed in the Art and Music Division. Some of these books are circulating, some non-circulating.

VIII. GUIDELINES FOR SELECTION OF YOUNG ADULT MATERIALS

The objectives of library service to young adults have been stated earlier in the policy, and materials chosen for this group must meet the same selection criteria as do all other library materials; however, certain areas of concern require further definition.

A. General Guidelines

   To be selected for the YA collection, books must usually be recommended specifically for this age group in at least one professional review; however, a book which is sure to be recommended for teens at a later date (e.g., the autobiography of a popular sports figure or a book by the author of many standard YA titles) may be ordered on the basis of one good adult review. Books which have not been reviewed for YA but which appear on the YA acquisition lists of other libraries are also considered.

B. Special Topics

   1. Junior Novels and Easy Non-fiction

      Although 80-90% of the Young Adult Collection consists of adult books recommended for YA, fiction and non-fiction written especially for teens are included on their particular merits. Simple teen-age stories of adolescence, as well as simply written non-fiction on popular subjects, often teach young and reluctant readers a love of reading. These titles would be the only books in the Young Adult department that might not be duplicates of books found elsewhere in the Library. In the case of books whose age or interest level is questionable, the opinion of the Children's Librarian is solicited.

   2. Paperbacks

      A large and current collection of paperbacks is a necessity in the Young Adult area, since the format has special appeal to teens, including even reluctant readers. Although the paperback collection is largely made up of duplicates of hardback editions already in the YA collection, other well-reviewed books are added in paperback editions only.

   3. Magazines

      A current collection of periodicals is maintained by the YA department. Although many of these titles are duplicates of magazines in Main Subject Divisions, several titles of particular interest to teens, ephemeral and not indexed, are also included. Back files of such titles are not maintained, while back files of standard periodicals are given by YA to the appropriate Subject Division.

   4. Career Pamphlets

      Since the investigation of possible careers is an important concern of young adults, every effort is made to keep available a large and up-to-date file of materials on a wide variety of vocations. Due to the changing nature of this material, as well as the ready availability of free and inexpensive career pamphlets, almost no career books are purchased. Exceptions are occasionally made in the case of extremely popular fields, such as teaching and nursing, or of broad surveys in such general areas as civil service or medicine.

All pamphlets in the YA department concern careers or employ-ment. Pamphlets in all other subject areas, despite their interest to teens, are more accessible to all age groups when located in the appropriate subject division.

5. Unconventional Language

The use of incidental profanity or frankness in dealing with sex and social issues is present in some works of literature and con-temporary problems. The value and impact of materials which con-tain controversial passages must be examined as a whole since the significance of an entire work often transcends the words, phrases or incidents out of which it is made.

6. Sex

Books about sex information appropriate for teen-agers are added to the open shelves of young adult collections. These mate-rials are carefully selected in order to provide sound and reliable information for the understanding of sex.

IX. GUIDELINES FOR SELECTION OF CHILDREN'S MATERIALS

A. General Guidelines

1. New Titles

Reviews are gathered from a number of authoritative sources. New books for children must normally have two favorable reviews to be accepted for the collection. In the case of a difference of opinion among the reviewers an attempt is made to obtain the book from the Cooperative Children's Book Center and to read it before a decision is made. The children's librarians and the branch librarians may re-quest the consideration of any book and the reconsideration of any title once passed.

Criteria for selection include literary and artistic worth, suita-bility of content and vocabulary to the age of the readers, and the contribution of the book to the balance of the total collection. In-formational books are chosen because of their interest to children and the quality of the writing and illustrations, not because of any relation to school curriculum.

A copy of each new title selected for the system is purchased by the Main Children's Room. Eventually through loss or discard the Main Children's Room may not have every title that the branches still own.

2. Exclusion of Materials

If a title in the collection is criticized or questioned by patrons or in the professional literature, a re-evaluation by the children's librarians and the branch librarians is made. Should this evaluation substantiate the original decision the title in question remains on the shelves. If the criticism is considered valid the title is removed from the circulating collection.

B. Special Collections

1. Children's Historical Collection

Books of value in a comprehensive children's collection, though of slight current use, are retained in an historical collection in the Main Children's Room as they illustrate trends in writing for children.

2. Child's Own Library

A small collection of non-circulating children's books is kept in the Main Children's Room to guide parents in selecting books for their children and for reading aloud. Some of these books are useful for satisfying current interests; others have a timeless quality that provide a family with a literary heritage.

3. Reference Collections

The reference collections consist primarily of standard children's encyclopedias and dictionaries. Other books on popular subjects are also included as are a few adult reference books.

C. Principles of Selection in Specific Areas

1. Books

a. Encyclopedias

Children's encyclopedias are a part of the children's reference collections. Sets of books designed primarily for home use and of little or no value as reference tools are not purchased.

b. Readers

Readers, that is, books used in primary grades to teach reading skills, are acquired only when they are particularly happy choices to furnish easy and enjoyable reading; preference is given to trade books which are on the same vocabulary levels as the readers. The teaching manuals or workbooks that supplement readers are not purchased.

c. Textbooks

In general, textbooks are added to the collection only when there is little or no material available from any other source. The Library assumes its responsibility to be that of providing books which will broaden the interests stemming from a textbook rather than in providing the textbook itself.

d. Series Books

Books published as part of an author's series or publisher's series are purchased with care. Long series frequently tend to be below standard in literary merit; consequently, each book is evaluated separately before it can be included in the collection.

e. Abridged Classic

(1) Abridged adult classics are seldom purchased, the exception being either some long accepted literary editions of "Canterbury Tales," "Don Quixote," "Pilgrim's Progress," etc. or a new presentation of such excellence that it does not destroy the spirit of the original.

(2) Abridged children's classics, such as "Alice in Wonderland" "Hans Brinker," and "Treasure Island," are not purchased because the original style and character portrayal, rather than the plot alone, have kept these titles alive for generations. The recommendation to patrons requesting "simple versions" of the children's classics, is to postpone their reading until the child is of proper age to appreciate the style, vocabulary, and flavor of the whole story as written.

(3) In the area of folk literature and legend, such books as "Robin Hood" and "King Arthur" are occasionally purchased in "simplified versions." In any such instance a careful evaluation is made for literary merit before a title is included in the collection.

f. Large Print Books

Books in large print are purchased for the Children's Room for handicapped children. They are duplicates of regular editions in the collection.

g. Paperback Books

Circulating paperbacks for younger and older readers are purchased for Children's Collections. Most are duplicate copies of popular titles or appealing editions of less popular titles.

h. Foreign Language Books

Books in foreign languages are purchased for the Children's Collections where there is demand. These include foreign publications, books by foreign authors issued by American publishers, and American books in translation.

2. Pamphlets

Circulating pamphlets are purchased to supply material in fields in which few books are available. Of ephemeral value, these are not catalogued and are discarded when more recent or better material becomes available. The Main Children's Room maintains a file of non-circulating professional pamphlets for librarians and adults working with children's literature.

3. Periodicals

A limited number of popular children's periodicals are purchased, and are circulated as long as there is a demand. The Main Children's Room maintains back files of these periodicals and all the professional journals used in book selection.

4. Phonorecords

The Main Children's Room has a collection of musical, activity, and story phonorecords which may be borrowed by adults and children. Selection standards are: interest of the content for a young audience, skill in performance, reading or interpretation, technical quality of the recording.

A special collection of recordings appropriate for use by librarians in story hours is available in the Main Children's Room office.

5. Films

Films for children are purchased by the Art and Music Division in consultation with the children's librarians and the branch librarians. Films of informative and imaginative content are acquired, checked for accuracy, artistic treatment and technical merit.

D. Special Topics

1. Guns

Because it is felt that children should not assume the responsibility of handling guns without the direct supervision of an adult, books which describe the mechanism of guns and which provide instruction in shooting are excluded from the children's collections.

2. Judo and Karate

Books describing the techniques of judo, karate, and similar combat techniques are primarily written for adults and young people above the age of fourteen years. Since children may not be mature enough to understand or abide by the cautions given in the text, this material is not acquired for the children's collections.

3. Automotive Mechanics

Instructional materials on car repair or maintenance, hot-rod mechanics, and driving technique are not added to the children's collections. The responsibility for the borrowing of such material for children's use should be assumed by parents.

4. Sex

Books written in a simple, dignified, and scientific manner on the processes of human physical development and reproduction are provided in children's circulating collections.

5. Human Relations

Books relating to countries, races, nationalities, religious groups, and social issues are carefully selected, and those which reflect any inherently discriminatory attitudes are not purchased. Books which are recognized as children's classics and which are of considerable literary merit are retained even though they may contain words of episodes which are today unacceptable. Current books which are well written and portray authentically a period or incident or way of life are accepted despite the occasional use of an unacceptable term, provided the total quality of the book meets the standards maintained in the children's collections.

Reprinted by Permission of Madison Public Library, Mr. Bernard Schwab, Director.

Minneapolis Public Library
Minneapolis, Minnesota
Adopted May 20, 1965

ADULT BOOK SELECTION POLICY

The purpose of the Minneapolis Public Library book selection policy is to guide librarians and to inform the public about the principles upon which selections are made.

A policy cannot replace the judgment of librarians, but stating goals and indicating boundaries will assist them in choosing from a vast array of available materials.

The Library sets as its major goals in book selection: the advancement of knowledge, the education and enlightenment of the people of the community, and the provision of recreational reading. Basic to the policy is the Library Bill of Rights as adopted by the American Library Association, which states among other things:

> "As a responsibility of library service, books and other reading matter selected should be chosen for values of interest, information and enlightenment of all of the people of the community. In no case should any book be excluded because of the race or nationality or the political or religious views of the writer. There should be the fullest practicable provision of material presenting all points of view concerning the problems and issues of our times--international, national and local; and books or other reading matter of sound factual authority should not be proscribed or removed from library shelves because of partisan or doctrinal disapproval."

I.   DEFINITIONS

The words "book," "library materials," or other synonyms as they may occur in the policy have the widest possible meaning; hence, it is implicit in this policy that every form of permanent record is to be included, whether printed or in manuscript; bound or unbound; photographed or otherwise reproduced. Also included are audio records on tapes, discs or otherwise; films and pictures in the form of photographs, paintings, drawings, etchings, etc.

"Selection" refers to the decision that must be made either to add a given book to the collection or to retain one already in the collection. It does not refer to reader guidance.

II.   RESPONSIBILITY FOR BOOK SELECTION

Final responsibility for book selection lies with the Librarian. However, the Librarian will delegate to staff members authority to interpret and guide the application of the policy in making day-to-day selections. Unusual problems will be referred to the Librarian for resolution.

III. OBJECTIVES

The primary objectives of book selection shall be to collect materials of contemporary significance and of permanent value. The Library will always be guided by a sense of responsibility to both present and future in adding materials which will enrich the collections and maintain an over-all balance. The Library also recognizes an immediate duty to make available materials for enlightenment and recreation, even though such materials may not have enduring interest or value. The Library will provide, too, a representative sampling of experimental and ephemeral material, but will not always attempt to be exhaustive. The Library does not consider it necessary or desirable to acquire all books on any subject if these books tend to duplicate each other.

IV. DUTIES OF LIBRARIANS

All staff members selecting library materials will be expected to keep the objectives in mind and apply their professional knowledge and experience in making decisions.

V. USE OF THE LIBRARY'S BOOKS

The Library recognizes that many books are controversial and that any given item may offend some patrons. Selections will not be made on the basis of any anticipated approval or disapproval, but solely on the merits of the work in relation to the building of the collections and to serving the interests of readers.

Library materials will not be marked or identified to show approval or disapproval of the contents, and no catalogued book or other item will be sequestered, except for the express purpose of protecting it from injury or theft.

The use of rare and scholarly items of great value may be controlled to the extent required to preserve them from harm, but no further.

Responsibility for the reading of children rests with their parents and legal guardians. Selection will not be inhibited by the possibility that books may inadvertently come into the possession of children.

VI. GUIDELINES FOR SELECTION

A. The Library takes cognizance of the purposes and resources of other libraries in the Twin Cities and shall not needlessly duplicate functions and materials.

B. The Library does not attempt to acquire textbooks or other curriculum-related materials except as such materials also serve the general public.

C. Legal and medical works will be acquired only to the extent that they are useful to the layman.

D. The Library acknowledges a particular interest in local and state history; therefore, it will seek to acquire all state and municipal public documents, and it will take a broad view of works by and about Minnesota authors as well as general works relating to the State of Minnesota, whether or not such materials meet the standards of selection in other respects. However, the Library is not under any obligation to add to its collections everything about Minnesota or produced by authors, printers or publishers with Minnesota connections if it does not seem to be in the public interest to do so.

E. Because the Library serves a public embracing a wide range of ages, educational backgrounds and reading skills it will always seek to select materials of varying complexity.

F. In selecting books for the collections, the Library will pay due regard to the special, commercial, industrial, cultural and civic enterprises of the community.

VII. GIFTS

The Library accepts gifts of books, but reserves the right to evaluate and to dispose of them in accordance with the criteria applied to purchased materials. Gifts of books which do not accord with the Library's objectives and policies will be refused. No conditions may be imposed relating to any book after its acceptance by the Library.

VIII. MAINTAINING THE COLLECTIONS

Librarians are expected to use good judgment to remove from the collections whatever no longer serves a need, and to refurbish by rebinding or other means books which might suffer deterioration if not so cared for.

IX. REVISION OF POLICY

This policy will be revised as times and circumstances require.

Reprinted by Permission of Minneapolis Public Library, Mr. Ervin J. Gaines, Director.

Oak Park Public Library
Oak Park, Illinois
Approved April 21, 1970

SELECTION POLICY FOR LIBRARY MATERIALS

The Public Library is a community institution that attempts to meet the informational, cultural, recreational, and educational needs of all of the community's residents regardless of age or formal schooling.

I. ROLE OF THE OAK PARK PUBLIC LIBRARY

   A. The Library assembles, preserves, organizes, and offers guidance in the use of printed and audio-visual materials that enable Oak Park residents to:

   1. Find reliable and current information and keep pace with significant ideas and with progress in all fields of knowledge.

   2. Become more familiar with their cultural heritage and with the history and literary heritage of Oak Park.

   3. Supplement formal study and encourage informal self-education.

   4. Become more enlightened citizens.

   5. Become more capable in their occupations.

   6. Develop their creative capacities and increase their appreciation of the arts, literature and sciences.

   7. Promote personal and social well-being through an enjoyment of reading.

   B. The Library sponsors and co-sponsors programs that help fulfill the above aims.

   C. The Library provides materials and offers services that are of use to organizations, business firms and government agencies of Oak Park.

   D. The Library works with other agencies in order to realize more fully its aims:

   1. By cooperating with schools in order to:

      a. Encourage good reading habits among young people.

      b. Orient young people in the proper use of the library.

      c. Help meet the supplementary reading needs of students in elementary, secondary, college and adult education classes.

   2. By entering into cooperative ventures with other libraries to provide better library service for Oak Park residents.

   3. By providing materials and services to local community organizations.

113

II. GENERAL CRITERIA FOR THE SELECTION OF MATERIALS

A. To enable citizens to understand the world in which they live, the library will attempt to provide materials that present widely diverse points of view, including those which may be controversial or unorthodox.

B. The library makes an effort to provide materials of excellence and lasting value. Ephemeral topical materials of current interest will also be added. An attractive useful collection will be maintained through a continual discarding and replacing process.

C. A special attempt is made to collect appropriate titles listed in bibliographies of notable books and standard library indexes.

D. The selection of materials is influenced by the following factors:

1. Relevance to community interests and needs.
2. Current or historical significance.
3. Attention of critics and reviewers and public.
4. Number and nature of requests from the public.
5. The need for additional or duplicate materials in the existing collection.
6. The physical limitations of the building.
7. Budgetary considerations.
8. Availability of materials in the Suburban Library System collection, in the library's rental collection, through inter-library loan, and in special or more comprehensive library collections in the area.
9. General commercial availability of library materials.
10. Common sense.
11. Suitability of format of the material for library purposes.

E. Books received as gifts that meet the standards of selection and require no special handling or housing may be added. If they are not suitable or useful, they may be sold or given away.

F. Non-book materials will be added as they become available and can be incorporated into the library's collection.

III. COLLECTIONS AND CRITERIA FOR SELECTION

A. Fiction

1. While it is not possible to set up a single standard of literary quality, it may be said that the library generally will acquire fiction which is well written and based on authentic human experience and will exclude weak, incompetent, cheaply sentimental or solely sensational works.

2. Characterization and language must be evaluated in relation to the work as a whole and can not be considered out of context.

3. Novels which contain experimental writing and reflect new trends will be considered for purchase.

4. The literary reputation of an author will be considered.

5. The prominence of an author and the extent of public interest in a given title will also be taken into consideration.

B. Non-Fiction

1. The author should be qualified on the basis of knowledge and experience.

2. Information should be accurate and presented in a clear, readable style.

3. Technical books are evaluated in terms of suitability of style and content for the intended users.

4. Medical, health and nutrition books will be selected with special care, consideration being given to the author's credentials, position, manner of treating the subject and adherence to generally accepted medical principles. Favorable evaluation by one or more reputable reviewers will be required. Books purchased will be at levels suitable for students, adult laymen, and such professional workers as teachers, social workers and nurses. Clinical texts on diagnosis and treatment and case histories suitable primarily for professional medical libraries will usually not be purchased.

5. Books on law will also be selected with special attention to evaluation by responsible reviewers.

6. Special care will be taken in the consideration of pseudo-scientific and occult materials with avoidance of titles which are sensational or exploitative in nature.

7. An effort will be made to keep the non-fiction collection as up-to-date as possible and to provide materials on all subjects of current interest.

8. The library will not attempt to supply materials required for course work of elementary or secondary schools or of institutions of higher learning. The public library has materials for supplementary reading and self study, but it is not primarily designed to furnish reading material required for academic course work.

C. Reference

Reference materials are acquired to satisfy the general requests and the more frequently expressed special informational needs of the Oak Park community. These materials are augmented by more specialized titles, selected by the Reference staff but paid for by the Suburban Library System. These materials are housed in the Oak Park Library to enrich the informational capabilities of the Reference staff in its service to Oak Park patrons and to other SLS member libraries.

D. The library through its local history collection preserves books and source materials which document the history of Oak Park and provide a record of current happenings in the community.

E. To preserve Oak Park's contribution to the world of letters, the library maintains a local authors collection of books and manuscripts by:

1. Persons born in Oak Park or in River Forest.

2. Those who graduated from a local elementary or high school.

3. Persons who have lived here for at least a year or who have gained local prominence.

Because of the significance of the work of Frank Lloyd Wright and Ernest Hemingway, the library endeavors to have a comprehensive collection of critical works about those men, to collect many editions of their works, and to collect such other items as photographs and miscellaneous printed materials concerned with their lives and work.

F. Periodicals are selected as the most current source of news, information and opinion; for their value in research work; and for recreational reading. An attempt is made to collect those titles listed in the various indexing services such as Readers' Guide to Periodical Literature, Education Index, Business Periodicals Index, etc.

G. Microfilm is to be acquired to augment the periodicals collection and to provide specialized materials not otherwise available.

H. Pamphlets from reliable sources and a selection of government documents supplement the book collection.

I. A record collection of monophonic and stereophonic 33-1/3 rpm discs includes classical music, ethnic and folk music, musical comedies, opera, jazz, contemporary music and non-musical recordings of many kinds. Selections are made on the basis of favorable reviews in standard reviewing media.

J. The film collection consists of 16 mm sound, 8 mm and Super 8 mm silent films. Super 8 and 8 mm films are purchased according to availability and general interest. 16 mm sound films are purchased on the basis of reviews and after previewing to supplement the collection available through the Suburban Library System.

IV. SELECTION PROCEDURES

A. A Book Selection Committee, under the chairmanship of the Assistant Librarian, is responsible for selecting all adult and young adult circulating books, films and recordings. The Reference Department staff selects reference books, pamphlets, government documents and periodicals; the Children's Department head is responsible for the selection of children's books.

B. In order to provide the best possible range of subject knowledge and awareness of community interests it is desirable to have all professional staff members participate in the selection process.

C. The library invites suggestions for purchase from patrons and may ask for the specific advice of subject experts on book selection matters.

D. Since it is impossible for the library staff to review personally the large number of books published, reviews found in professional, literary, specialized, and general periodicals are used as a basis for evaluation.

E. In the event there is considerable disagreement among the published reviews and the Book Selection Committee finds it difficult to reach a decision concerning the selection of a book, one or more staff members will be asked to read and review the work and report back to the committee.

    F.   The ultimate responsibility for selection of library materials rests with the Librarian.

V.   This policy is in accord with the Library Bill of Rights, adopted by the Council of the American Library Association, June 27, 1967, and with the Freedom to Read Statement adopted by the American Library Association Council June 25, 1953. The Board of Library Directors of the Oak Park Public Library endorses both of these statements.

BOOK SELECTION POLICY
CHILDREN'S DEPARTMENT

In selecting books for children, the library's objective is to make available a collection that satisfies the informational, recreational, and cultural reading needs and potentials of children from infancy to early adolescence. In an age of rapid, widespread development and communication of events and ideas, it is recognized that children's needs include access to: the accurate, responsible presentation of information about topics and issues of current interest in our society; the sensitive, realistic portrayal of the values and complexities of human relationships; and the imaginative, creative use of language and art.

All librarians in the Children's Department participate in the selection of children's books under the chairmanship of the head of the department. In general books are selected with the aid of reviewing periodicals, The Children's Catalog and The Junior High School Catalog, and lists compiled by the children's departments of large libraries. Occasionally books may be ordered on approval because of the reliability of the publisher and reputation of the author or illustrator. It is helpful for staff members to examine books before purchase whenever possible.

Criteria for selection and replacement of books include literary and artistic worth, accuracy and clarity, suitability of content and vocabulary to the age of the readers, and the contribution of the book to the balance of the collection. Duplication is largely contingent upon the size of the book budget and the demand of the children for the material.

In general, textbooks are added to the collection not to satisfy school demands but to provide information on subjects when there is little or no material available in any other form. The school reader is considered primarily a stepping stone in the mastering of reading skill, and an attempt is made to provide trade books which will have the same vocabulary and interest level of the reader and also meet library standards of literary and artistic quality. The library considers that its responsibility lies primarily in supplementing the reader.

In that the original style and character portrayal, rather than the plot alone, has kept some titles alive for generations, the library purchases the classics only in standard editions for circulation to children. The only abridged editions purchased are those that have long been accepted as literary presentations of adult classics such as

"Canterbury Tales," "Don Quixote," and "Pilgrim's Progress." Abridged versions of children's classics are not purchased.

Books in series are evaluated as individual titles and are added or rejected as they do or do not meet the basic quality standards for children's books.

Books on certain aspects of guns, jujitsu, karate, and hypnotism are not included in the children's collection, since a certain amount of maturity or adult supervision is necessary for wise use of such information.

Books which will help adults in gaining a knowledge of children's literature will be considered appropriate purchases for the children's collection, as will books on the techniques of storytelling. Books on the mechanics of teaching are considered outside the scope of this department.

Non-circulating materials purchased for the children's collection will include reference items, a complete set of the Newbery and Caldecott award books, and a collection of the folk tales and picture books most often used by staff members for storytelling programs.

Non-book materials currently purchased for the children's collection consist of magazines and recordings. These are selected by the same standards of quality, suitability, interest, and balance that apply to the book collection.

Children's collections in the branch libraries are intended to comprise an up-to-date, well-rounded book stock which is as extensive as required by community interest and need and as permitted by space and budget limitations. The advice of branch staff is sought in selection of materials.

Reprinted by Permission of Oak Park Public Library, Barbara Ballinger, Librarian.

Palo Alto Public Library
Palo Alto, California
no date

BOOK SELECTION POLICY

I.   GENERAL STATEMENT

This memorandum is concerned with that basic function of the Library dealing with the evaluation and selection of library materials--books, pamphlets, newspapers, periodicals, government publications, maps, music scores, picture and other printed material, microcard, microfilm and phonograph records. The selection of these resources must be inclusive rather than exclusive by the very nature of the demands made upon the collections. Therefore, the selection process aims to provide books and materials which will facilitate informal self-education of all people in the community; enrich and further develop the subjects in which individuals are undertaking formal education; keep pace with progress in all fields of knowledge; support the educational, civic and cultural activities of groups and organizations; develop greater efficiency in the performance of their work; discover and develop creative capacities for and powers of appreciation of arts and letters; and encourage wholesome recreation and constructive use of leisure time.

It is an objective of the Library Department to provide a resource where the free individual can examine many points of view and make his own decisions. Physically, this resource covers a variety of forms, together they provide a reservoir of knowledge which supplies inquiring minds with materials which are accurate, objective and sincere, diligently avoiding those which are consciously sensational. In fulfilling its responsibility, the Library strives to include:

(1) Great works which are the basis of our civilization;
(2) Thoughtful interpretations of the ideas of the past;
(3) A record of the times which is of current interest and provides material of future significance . . . including books which present conditions and mores and those which reflect varying trends of thought;
(4) Personal accounts of personal opinion on a subject of interest, counter-balanced by expressions of other and contrary opinions if they are available;
(5) Contemporary and standard works for recreation and leisure, which includes the novel and other writings of more ephemeral nature in demand because of a certain timeliness, surface originality and fashion.

II.   FACTORS AFFECTING BOOK SELECTION

The evaluation, selection and purchase of library books and materials is based on four controlling factors: the community, the individual merit of each book, the Library's existing collections, budget and services, and common sense.

    A.   The Community

        To do an adequate job, the Library staff must know the community, and the community must be aware of the Library and its services. Palo

Alto is situated in the northern part of Santa Clara County adjacent to the campus of Stanford University and the foothills of the Coast Range mountains. The City was founded in 1889 and incorporated in 1894.

The Library Department serves the residents of the City of Palo Alto and those interested non-residents privileged to use its materials and services. The March 1960 census recorded a population of 52,287. As in other areas facing the problems of population growth, the City of Palo Alto, with its 105.9% change in total population from 1950 to 1960, numbers 9.7% in the 60-and-over age group, 54.3% in the middle age group, and 35.9% in the 19-and-under age group. Palo Alto is essentially a suburban-residential community with well-planned research centers, light industrial and trading areas. It serves as a metropolitan sub-center for the peninsula. The educational and cultural attainments of a great number of residents is an important factor in book selection. The 1950 census lists the educational background of the population at a median of 13 years of school completed (male 13.2; female 12.7). Cultural and educational institutions include Stanford University, the Hoover Institution and Library, Palo Alto-Stanford hospital and medical center, a military academy for boys, two schools for girls and ten nursery schools. Many formal and informal classes are held in the Adult Education Division of the Palo Alto Unified School District with interests both practical and cultural. Several organizations are active in the fine arts field, with music and art being generally the most popular. Diversified recreational activities are available through the City's Recreation Department, which maintains the nationally known Community Center; 16 parks and the 1,194 acre Foothills Park recently acquired for future recreational needs. The City has one radio station. Two hospitals are in Palo Alto; the Palo Alto-Stanford Hospital Center with 627 beds and the U. S. Veterans Administration Hospital with 1,000 beds. Industrial, financial and business interests exist in the community and an active Chamber of Commerce supports the numerous organizations: special interest groups; trade and professional groups; men's and women's service clubs; women's clubs; garden clubs; and other organized groups with civic, recreational, cultural and educational activities. The Library strives to achieve a balance among the various group interests as a primary goal in the selection process.

Large industrial libraries plus several smaller ones exist in the area in addition to the scholarly and professional collections of the Stanford University Libraries. The libraries of the Palo Alto Unified School District have collections designed to meet the curriculum needs of the boys and girls enrolled with fairly large collections in the Junior and Senior High Schools, and smaller collections in the twenty-plus elementary school libraries.

General social patterns are characterized by the following: over sixteen thousand housing units (homes and apartments) which have attracted men and women of the arts, sciences and professions, who enjoy the advantages of an university community; an emphasis on home and family life; and an estimated church membership of 52% of the total population (15,000 Protestant, 9,000 Roman Catholic, 3,000 Jewish, 1,000 other denominations).

B.   The Individual Merit of Each Book

The basic criteria outlined in the ACQUISITION CODE (I-41) apply to all acquisitions whether purchased or donated. Helen Haines in her book LIVING WITH BOOKS noted two principles that related to the books themselves: (1) Select books that will tend toward the development and enrichment of life, and (2) Let the basis of selection be positive, not negative. Remember, each book should be of potential service to somebody . . . "if the best that can be said for a book is that it will do no harm, there is no valid reason for its selection."

The Library Department does not promulgate particular beliefs or views, nor is the selection of any given book equivalent to endorsement of the viewpoint of the author expressed therein. With the framework of the LIBRARY BILL OF RIGHTS and the FREEDOM TO READ statements adopted by the American Library Association, the Library does strive to provide materials representing all approaches to public issues of a controversial nature.

C.   The Library's Existing Collections, Budget and Services (See also I-1)

Three factors are considered in evaluating existing collections:

1.   What kinds of books are in the collection and how valuable each is in relation to other books in its subject which are not in the Library;

2.   The kind of community served, in order to decide whether the books in the collection are actually appropriate to our residents, regardless of how valuable the books may be in terms of an abstract evaluation of their worth;

3.   The purposes which the collection is to achieve.

The Library's bibliographical resources budget (books, periodicals, binding, phonorecords, etc.) is the controlling limitation in the acquisition of books and library materials. Constant attention to the several criteria is important to insure coverage in all fields. "If you buy this, you cannot buy that," is the unspoken warning that becomes a sort of "inner check" to all evaluators. The Library's book budget is based on the population of the City, taking in account cost and life factors of the collection. Thus, the requested sum for books and library materials will vary with the growth of the community.

In line with this, it must be remembered that the character of the Library's service is largely determined by the character of the books and materials made available to our residents. The objective of the Library is to serve the residents with its collections within the budgetary limitation through its service functions of assembling, preserving and making available its resources as well as interpreting and guidance in the use of the collections. If this is done well, the Library fulfills its responsibility of communicating experience and ideas from one person to another.

D. Common Sense

Common sense is necessary and must be applied consistently by all evaluators to extend the collections and services beyond the dictionary definition of a Library to a vital living force in the life of our community.

III. CONCLUSION

The selection of books and library materials shall be based upon principle rather than personal opinion, reason rather than emotion, objectivity rather than prejudice, and judgment rather than censorship.

These policies are subject to periodic review.

Reprinted by Permission of Palo Alto Public Library, June Fleming, Director of Libraries.

Free Library of Philadelphia
Philadelphia, Pennsylvania
Revised 1970

SELECTION POLICIES FOR LIBRARY MATERIALS FOR CHILDREN

I. GENERAL STATEMENT OF OBJECTIVES

The Library's primary objective is to inculcate in children an enjoyment and appreciation of reading for "reading's sake" and to provide books of literary quality and those materials which will satisfy a child's recreational needs and natural curiosity, thus contributing to his growth as an intelligent world citizen. Since children's work in the public library services a wide range of age and mental development--from preschool through the eighth grade--books and non-print materials are purchased for use by parents with young children as well as for the needs of seventh and eighth grade boys and girls who read above their grade level.

A. Objective as a District Library Center

Under the Pennsylvania State Library Code (Pamphlet Law 324), the Free Library serves as a District Center and is responsible for lending to local libraries in the Philadelphia District, books and non-print materials not expected to be included in the local library, for the special reader for loan through the local library or for reference use at the local library.

B. Objective as a Resource Library

As one of the four resource libraries under the Pennsylvania State Library Code, special collections, such as Folklore and Fairy Tale, Historical, Illustrators, and Foreign Language for use by adults will be made available.

II. TYPES OF COLLECTIONS

A. Central Children's Department

Central Children's Department serves two functions:

1. as a service agency for children in the neighborhood and from other parts of the city in the same manner as a branch;

2. as a research center for adults interested in the field of children's literature, the illustration of children's books, and children's reading.

Therefore, the department maintains several collections:

1. Circulating and Reference Collection

Materials of current interest, covering a variety of subjects and reading levels, are bought for this collection. All children's titles reviewed and accepted by The Free Library are bought for the Central Children's Department. Useful adult titles, for advanced students, are also bought and may be bought by other agencies where the adult and children's areas are not adjacent; for example, Coffins' Coin Collecting.

2. Parent-Teacher Collection

This extensive circulating and reference collection for adults interested in children's books includes:

a. A basic collection of books for a child's library;

b. A basic collection of picture books for home use by parents;

c. A reference collection of Newbery-Caldecott award books;

d. Books of permanent value, such as Kingsley's The Water Babies, for which demand is slight;

e. Books on children's reading and children's reading books for use by parents, teachers, and students of children's literature; e.g., Duff's Bequest of Wings.

3. Special Collections

As the state depository of children's literature, The Free Library maintains an extensive, non-circulating collection of important children's literature and emphasizes books by Pennsylvania authors and illustrators and books about Pennsylvania. The six separate types of collections included are:

a. Historical Bibliography

Copies of all the bibliographic tools and their various editions relating to children's books are contained in this collection and arranged by author.

b. Kathrine H. McAlarney Collection of Illustrated Children's Books

Based on Mahoney's Illustrators of Children's Books, 1744-1945 and the supplements by Miller and Kingman, this collection represents the work of outstanding illustrators in the field of children's books and includes all Caldecott medal winners and runners-up. It is arranged by illustrator.

c. Folklore Collection

Based on Eastman's Index to Fairy Tales, Myths and Legends and its supplements, this collection is not selective but an attempt to have a comprehensive collection and is arranged in Dewey Decimal order.

d. Historical Collection

Based on Meigs' A Critical History of Children's Literature and containing books dating from 1837 to the present year, this

collection is a continuation of the Collection of Early American Children's Books housed in the Rare Book Department which ends with the year 1836. It includes:
(1) Series books;
(2) Children's magazines;
(3) Books selected annually for the ALA Notable Children's Books list;
(4) Books by Philadelphia and Pennsylvania authors;
(5) Books about Philadelphia and Pennsylvania people and places;
(6) Books published in Philadelphia and Pennsylvania.

It is arranged by year of publication.

e. Foreign Language Collection

An attempt to represent all areas of the world (excluding English-speaking countries), with priority given to:

(1) Picture books and easy reading for all but the most prominent languages;
(2) Major children's award books;
(3) Books written in the original language of the authors.

Unlike the other special collections, these books may be borrowed by an extension agency or District Libraries, and by individuals.

f. Collection of Framed Original Illustrations

Contributions by artists of original artwork for children's books are framed and allowed to be exhibited in extension agencies and in District Libraries. These illustrations are arranged by illustrator.

State funds for resource libraries are used to buy books for the special research and resource collections in the Central Children's Department.

B. Rare Book Department

A special collection of early children's books, including the famous Rosenbach Collection of Early American Children's Books and the American Sunday School Union Collection of Historical Children's Books are shelved in the Rare Book Department. An extensive collection of Arthur Rackham, Kate Greenaway, the Elisabeth Ball Collection of horn books, the Beatrix Potter collection, the Thornton Oakley collection of Howard Pyle, and the C. Barton Brewster collection of A. B. Frost are also housed in this department. These children's books are listed by author in the Central Children's Department master file of special collections. Special editions published after 1836 may be bought by Central Children's Department and housed in the Rare Book Department when desirable.

C. Extension Division

1. Regional Libraries

The Regional Library serves as an area as well as a neighborhood agency and has a reference and circulating collection suited to the needs of the community. It provides not only duplicates of unusual titles that might not be bought by the branches in the area but many reference materials for use by students of children's literature that would save them a trip to the Central Library. Except in unusual situations, the Regional Library must have at least one copy of each title bought by the branches in the area.

2. Branch Libraries

Depending upon the size of the branch and the needs of the community, these collections are intended to comprise a well-rounded bookstock which, supplemented by adult and young adult titles selected under the supervision of a librarian, will satisfy any child's need whether in the recreational or informational field.

When the children's room and adult and young adult rooms are on separate floors, certain titles may be duplicated that would not be when collections adjoin one another.

3. Stations Department

a. Deposit Libraries

These collections serve schools and agencies working with children located outside the branch area for children. (This area is a radius of one-half mile from the branch building.) They are collections of books for informational and recreational reading which have a high frequency of use. Books that cannot be supplied by Deposit Libraries may be borrowed on special request from the Central Children's Department, the Regional Libraries or from branches.

b. Bookmobiles

Because of the limitations of space, books for bookmobiles are selected to meet the demand for informational and creative recreational reading. Informational books included are chosen because of the children's natural interest in the subject and the value of the writing or illustrations.

III. GENERAL POLICIES

To meet the varied reading abilities and interests of children, the Library strives to purchase titles covering a wide range of knowledge, from the earliest rhythmic poetry, such as Mother Goose, to the latest book on space or drugs suitable to a child's understanding. In the field of purely recreational reading, stress is laid upon those books which develop the imaginative faculties, promote understanding and cultivate worthwhile ideals and values.

A. Current Book Publications

Children's Librarians review all children's books received as publisher's gifts or under the Library's contract plan, before the books are accepted or rejected for the collection. In addition, other titles which seem worthy of examination are ordered for review.

1. Factors to be Considered in the Selection or Rejection of Books

In judging books, several factors blended with common sense and experience in book selection must be kept in mind:

a. Literary quality;

b. Suitability in content and vocabulary for children;

c. Need for the subject matter (are there better books of like content in the collection, or does this title present a new approach?).

Factors which determine the exclusion of certain books for children are:

a. Lack of good taste or sufficient literary merit;

b. An inaccurate, unfair or unhealthy picture of the subject;

c. Insufficient need or value to collections to justify expenditure;

d. Textbook material that should be provided by the schools in line with the curriculum needs and materials used only for teaching the techniques of reading;

e. Material, such as judo or karate, which requires appropriate supervision.

2. Specific Factors Noted in Staff Reviews

a. Brief plot and setting if fiction

b. Style of writing

c. Questionable scenes, illustrations, or controversial points

d. Format and illustrations

e. Comparison with other works on same subject or by the same author

f. Practical use in regard to indexes, maps, etc.

g. Use in library

h. Grade and interest level for reader

i. Recommendation for purchase or rejection:

(1) General
A book of unusual quality or importance to the collection, at least one copy of the title must be bought by each agency.

127

(2) Limited
Books suitable for purchase by any agency that needs the particular title.

(3) Central Children's Department and Regional Libraries
Titles which should be represented in the Free Library collection because of importance of author, illustrator, publisher, content, or format. Books in this category may be bought by regional libraries or individual agencies if need is shown for the particular title.

(4) Central Children's Department Only
Titles chosen for the special collections described in Section III-A-3 which are not being added to the circulating collection.

(5) Adult or Young Adult Consideration
Books considered too mature for children in writing or concepts which have been accepted for the Adult or Young Adult Collection or which should be considered for these collections.

(6) Not Recommended
Books may be rejected for many reasons: poor or mediocre writing, and/or illustration; inaccurate statements or facts; adequate material on the subject already in the collection; inadequate funds.

A rotating committee of children's librarians meets with the Head of Book Selection, ten times a year to discuss new titles and to recommend for disposition as listed under Section III-A-2. The books are then made available for the children's librarians who order according to their branch budgets and the needs and interest of their communities.

The Coordinator of Work with Children is responsible to the Director for the final inclusion of any title. In case of a difference of opinion between the reviewer and the Coordinator, the book is generally read by other children's librarians but the Coordinator makes the final decision. The children's librarians may request the consideration of any book published and the reconsideration of any title once rejected.

B. Duplication

Duplication is to a great extent contingent upon the number of children served, the size of the book fund, and the demand by the children for the material, always keeping in mind the state of the collection as a whole and the comparison of the particular book with other titles. The Library cannot, at all times, meet the great demand for curriculum material such as plays, poetry, books and holidays and geographical information on foreign countries because of budget limitations. Therefore, it concentrates on duplication in the recreation and general subject fields. The type of community which the library serves also influences the duplication of titles—for example, to meet the demand in areas with a large Negro population, children's books on the Negro are duplicated heavily.

Because of the overlapping of interest and reading abilities, titles in the young adult collections, as well as the adult collections, are occasionally duplicated. The extent of this duplication is largely determined by the need, budget limitations and proximity to other collections. The decision for such duplication is left to the discretion of the branch and children's librarians with the advice, if necessary, of the Head of Book Selection. To fill requests from District Libraries, the Central Children's Department may duplicate titles which because of price, subject matter, makeup or style of writing, would normally be bought in single copies.

C. Replacement

All titles to be replaced are checked against the approved replacement lists and careful consideration given to their value to the collection as a whole. The replacement lists are compiled by committees of children's librarians whose responsibility is to re-evaluate, the titles already in the children's collection, in regard to use, up-to-dateness, literary value, etc. The complete collection is re-evaluated every two years. Last copies of all withdrawn children's books not in Books in Print are sent to the Coordinator of Work with Children. If the title is needed in the collection from an historical point of view, it can be added to the Central Children's Department's Historical Collection. Every effort is made to keep in the collection certain standard children's books, although in some cases if the title is available in the Central Children's Department Collection, it will not be replaced in a branch. Many titles are out of print and cannot be replaced. In areas where the information in such titles is needed by the children, an effort is made to locate substitute material in pamphlet form if it is unavailable in book form.

D. Weeding

The weeding of a book collection is a form of book selection--perhaps it could be called book selection in reverse--and is thus an important policy to define. Weeding is a thorough and conscientious effort to achieve a well-balanced collection suitable to the clientele served and should be a continuous, consistent process. Factors to consider in weeding are:

1. The physical condition of the book;

2. Slow moving material not listed in standard sources; e.g., Children's Catalog;

3. Books containing subject matter no longer of current interest;

4. Multiple copies of titles no longer in demand;

5. Old editions replaced by later revisions of non-fiction titles;

6. Retention of local material and books by Pennsylvania and Philadelphia authors.

More explicit instructions are given in C-PS #61 WEEDING BOOK COLLECTIONS IN BRANCHES--CHILDREN'S BOOKS (February 17, 1966).

IV. PRINCIPLES OF SELECTION IN SPECIFIC AREAS

The service which the Library gives to children cuts across many areas, from the parent who wishes to familiarize himself with children's books before the child is born and during its earliest years to the teacher and social service worker who, in developing the child's mental and emotional stability, recognizes the value of using children's books.

A. According to Types of Readers Served

1. Children

   a. Preschool

   Children's books for use with infants and preschool children include books of jingles, rhymes, poetry, simple animal and fairy tales, ABC books, handicraft books for kindergarten age and childhood classics, such as Brooke's <u>Johnny Crow's Garden</u>; Gag's <u>Millions of Cats</u>; and Lenski's <u>The Little Train</u>.

   b. Elementary School

   Children's books are sought which will keep pace with the wide range of children's interests in the elementary grades. The Library considers it a responsibility to provide, whenever possible, books on all subjects of major interest to children and at an appropriate reading level which includes modern fiction and fantasy as well as factual books. However, because of the variety of interests and the great difference between chronological and mental development of children, it may be impossible to find books on some subjects at certain reading levels. In areas such as social sciences, for example, books are not published rapidly enough to meet children's widened horizons at the grade or reading level needed. Therefore, at times, some children will have to be served from the young adult or adult departments, or they may have to depend upon encyclopedias, pamphlets and periodicals.

   c. Junior High School Students through the Eighth Grade

   Service to children includes the eighth grade of school. To this end, fiction with plot and subject matter of interest to older children is sought--career, sport, mystery, adventure, and love stories--as well as biography, history, and material in the field of science.

2. Adults

   a. In the Central Children's Department and in many of the branches, separate collections entitled Parent-Teacher Collections are maintained. If a book recommended for this collection is available in many editions, as far as funds permit, an attempt is made to include several editions to enable the parent to acquire a taste for and a knowledge of the well-designed and illustrated children's book.

b. In addition to the Parent-Teacher Collection at the Central Library and the special Parent-Teacher collections in the branches, the children's librarian works closely with the adult in the selection of reading materials which will further the development of the child's literary background. It is not the function of the Library to advise the parent on how to assist the child in the mechanics of reading or to provide textbooks which will contribute to this end.

c. Books which will help the adult in a knowledge of children's literature, such as Eaton's Reading with Children and Duff's Bequest of Wings, are, however, purchased for children's collections, even though the titles are duplicated in the adult collections.

It is seldom necessary to duplicate such titles in branches, since the physical layout of the majority of branches permit easy borrowing from all collections.

B. According to Form or Nature of Material

The distinct form or nature of the material influences the purchase or selection within a particular area. Each type of material is judged according to its own particular characteristics, and its relation to the whole field of library service to children is carefully considered.

1. Books (Hardcover)

a. Encyclopedias and Reference Sets

Encyclopedias, which provide information to assist in the answering of reference questions, are a part of each agency's collection. Encyclopedias are judged according to the qualifications of their editorial board, for their accuracy, the general breadth of material included, and the inclusion of current material. Other criteria in considering encyclopedias are the reading level and concepts understandable to and suitable for children, the choice, quality, number and reproductions of pictures, maps, graphs and diagrams, the arrangement of the material, bibliographic sources, cross-references, and the authority of the author of signed articles.

Insufficient funds may limit the buying of sets of books approved for home buying or as supplementary library materials. If possible, such sets are bought for the Central Children's Department and/or for the Regional Library for examination and use by parents, teachers and librarians. They may be loaned to individuals or other agencies for a limited period of time.

b. Picture Books and Easy Reading

Picture books and easy reading materials are bought in large quantities. The same standards of selection are applied, with the Library's aim uppermost, i.e., that of creating satisfaction and delight in reading in the formative years. Since the function of the schools is to teach the mechanics of reading and to provide readers, only one set of readers (for use by parents) may be purchased by an agency. The reader is considered primarily a stepping stone in the mastering of reading skills, and an attempt is made to provide trade books which will have the same vocabulary and interest level of the reader. The Library considers that its responsibility lies in supplementing the reader rather than in including such titles in the collections.

c. Textbooks

Textbooks are not added to the collection unless there is little or no material available from any other source. The Library assumes its responsibility to be that of providing books which will broaden the child's interest in a particular subject that may stem from the use of a textbook, rather than in providing the textbook itself. Specific information from textbook type materials needed for class assignments should be provided by the school library. In certain areas, namely, the social sciences, little material has been written on the necessary grade levels, with the result that some textbooks are purchased to round out the collections.

d. Informational Books

The criteria for information books include readability, accuracy of fact, lack of bias in presentation, and the need for the subject in a children's collection. Books on controversial subjects or issues are selected carefully and must inform by stated fact rather than by implication. As with adults, tempered with awareness of the limitation of children's knowledge, the Library strives to assist in the development of a thinking, evaluating citizen.

e. Recreational Books

Recreational books of all kinds, whether story or fact, are purchased with a view toward giving pleasure in reading and developing healthy attitudes toward the individual, the family, the community, the nation and the world. Those titles which present a fair picture of various religious, ethnic, or national groups are purchased providing always that their primary value lies in their story content.

f. Series

Books in a series are considered on their individual merit since long series frequently tend to be below standard in taste and literary merit.

g. Reference Collections

The reference collection in each agency is determined by the children's librarian and usually includes the latest editions of encyclopedias, dictionaries, atlases, and other titles deemed useful. One copy of certain titles, which because of seasonal or other temporary demand are in constant use, may be made temporary reference to insure the fair and impartial use of the book during the rush period.

h.   Adaptations, Abridgements and Retellings

Careful consideration is given to adaptations, abridgements, and retellings. Whether the book is by a living author or not, only those books that remain true in literary quality as well as mood of book are selected. Since folk literature is oral by tradition, anyone can retell a folk tale, but only the best are selected for the Library. In general, adaptations are not bought and abridgements are selected only when the story and concepts are considered suitable for children and the style of writing is too involved for the average child.

2.   Paperbacks

Paperbacks available in hardcover and already in the collection may be bought to supplement the collection. Paperbacks not available in hardcover may be bought after going through the reviewing process, with at least one copy being reinforced and cataloged in order to be listed in the Book Catalog.

3.   Pamphlets

For certain areas of knowledge where up-to-the-minute information is important and not available in book form, pamphlets are purchased for circulation and/or reference. One pamphlet file serves an agency except for buildings where the children's room is on the second floor or remote from the adult area.

4.   Periodicals

A dearth of satisfactory periodicals for children limits the number of titles accepted. The Central Children's Department subscribes to each title approved for children. Any children's periodical may be added to an agency if it is on the Library's approved list and funds are available.

5.   Non-Print Materials

It is the responsibility of the Library to provide such non-print materials as will aid the child in developing and increasing awareness of himself and his world.

a.   Films

Films of particular interest to children are purchased by the Regional Film Center in consultation with the Children's Audio-Visual Committee. Certain films of interest to adults that are effective in use with inservice training classes or are in constant demand for use with parents may be recommended for purchase by the Regional Film Center.

All children's films recommended shall meet the standards set forth in the criteria for any materials for children: appropriateness of subject, excellence of technical factors, faithfulness to text if book-related, general aesthetic qualities and creative and appropriate use of medium.

b. Recordings

Recordings, both disc and tape, shall be purchased especially for use of the libraries and others involved in library programming.

For children, titles are ordered for previewing by the Children's Audio-Visual Committee with the approval of the Head of Book Selection Unit from reviews in professional literature and audio-visual catalogs. A reference collection of such titles is maintained by the Central Children's Department. Basic circulating collections shall be maintained by branches and regional libraries where funds and personnel permit. The collection shall include important general musical compositions, interpretations of children's literature, suitable ethnic material and recordings specifically designed for young audiences. Such materials are judged on the general criteria of excellence in sound quality and technical reproduction, appropriateness of subject and presentation and usefulness in relation to the purpose of the collection.

C. According to Subject

1. Religion

The Library considers the child's spiritual development primarily the responsibility of his home and his church, but with the realization that the spiritual side of man is all important to himself and to his fellow man, supplies certain books on religious subjects for children. Bible stories, lives of saints, biographies of religious characters are bought when the particular title meets the required standards for children's books generally. Books on customs and traditions of religious faiths are occasionally purchased, such as Fitch's One God, and titles of general spiritual content, such as Jones' Small Rain. Books or pamphlets of specific religious teaching or practice, except where the book may be used for information on a career or to give historical background, are not purchased for children's collections, but in many cases may be found in the Education, Philosophy, and Religion Department of the Central Library.

2. Foreign Languages

Teaching of foreign languages at the elementary level, increased travel by families for pleasure and business, and the interest of the Library in fostering knowledge and understanding of people of other lands and other cultures have created quite a demand for children's books in foreign languages.

The Central Children's Department is the only agency which buys children's foreign language books (see Section II) except where a predominant language is part of a branch's community. Popular titles with exact English translations that are sold through regular trade book channels, e.g., Here is Henry! (Voici Henri!) may be bought in both the English and foreign language version for any agency.

3. Folk and Fairy Tale Literature

In the belief that this type of book frequently forms the basis of a child's literary heritage in addition to advancing an understanding of the world's peoples, the Library considers it a responsibility to include titles which will provide as complete coverage of this area of literature as is possible. Each new title in this classification is evaluated against previous titles of the same subject or format, as well as in relation to its ability to fill gaps in the folk literature of the world. An effort is made to include a variety of editions particularly when the compiler, translator, or illustrator is of sufficient distinction to add to the stature of the book.

All children's fairy tales, books of folklore written for children to read themselves, for adults to read to children, or for adults to use to develop a background in the subject, will be cataloged for the children's collections. All books about folklore may be cataloged for the adult or Central Children's Department special collections. Any question of duplication will be decided individually by the departments involved.

4. Human Relations

The Library considers the removal of prejudice and ignorance regarding racial, ethnic, or religious groups of peoples one of its major responsibilities, and to this end makes a continuous effort to include in its book collections for children titles which will foster healthy attitudes along these lines. Books on other countries, races, nationalities, and religious groups are carefully selected; and, in general, those which bear discriminatory remarks or attitudes are not purchased. If possible, books on these subjects are reviewed for accuracy by a member of the particular national, religious, or racial group involved.

5. Human Physical Development and Reproduction

Books which deal with the process of human physical development and reproduction are purchased, providing the title presents the subject in a dignified and scientific manner. These titles are shelved with the regular children's collection to make them easily accessible to children and parents. However, when in the selection of a particular title, the recommendation is made that it be used by or with an adult only, or has been or might be subject to mutilation or theft, the book will be shelved in the reference section or on the Parent-Teacher shelf.

6. <u>Judo, Karate and Hypnotism</u>

The Library has a responsibility to prevent physical, as well as mental and emotional, injury to a child through the materials selected for the children's collections. The practice of the techniques of judo, karate and hypnotism taken from a book can cause serious injury to the reader and/or others unless carefully supervised by an expert. Therefore, no "how-to-do-it" books on these subjects will be bought for children's collections. The circulation of these books from the adult or young adult collections on a child's card may be done only when the parent or guardian accompanies the child to the Library and gives permission to the Library Assistant at the charging desk.

Reprinted by Permission of The Free Library of Philadelphia, Mrs. Peggy Glover, Coordinator, Office of Work with Adults and Young Adults.

BOOK SELECTION POLICY

The St. Mary Parish Library aims to provide material that will meet day-to-day educational, informational, cultural, and recreational interests and needs of the community.

The purpose of the selection process is to obtain materials which will assist the children, young people, and adults of St. Mary Parish to:

"Educate themselves continually
Keep pace with progress in all fields of knowledge
Become better members of home and community
Be more capable in their daily occupations
Develop their creative and spiritual capacities
Appreciate and enjoy works of art and literature
Make such use of leisure time as will promote personal and social well-being
Contribute to the growth of knowledge."*

I. Criteria--One or more of the following standards will be applied in selecting the material best suited to the St. Mary Parish Library.

1. Importance of subject matter to collection
2. Permanent or timely value
3. Purpose or intent of book
4. Historical value
5. Scarcity of material on subject
6. Reputation and significance of author
7. Reputation and significance of illustrator
8. Popular appeal
9. Reputation and professional standing of publisher
10. Price

II. Selection must meet not just the needs of those who use the library regularly, but anticipate the needs of the non-users.

III. The needs of the various age and interest groups in the community must be reflected in the library's acquisitions.

IV. The collection should contain opposing views on controversial topics of interest to the citizens and should represent the best possible balance between an honest presentation of both sides of public questions.

---

*American Library Association, Public Library Service, 1956.

V. Non-book materials (recordings, microfilm, films, paintings, etc.) are an integral part of the public library's holdings and will be provided as far as possible within the budget.

VI. Systematic withdrawal of lost, damaged, worn or out-dated materials which are no longer useful in maintaining an active, accurate collection is expected.

VII. The request of an individual or group to withdraw from the library shelves material which has been selected in accordance with the principles of this policy shall be referred to the Parish Librarian. The library welcomes the opportunity to discuss with the citizens of St. Mary Parish the interpretation and application of these book selection principles.

VIII. The same standards will govern the addition of all gifts to the collection. Acceptance of a gift, therefore, does not imply that it meets these criteria.

IX. **Books and library materials selected under this Book Selection Policy shall be held to be selected by the Board.

X. **This Board defends the principles of the freedom to read and declares that whenever censorship is involved no book and/or library material shall be removed from the library save under the orders of a court of competent jurisdiction.

XI. **The Library Bill of Rights as adopted by the Council of the American Library Association is considered as part of the Library's book selection policy.

RESPONSIBILITY FOR SELECTION

The initial responsibility lies with the professional staff of the Library operating within the areas of service to children, young adults and adults. All staff members and the general public may recommend materials for consideration.

The ultimate responsibility for book selection, as for all library activities, rests with the parish librarian who operates within the framework of policies determined by the Library Board of Control.

**As amended by the Board, May 21, 1970.

Reprinted by Permission of St. Mary Parish Library, Mrs. Lola Thompson, Librarian.

Finkelstein Memorial Library
Spring Valley, New York
1968

MATERIALS SELECTION POLICY

I.   GENERAL LIBRARY OBJECTIVES

The Finkelstein Memorial Library renders free library service to all individuals and groups in Ramapo Central School District No. 2. Its basic objectives are to provide and service expertly selected books and other materials which aid the individual in the pursuit of information and in the creative use of leisure time.

The primary function of the Library is service to adults for whom the use of books is a necessary and natural part of intelligent living. In addition, it provides special services for young adults and seeks to direct and stimulate these readers by affording them selected books and skilled individual and group guidance.

For school children, the Library's objectives are to provide books, related materials, and special services which amplify and potentiate the information these children are in the process of receiving in the classrooms and excellent school libraries of Ramapo Central School District No. 2, and to encourage them to engage in selective reading during their leisure time. In the case of pre-school children, an important function of the Library is to stimulate in them an interest in learning to read. The Library works closely with parents, teachers, and other adults, as well as with the children themselves, to obtain and provide expert guidance in these areas.

II.   OBJECTIVES OF SELECTION

Within the limitations of its available space and approved budget, the Library selects books from among those which supply specific information, enlarge experience, broaden horizons, stimulate imagination, promote aesthetic appreciation, and provide recreation.

Selection is based more specifically on the particular needs and interests of the community. Typical of such needs are books dealing with personal development, economic competence, satisfactory social relationships, citizenship responsibilities, wholesome family living, and the creative use of leisure time.

The importance of both basic, permanent value books and timely materials on current issues and problems is recognized, and has been considered.

III.   RESPONSIBILITY FOR SELECTION

Ultimate responsibility for book selection, as for all Library activities, rests with the Director, who operates within the framework of policies determined by the Board of Trustees.

IV. SELECTION POLICIES

The Library is the reservoir of books for the area and will be the permanent collection for future use. In selecting material, this fact is of paramount importance.

V. GENERAL POLICIES

The Library attempts to provide a general collection of reliable materials embracing the broader fields of knowledge, with due regard for variations in educational level, reading ability, and reading interest.

General criteria for book selection include: readability and popular appeal, quality of writing, reputation and significance of the author and publisher, and timeliness or permanence of the book. Materials to satisfy highly specialized interests are bought if real or potential demand exists. While suggestions from readers are welcome and are given serious consideration, the Library cannot, of course, include in its permanent collection every specialized book desired by individuals nor can it answer every obscure or specialized question. In certain cases, the most satisfactory service to a reader is to obtain the book on loan from a state or national library, or to refer the individual to another institution or to an expert in that field.

Gifts of books or other materials are accepted by the Library with the explicit understanding that they are not necessarily to be added to the collection, but will be used if possible.

VI. DUPLICATION

The duplication of books will be held to a minimum at all times.

Current popular books are duplicated to meet demand by renting copies for limited periods of time. An additional copy is rented for every three reserves taken. These books are returned when the demand ceases.

Since the Library accepts responsibility for the provision of supplementary materials for school and college students, some duplication of such materials is needed. However, it is the policy of the Library to hold this type of duplication to a minimum in the expectation that school and college libraries will assume greater responsibility for the needs of their own students.

VII. REPLACEMENT

It is not the Library's policy to replace automatically all standard and important books withdrawn because of loss, damage, or wear. In each case, need for replacement is weighed with regard to several factors: number of duplicate copies; extent of adequate coverage of the field; other similar material in the collection, especially later and better material; and demand for the particular title.

Every effort is made to replace important, out-of-print titles from second hand dealers. If satisfactory reprint editions of titles to be replaced exist, these may be preferred to the more expensive trade editions. In some cases, replacement by reprint edition is preferred to rebinding, when cost, estimated wear, and sturdiness of the reprint warrant it.

VIII. SELECTION FOR ADULTS

The aim of the Library is to provide, for the mature, adult reading public, the books they feel that they need for general reading, reference work, and recreation.

The following criteria apply to the selection of books for adults: general interest, special interest by a substantial segment of the reading public, scholarly works needed to round-out the collection, and books which enable the individual to investigate, as far as possible, all sides of debatable questions.

The Library will also maintain and continually enlarge, its collection of general and special standard reference books and non-book materials.

IX. SELECTION FOR YOUNG ADULTS

The ultimate aim of library work with young adults is to contribute, through books, to the development of well-rounded citizens with an understanding of themselves and other people, at home and abroad.

Readable adult titles, keyed to young adult needs and interests, are selected, as well as books that will tend to open up new interests in cultural, economic, scientific, and social fields.

Since readers of teen age vary widely in ability and background, the books selected for them will, of necessity, vary in content and reading difficulty, but all titles are purchased in the hope they will lead to continued reading in adult fields on as high a level as possible for each individual participant.

Since the collection is selected for general and recreational reading, no attempt is made to maintain a separate reference collection. Young adults use the regular adult reference and informational services.

X. SELECTION FOR CHILDREN

In selecting books for children, the Library's objective is to make available a collection that satisfies the informational, cultural, and recreational reading needs and potentials of children from pre-school age to fourteen. Books are included which meet the general demands of the majority of children as well as books with special qualities which make them valuable to children with special needs, talents, problems, or interests.

Criteria for the selection of children's books include literary and artistic worth, suitability of content and vocabulary to the age of the readers, and the contribution of the book to the balance of the total collection.

School curriculum demands are considered, insofar as they do not obscure the public library's general contribution to the community or attempt to substitute for the development and use of school library resources.

In general, textbooks are added not to satisfy school demands, but to provide information on subjects when there is little or no material available in any other form, or when the textbook makes a significant contribution to the collection.

Abridged adult classics are not purchased except where the abridgements are accepted literary works, as in the case of editions of "Don Quixote" or "Pilgrim's

Progress." Abridged versions of children's classics are not purchased. In the case of classic folk literature, editions for children are evaluated for literary merit before they are purchased.

Books in series are evaluated as individual titles and are added or rejected as they do or do not meet the basic quality standards for books.

Books on human physical development and sex are carefully selected as to scientific accuracy, and simplicity and dignity of presentation.

Books relating to religious groups, nationalities, countries, and races are carefully selected so that objectivity, fairness, and balance is maintained in the collection.

Books which are recognized as children's classics and are of considerable literary merit are included in the collection even though they may contain a word or phrase which is, today, unacceptable.

Current books which are well written and portray authentically and meaningfully a period, or incident, or way of life, are purchased despite the occasional use of an unaccepted term, provided the total impact of the book meets the standards maintained in the collection.

Children's books in foreign languages are purchased in limited quantity. These books are chosen for distinction in illustration and format, as examples of the best children's books of other countries.

XI. BASES FOR EXCLUSION

It should be noted that the absence of a particular book from the Library's collection does not necessarily mean that it is not available. The Library is always glad to borrow books from other libraries, if such books are not in its own collection.

However, every library which does not acquire all printed materials must, of necessity, employ a policy of selectivity in acquisition. The criteria for selection of books have been discussed. Criteria for exclusion are as follows:

A. Books which offend good taste or are contrary to generally accepted moral and ethical standards, and

B. Books on public questions presenting one side only, and written in a violent, sensational, inflammatory manner.

It should be remembered that books in the adult collection are selected for the use of mature readers. Books recognized as classics are purchased. Serious works which present an honest picture of some problem or aspect of life are not necessarily excluded because of coarse language or frankness. However, books written obviously to trade on a taste for sensationalism are not purchased, nor are purely pornographic works.

It should also be remembered that freedom of speech and freedom of the press, with certain exceptions defined by law, are a part of our national heritage and are accepted and defended by the courts. As an agency supported by public funds, the public library must heed these recognized principles of custom and law.

On questions on which there are two or more widely supported opinions or theories, or about which definite facts have not been established, or which by their very nature are not susceptible of factual proof, the Library will provide material on both or all sides as far as availability permits. An attempt will be made to provide books that give evidence of a sincere desire to get at the facts and seem to be written in a reasonable fashion, and as a result of careful study. However, but for the exceptions noted below, the Library may exclude sensational, violent, or inflammatory books, those that contain undocumented accusations and demonstrably false statements, and those regarded by a consensus of responsible opinion--civic, scientific, religious, and educational--as unsound, and have been so regarded over a period of years.

> Exceptions: for the use of scholars and students, the Library collection may include a few representative and prominent books which, when published, favored practices which have since come to be regarded as either anti-social or positively illegal. For their historical value, the Library may also purchase works of world or national figures whose views, though they may be widely rejected, have affected events.

Decision to exclude a book is made after review and consultation among the Library staff and, in doubtful cases, after referral to the Director.

The Library is opposed to the withdrawal or addition, at the request of any individual or group, of books which have been chosen or excluded on the basis of the foregoing principles. The Director welcomes the opportunity to discuss the interpretation of these principles with the individual or with representatives of such groups.

XII. THEFT AND MUTILATION

Since any book in the Library is liable to theft or mutilation, the possibility of theft and mutilation becomes only a secondary consideration in excluding materials. Experience has shown, of course, that materials in some subject fields, e.g., books on marriage and sex, as well as textbooks, reference books and illustrated books in many fields, are more often subject to mutilation and theft than others. If the material is essential in a well-rounded collection, the Library prefers, instead of excluding such books, to protect them by various precautionary measures, such as making them reference or placing them in closed stacks. However, in the case of some individual books on less important subjects which are regularly lost or stolen, it may be decided that no further duplicates are to be bought.

XIII. STUDENTS--SECONDARY AND HIGHER INSTITUTIONS

General student use of the Library on the high school level cannot be questioned. Since, however, limited funds must be stretched to cover the most urgent needs of a very diversified clientele, especially those without other library facilities, and since the obligation of providing duplicate copies for students is primarily that of an institution's own library, the Library functions only as a supplementary source for students' reading or reference purposes. It expects the college or school library to provide a working collection containing adequate copies of reference tools which are used over and over by large groups of students. It does not undertake to meet the demands for large class assignments which tend to monopolize the facilities of the Library to the detriment of its use by the general public.

XIV. INFORMAL STUDY

In serving as a supplementary source for student use, the Library selects, other things being equal, those texts or other books which will also be useful for the general reader. Though in practice it is difficult to discover the purpose of each reader, the aim is to serve specifically the non-academic student who does not have direct access to the resources of a school or college library. In initial purchase or in duplication first consideration, within budget limitations, is given to the needs of these students. This includes persons engaged in self-education programs such as study and discussion groups in clubs, civic organizations, churches or other agencies, or courses or institutes sponsored by such agencies, or presented on radio and television.

Special attention is also given to providing an adequate supply of suitable introductory texts for adults who wish to review a subject or pursue independent study.

XV. READERS OF LIMITED SKILL

The Library is alert to the need for easy reading materials for the less skilled adult reader, both native and foreign-born. Pamphlets, duplicates of useful children's books, books with many illustrations, simplified classics, etc., are provided for this purpose.

XVI. FICTION

Involved in the problem of selecting fiction is the existence of a variety of types of novels and the need to satisfy readers of differing tastes, interests, purposes, and reading levels. The Library's collection, therefore, includes representative novels of the past and present, notable for literary quality and cultural value; historical and regional novels; character studies, biographical and psychological novels; novels relating to the fields of art, industry, science, social problems, and the professions; satire, fantasy, and humor; mystery and suspense, science fiction, western, and other adventure stories; the better light fiction; and short stories.

The novel has assumed an important place as an educational tool. It is recognized as a medium for recording and molding public opinion and as an instrument for changing individual attitudes. The sound treatment of significant social and personal problems or of racial and religious questions through novels of many-reader appeal may contribute much to the betterment of human relations. For this reason, a substantial number of novels of serious purpose are purchased in preference to many titles of light fiction and adventure. Due attention is paid to maintaining a basic collection in attractive editions of standard novels, the classics, and the semi-classics of world literature.

Since each novel is ordinarily judged on its individual merits, there is as a rule no attempt at completeness in the Library's holdings of authors' works. Exceptions are made, however, of the great novelists of the past, all of whose works (including minor and fragmentary writings) are obtained if possible, and of the outstanding contemporary novelists.

In selecting fiction the Library has set up no arbitrary single standard of literary quality. An attempt is made to satisfy a public varying greatly in formal education, social background, and taste. Under these circumstances fiction selection does not mean choosing only the most distinguished novels but also the most competent, pleasing, and successful books in all important categories of fiction writing. Staff members, when reviewing new books, consider a title in comparison with the good work which has been done in the writer's specific field. Naturally the literary criteria applied in the case of an experimental novel, for example, will differ from those by which a detective story is chosen.

However, it is the experimental novel rather than fiction written purely for entertainment that usually poses problems in book selection. The novel is a vigorous literary form, subject to change and innovation by writers to suit their differing aims. The author's purpose and his success in achieving it are the best guides in judging a novel at a time when ideas about structure and styles are so varied and conflicting. In the past, plot and characterization have been considered essential to the novel, but in recent years plot has been almost abandoned by many leading novelists. The major interests among writers of serious fiction today are character and ideas, although plot may be said to survive in the development which takes place in the leading character.

Readers, however, do not always look with favor on experimentalism, and the Library's staff is aware that a novel distinguished for characterization and style must also possess a well-constructed plot, in order to be sure of a favorable reception among large numbers of readers. Titles that combine these qualities are sought and duplicated, although care is taken to include representative works of experimental novelists, examples of new trends, and the like.

The Library rents books to meet this demand. After all reserves have been filled, the books are returned to the rental agency.

Novels, even though widely advertised, are not purchased if they fail to measure up to the Library's rather broad standards of literary quality. A book in which the plot is trite, the characters stereotyped, or the writing dull or trivial is not purchased.

Although no single standard of literary quality can be set up, it may be said that the Library's policy is to acquire fiction, whether serious or amusing, realistic or imaginative, which is well written and based on authentic human experience and to exclude weak, incompetent, or cheap sentimental writing, as well as the solely sensational, morbid, or erotic.

The Library purchases new as well as standard titles in Hebrew. This includes some reference materials.

The Library also purchases standard and a few modern novels and plays in French, German, Italian, Spanish and Russian.

XVII. STUDY OUTLINES, "SHORT-CUT" MATERIALS, ETC.

Selection of materials of a "short-cut" type is based on the following factors: potential usefulness to general readers, responsibility of other agencies, and practicability of library use of the materials.

A.   Study Outlines

The study outline, when compact but fairly complete and prepared by a competent scholar in the subject field, provides a quick survey of a subject useful in many ways for both self-teaching adults and students: as a study aid when reviewing for examinations and organizing subject matter; for brief background reading and reviewing; and for introduction to a new subject.   The excellent <u>College Outline Series</u> is a good example of the best type of study outline.   These and others of similar quality make extremely useful and worth-while additions to the book collection of the Library.

B.   Laboratory Manuals and Work Books

Since this type of materials is almost useless apart from laboratory practice, it is seldom purchased.

C.   Examination Manuals

Although many Civil Service and other examination manuals are far from satisfactory, they are purchased to satisfy a need not otherwise met.

D.   Synopses, Summaries, Etc.

Synopses, summaries and similar short-cut materials are purchased for reference purposes or in some cases for circulation, since they have many uses beyond their sometimes questionable use by students. For example, plot outlines of plays, novels, etc., serve as play selection aids to little theater groups, as legitimate study aids for quick reviewing, and for quick brush-up on books read previously but partially forgotten.

XVIII. PAPERBACKS

The term paperbacks includes all separates of the type ordinarily considered as books rather than pamphlets, bound in paper and other inexpensive bindings.

Paperbacks may be bought for any of the following reasons:
(1) If a title is out of print or otherwise unobtainable in better format.
(2) If the title is one which has never appeared in any other edition.
(3) If it is a title in heavy demand.
(4) If it is an older title, useful only occasionally which has become available in a paperback edition.

XIX.   MATERIALS OTHER THAN BOOKS

A.   Pamphlets

Selection of pamphlets follows the general policies outlined for the selection of books, but the nature of pamphlet material requires certain changes in procedure. Principal sources are regularly checked.

Since they are usually free or inexpensive, useful pamphlets may be duplicated heavily at slight cost. Frequently their attractive format, brevity, and simple presentation make them ideal for use with self-educating adults. Their use as a medium for propaganda or advertising, however, makes it necessary that pamphlets be examined with some care before being added to the collection. It is not the Library's policy to exclude propaganda or advertising publications, but obviously undesirable items must be eliminated, and a proper balance of viewpoints must be sought in controversial subjects.

Those advertising pamphlets which distort facts, intrude commercial messages unduly, or contain misleading statements are not added. Propaganda pamphlets are naturally expected to be one-sided, but those whose propagandist intent is clearly indicated by the publishers' names or statements of purpose are preferred to those which appear under imprints whose sponsorship is not clearly defined. Clear, moderate statements of viewpoint are sought on controversial subjects to balance partisan points of view. An effort is also made to avoid overloading the files with free publications of aggressive propaganda organizations to such an extent as to destroy the balance of viewpoint.

B. Periodicals

Periodicals are purchased or accepted as gifts, chiefly for one or more of the following reasons: (1) to keep the Library's collection up to date with current thinking in various fields, and to provide material not available in books; (2) to supplement the book collection; (3) to supply recreational reading; (4) to serve the staff as book selection aids, book reviewing media, and professional reading. Those which are most needed for reference or research are duplicated in microform for long-term use as they become available in this form and as budget permits.

The type of periodical most obviously needed as a source of material not in books is that which deals with current affairs, either generally or in a special field. Periodicals of this type are needed both for reference work and for general reading. Individual titles are chosen for the following reasons: accuracy and objectivity; accessibility of content through indexes; ease of consultation; demand; need in reference work; representation of point of view or subject needed in the collection; local interest in subject matter; price.

In most fields of scholarship, technical research, and creative writing, important new theories, discoveries, trends, and viewpoints appear first in journals, and frequently do not find their way into published books for many years. Even when they are later incorporated into books, they are not usually dealt with in such detail as in the original periodical treatment. As a result, the periodical references are often cited in footnotes and scholarly bibliographies. In those fields in which the Library provides books of even a fairly scholarly nature, the important journals are therefore needed. In selection of individual titles, the following factors have considerable weight: issuance of the journal by a well-known organization; indexing in periodical indexes; authority and reputation of editors and contributors.

In selecting periodicals for purchase the various groups in the community are considered. For example, the leading Negro periodicals, journals of trades and professions and the like.

C. Newspapers

Since local papers are indispensable sources for local information, some of it available in no other printed work, the Library acquires all known Rockland County newspapers. Before the purchase of old files, offered at a considerable price, availability of files elsewhere and of other papers of the same locality are taken into consideration. In order to build up back files an effort is made to acquire microfilm files of local newspapers.

For reference purposes, a complete file of the New York Times, on microfilm is indispensable, along with its index. This file is gradually being built up as funds are available. Because of heavy use, newsprint files of the New York Times are also maintained for three months. A file of the Wall Street Journal on microfilm, along with its index, is also a part of the Library's collection.

D. Government Publications

The Library buys selectively but consistently those government publications that are important as reference materials or for popular reading and study.

All official publications of Rockland County and its Towns and Villages are acquired if possible.

E. Manuscript Materials

The few manuscripts in the Library are of local interest. It is the policy of the Library to emphasize printed material and to leave to other institutions, particularly the Historical Society, the collecting and care of original manuscripts relating to local history.

F. Microforms

The Library acquires, in microform, needed materials not available in any other form, materials preferred in this form because of lower cost or reduced bulk, and duplicates of materials available in other forms but desirable also in microform for reasons of preservation or space.

Space considerations, as well as preservation, dictate the acquisition in microform of newspaper files for permanent use and long runs of periodicals. Frequency of use is not a major factor in the decision to purchase in microform when there is a choice, but material likely to be in demand for circulation is still preferred in book form.

Because of the lack of standardization in the field of microforms, and in view of the many expected advances in the whole area of micro-reproductions, no one form is preferred. When there is a choice, selection is based on clearness of copy, availability of adequate machines, ease of servicing, and the form of micro-reproduction of related materials which are already in the library collection.

148

XX. AUDIO-VISUAL MATERIALS

A. Recordings

Several types of recordings are acquired by the Library either from regular funds or special grants.

Musical recordings are naturally the most numerous. Since a complete collection cannot be attempted, selection for both children's and adult use is based on composition, performer, recording quality, requests, and use. Predominantly classical music is purchased, orchestral and vocal recordings in about equal proportions. Representative folk music, outstanding examples of jazz, musical comedies, sound tracks of superior quality, and educational discs, e.g., demonstrations of musical instruments, are also acquired. No effort is made to supply various performances of a single work.

Non-musical recordings include poetry, drama, theatrical sound effects, speeches, teaching and practice records, e.g., language and business techniques, and prose readings, both fiction and non-fiction; story telling documentaries of historical events, nature, the physical universe, and the man-made world of sound. In the selection of verse, drama, and literary prose records, the importance of both authors and performers is considered. Recordings of poets reading their own works are preferred to those of professional readers, and poetry of permanent literary interest to the lighter and more ephemeral. In the field of drama, recordings of Shakespeare and other classics, performed by distinguished actors, are purchased. Recorded language courses, both foreign and English, are bought as funds permit. The aim is the inclusion of all important European and Far Eastern languages in the collection, with rather heavy duplication of the most popular. As the production of non-musical recordings in non-literary fields expands, selection is governed by the same general principles applied to acquisition of other library materials, plus consideration of the value of sound in conveying the subject matter to the listener.

Gifts are accepted if the recordings, musical and non-musical, offered are suitable for the collection.

B. Pictures

The Library expects to develop a general picture collection as time, space and staff permits.

C. Films, Filmstrips, and Slides

The Library does not purchase films, filmstrips or slides on a regular basis. Instead, it borrows these for library use and library users through the Ramapo Catskill Library System and other film suppliers. The Library may purchase a few seasonal films, children's films and adult films of permanent value.

The Library does attempt to build up a strong collection of film catalogs and information about films that will aid users in selecting the most appropriate films for their specific use.

D. Maps

Sheet maps of Rockland County and New York State are acquired by the Library to supplement those found in atlases and other books.

E. Music

The Library adds music of all kinds that is published in book form. At the discretion of the Director, the Library may add music in sheet form.

XXI. LOCAL HISTORY

The general aim of the Library with regard to local history material is to attain a fair degree of inclusiveness. It is the general policy of the Library to acquire, as far as is practicable, one copy for reference use of all printed items--fiction and non-fiction--contributing to a knowledge of local history. Its aim, however, is considerably broader in scope than the strictly historical, and emphasis is also given to the acquisition of those materials which will contribute to a knowledge of the social, civic, religious, economic, and cultural life, past and present. Genealogical material is not collected.

Duplicates of material likely to be useful for circulation, including standard works and current publications on subjects in demand, are acquired when available.

In accordance with the policy of concentrating on printed matter, certain types of material in the non-print category are generally excluded, e.g., manuscripts, paintings, and museum objects, but many types are included, e.g., photographs, photographic negatives, microforms, prints. Printed materials included are books, pamphlets, periodicals, newspapers, serials, documents, maps, atlases, clippings, and post cards.

The Library aims to have a representative collection of glossy photographs of outstanding local persons, buildings, outdoor views, and subjects such as agriculture, industry, etc., both past and present.

XXII. LAW

The Library recognizes an obligation to make available certain types of law materials. It provides a small collection of standard and popular books for the general reader on such subjects as jurisprudence, history of law, legal ethics, court procedure, jury duty, etc. Standard texts by recognized authorities are purchased.

The Library's law reference collection includes the laws of New York State, state and federal tax guides, encyclopedias, handbooks and other general reference materials.

XXIII. MEDICINE AND RELATED SUBJECTS

The Library recognizes its responsibility to supply authoritative, up-to-date, understandable material on health, hygiene, and common diseases. Books on medicine, surgery, psychiatry, and related fields are selected with care.

The books purchased are on several levels of difficulty: the junior and senior high school level and the level of the adult laymen. Material useful to the layman is sought in such subjects as psychiatry, geriatrics, obstetrics, space medicine, environmental medicine, atomic age medicine, and fallout hazards, drugs, cancer, heart and high blood pressure conditions, and therapeutic diets. Preventive medicine, personal health and hygiene, dietetics, and public health problems are emphasized. The Library also buys for the general reader and student a small but representative number of texts in such basic sciences as bacteriology, anatomy, physiology and physiological chemistry and, more extensively, in the fields of food, nutrition, and nursing. Textbooks for students and practitioners in medicine, dentistry, osteopathy, chiropractic, naturopathy, and optometry are not purchased.

In this whole area controversial and doubtful material is avoided. New books are reviewed carefully, with regard to the author's credentials, position, manner of treating the subject, and his adherence to generally accepted medical facts. Careful regard is given also to publisher, format, and type of illustration. Where any doubt exists as to reliability and suitability, final decision is deferred until authoritative reviews in professional journals are available.

XXIV. NARCOTICS

The Library recognizes its responsibility to provide for use of parents, teachers, social workers, and others legitimately concerned with the problem of narcotics, detailed and authoritative information on the subject such as the chemistry, history, and the origin of narcotic drugs, their physiological and psychological effects, and the treatment of addiction. While the Library is aware that certain books on this topic may be dangerous in the hands of the impressionable young, it does not exclude such works, if presented by qualified authors in unsensational style.

XXV. SEMI- AND PSEUDO-SCIENTIFIC MATERIALS

Special care is necessary in the purchase of books in those borderline areas of science in which subject matter or treatment is not recognized by reputable scientific authority. Careful review of such books may rule out those which are obviously unsound scientifically or potentially harmful. In doubtful cases, it is necessary to wait for authoritative reviews or to consult experts in the field.

Books catering to morbid interests, the esoteric, sensational, the rabidly reformist are not added. Material on such subjects as alcohol, tobacco and food fads are reviewed for reliability and objective presentation.

Books by well-established authors and scientists who hold ideas somewhat off the beaten track may be bought when the author's prominence makes his ideas of general intellectual interest. The reputation of the author, the tone of his work and the method of handling his subject are deciding factors.

The following rules of thumb are helpful in dealing with questionable scientific, health, and borderline materials: author (reputation, professional or academic position, other publications, etc.); publisher (whether book is privately printed by author, a bookshop, a small unknown press, or whether notice gives only P.O. box); source (whether sent unsolicited by author, distributor, or propaganda organization, especially when accompanied by high-pressure sales letter); content and purpose (whether authoritative, in accepted tradition of handling the subject matter, whether the book attempts to examine the subject objectively); literary style and vocabulary (whether nebulous, full of abstract or unusual jargon); typographic format (quality of paper, presswork, binding, general impression of the book as a book). While all of these factors may help to spot the pseudo-scientific, in the last analysis final decision must be based on expert opinion.

XXVI. RELIGION

Because religion is one of the deep concerns of man and theology is one of the major intellectual disciplines, it is essential that the Library have the standard works of the major world religions in so far as they are available in either the original language or translations likely to be familiar to potential readers. These include the Judaeo-Christian writings, ancient, e.g., Talmud, Church Fathers, medieval and Reformation, e.g., Summa Theologica, Luther, Calvin, and modern; and the sacred books of other religions such as the Koran and Mahabharata. Authoritative, well-written books on agnosticism and the psychology, philosophy, and history of religion are also represented. Standard versions of the Bible are included as are reliable commentaries, concordances, histories, and atlases. A number of long runs of periodicals of wide, scholarly usefulness and the most needed encyclopedias and reference and bibliographical tools are provided.

The following are bought if they meet the criteria of objectivity, good taste, clear writing, and scholarship: able and dispassionate presentations of comparative religion and of doctrine; books about the Bible; church histories; lives of Christ and Biblical characters; lives of saints and religious leaders; practical handbooks on religious education, missions, church administration, pastoral work; rituals and services for various occasions; collections of prayers; stories of hymns and hymnals; and books that offer inspiration. Since users of the Library vary widely in educational background and reading ability, an effort is made to choose material to fit differing needs while avoiding both the very specialized and abstruse, and the immature, over-simplified and saccharine.

As an educational institution the Library recognizes an obligation to identify and evaluate sectarian propaganda material which tends to foster hatred or intolerant attitudes toward other groups.

The Library includes information about the beliefs, practices, and ritual of many sects, if presented with authority, accuracy, and objectivity, and recognizes a special obligation to provide information about the major denominations represented locally.

XXVII. SEX

For some years social workers, ministers, physicians, and teachers have been teaching that social problems having their origin in sex may be at least partially solved by replacing the reticence of past generations by frank and open discussion, and by substituting for devious sources of information the clear and authoritative statements of well-written books. They believe that intelligent, directed reading will help solve many individual problems.

It is part of the functions of the Library to provide in adequate quantity for lay readers, books which are well balanced, authoritative, sound, sane, up to date, and scientific in treatment.

On the subject of sex deviations, the Library attempts to keep a stock of well-balanced materials including studies, reports, and some personal accounts for the serious reader in this subject.

Selection is made with regard to suitability for such varied groups as physicians, social workers, clergymen, parents, teachers, young people contemplating marriage, the newly married, adolescents, and children. Materials are provided which are adapted to several levels of educational background and reading ability as well as to differing social and religious customs.

Very scientific and technical works do not come within the scope of the Library's collection. Sensational, pseudo-scientific works, and books designed to gratify morbid interests are also avoided.

Reprinted by Permission of Finkelstein Memorial Library, Mr. Robert S. Ake, Director.

Tucson Public Library
Tucson, Arizona
Revised 1967

BOOK SELECTION POLICY

TABLE OF CONTENTS

PART 3 — CHILDREN'S BOOK SELECTION POLICIES

PREFACE

The book selection policies are the result of a cooperative effort on the part of many staff members of the Tucson Public Library. Inasmuch as they reflect procedure commonly practiced in the fields of librarianship, no claim is made for their originality. However, they have been formulated to meet the express needs of a particular system.

While these policies have been approved by the Tucson Public Library Board, and are offered as official guidelines to all staff members, they are by no means a static set of principles. They must constantly be subject to revision. As the system grows, needs and ideas change. Book selection policies must be adapted to changing situations. Suggestions that serve to clarify or strengthen these policies are always welcome.

November, 1967

PART 1

ADULT BOOK SELECTION POLICIES

I.   OBJECTIVES OF SERVICE

The Tucson Public Library is an educational institution serving all people who wish to profit from the recorded wisdom and experience of mankind. The library collects and organizes significant books and other printed, visual and recorded material so that they are easily accessible. Librarians are employed to help people locate information and select books they require for reading and study.

The library's services are available to all residents of Pima County without regard to race, creed, occupation, age or economic status. An active program that reaches all ages of people is carried on so that they cultivate a lifetime pattern and develop their voluntary enjoyment of reading. By providing recreational materials, the library encourages the creative use of leisure time. This library has a special responsibility to the community to act as an impartial center for cultural, educational and civic activities.

The library holds a responsibility for the conservation of the cultural and historical heritage of the community. It not only conserves but vigorously promotes the use of its resources through various programs and through extension of library facilities in the area. It seeks to maintain a balance of material on all sides of issues and accepts the responsibility to maintain the democratic principles expressed by the American Library Association in both the Library Bill of Rights and the Freedom to Read statement.

II. POLICIES GUIDING SELECTION OF LIBRARY MATERIALS

A. General Objectives

To implement the objectives of the library, major emphasis is placed on the educational and informational service of the library. One of the most important functions of the library is to provide reference materials for the direct answering of specific questions for individuals and groups, including business, industry, labor, church, professional and civic organizations. To be considered are the needs and interests of the individual as an individual and in his relationship to society as a whole.

Books in the adult collection are selected for mature readers. Separate collections are available to children and to young people. An attempt is made to buy books with due regard to the differences in education, interests and needs of all age groups. The Tucson Public Library is not a research library. It does not attempt to keep either fiction or nonfiction which has outlived its usefulness. In general, when a new edition of a work is published, the library discards the older edition, provided there has been extensive revision.

The general policy of the library is to have in the Central Library collection one copy of each book approved for purchase. However, because of lack of space in Central and budgetary limitations, there are times that Central cannot purchase a title that another agency needs. In such cases, the head of the agency may consult with the Coordinator of Work with Adults who may give permission for the agency to purchase the book.

In the case of controversial topics, an effort is made to see that all sides of the question are represented.

A request for specialized material or material for which there is only an occasional demand is met by interlibrary loan.

Multiple copies of books needed for class assignments will not be purchased. A book in popular demand will be duplicated, provided it is a book worth duplicating, at the ratio of one copy for every five reserves.

Books of a reference nature are not purchased for the circulating collection. Certain books which are not specifically of a reference nature will from time to time be placed in the reference collection.

The library will purchase at least one copy of a work by a local author or composer. Writers and composers born in Pima County who leave the area in childhood and others residing in the area temporarily are not considered as local authors or composers.

B. Criteria for Selection of Nonfiction

1. Qualification of the author in subject field
2. Scope and authority of subject matter
3. Quality of writing (style, readability)
4. Date of publication
5. Reputation of publisher
6. Arrangement of materials (indexes, bibliographies)
7. Relationship to collection
8. Physical qualities (binding, print, size, illustrations, margins)
9. Price

C. Criteria for Selection of Fiction

1. Style
2. Appeal: popular, limited
3. Characterization: constructive and true portrayal of character and life
4. Literary merit
5. Relationship to the collection, i.e., types: mystery, western, fantasy, science fiction, romance
6. Publisher
7. Price

D. Criteria for Selection of Materials Other Than Books

The same philosophy and standards of selection which apply to books apply to the selection of materials other than books. Need, demand and use are factors to be considered.

1. Pamphlets

The purpose of the pamphlet collection is to make available for use current material before it can be supplied in book form. Various viewpoints are represented on controversial subjects.

2. Periodicals

a. Periodicals are purchased to

(1) Supplement the book collection
(2) Provide material not yet available in book form
(3) Provide recreational reading
(4) Furnish professional reading for the staff
(5) Aid in book selection

b. Periodicals selected are

    (1) Those which are considered authoritative and objective
    (2) Those indexed in the standard periodical indexes
    (3) Those of local interest
    (4) Those frequently in demand

3. Newspapers

The Arizona Daily Star and the Tucson Daily Citizen are purchased currently and on microfilm as available. Out-of-town papers are selected on the basis of quality, geographical representation and demand.

4. Government Documents

The University of Arizona is the depository library for government documents in Tucson. Certain government documents which are considered necessary in a public library are added to our collection.

5. Audio-visual Materials

a. Recordings

Factors to be considered in the selection of musical recordings are: composition, performer, quality of musical interpretation, quality of record materials, requests and use. No attempt is made to supply popular song and dance music. Factors to be considered in the selection of nonmusical records are: author, performer, requests, use, and, in general, the same principles as those that apply to purchase of other library materials.

Types of recordings purchased:

(1) Classical, such as operas, symphonies, chamber music
(2) Semiclassical, such as show tunes, operettas
(3) Contemporary popular music, such as jazz, ragtime, dance music, except for current tunes
(4) Folk music
(5) Literature, such as books, poetry, plays
(6) Documentary and historical records
(7) Foreign language study records
(8) Religious, such as masses, hymns, oratorios
(9) Miscellaneous, such as bird songs, instruction (selling, typing)

Records for Special Programs--Branches scheduling programs that include records should, in most instances, purchase the recordings to be used. Before the recordings are ordered, the person in charge of selecting records for the Central Library should be consulted for the best recording currently available.

Basic Branch Collection--The Fine Arts section has available an order file for a basic branch collection of 1,500 records (discs). This file is available for those wishing to strengthen their collections. When using this file it will be necessary to check availability and price of the recordings due to rapid changes in this field. Additional checking of reviews will be necessary in many instances to insure ordering the best recordings available.

Regular Branch Orders--When the staff of the Central Library prepares a record order, this will be sent to the Book Selection Room to enable all agencies to select records at the same time. To conform with selection policies, the branches will make their selections only from recordings selected for purchase by the Central Library.

Gifts--To achieve uniformity in our material selection policy, gift records will be treated the same as gift books. If they are acceptable to the Fine Arts section, they will be kept at Central unless they are duplicate copies of records already in the collection. Duplicates will automatically be processed for the receiving agency if so desired.

b. Framed Art Prints

The library maintains a circulating collection of framed art prints for education and cultural enjoyment. An attempt is made to represent major artists as well as various periods and schools of art.

c. Maps

Accuracy, print and readability are considered. All types of maps are made available: political, geographical, topographical, pictorial, historical, geological and road.

d. Music (sheet music)

Works of standard composers, recognized contemporaries and folk music are included. No attempt is made to supply popular song and dance music for circulation. Vocal and instrumental music may be found in sheet music as well as in volumes.

e. Pictures

A circulating picture collection is provided for adults with the needs of commercial artists, teachers and other individuals and groups in mind. Authentic, clearly reproduced pictures are provided on a variety of subjects to supplement illustrations in books and periodicals.

6. Paperbacks

The same standards apply to paperbacks as to other books. Paperbacks are bought for the following reasons:

a. Title is out of print or unobtainable in other format
b. Title has not appeared in another edition
c. Title is in heavy demand for temporary current interest or information
d. Title is older and rarely used
e. Price

7. Telephone Directories

A collection of current telephone directories, including all Arizona cities, the larger cities of the United States and foreign countries is available.

III. TECHNIQUES AND SELECTION AIDS

A. Standard Selection Aids for Current Fiction and Nonfiction

1. Library Journal
2. Book Buyer's Guide
3. The New York Times Book Review
4. Kirkus
5. Saturday Review
6. Publisher's Weekly
7. Choice

These are but a few of the sources used. Bibliographies in scholarly magazines and lists prepared by various libraries and subject authorities are checked.

B. Techniques and Selection Aids for Materials Other Than Books

1. Pamphlets

a. Vertical File Index
b. Public Affairs Information Service
c. Monthly Checklist of State Publications
d. Booklist
e. Monthly Catalog of U.S. Government Publications

National periodicals are checked for lists of free and inexpensive materials.

2. Periodicals

The library considers for first purchase those periodicals indexed in:

a. Readers' Guide to Periodical Literature
b. Business Periodicals Index
c. Applied Science and Technology Index

The popular demand and interests of local groups and individuals are considered.

3. Newspapers

Newspapers of local, regional and national importance are purchased. As newspaper print is fragile and space is limited, permanent files of newspapers cannot be maintained. Microfilm files are maintained of The Arizona Daily Star, Tucson Daily Citizen and The New York Times. As a rule, back files of out-of-town newspapers are kept for one month at Central Library.

4. Government Documents

From time to time requests for government documents are sent to Arizona senators and representatives who are able to furnish to libraries certain documents free of charge. Those government documents that are necessary in all public libraries may be purchased when required.

5. Audio-visual Materials

a. Recordings

Reputable reviewing sources such as HiFi/Stereo Review, Library Journal, Notes, American Record Guide and High Fidelity are checked.

b. Framed Art Prints

Catalogs from authoritative sources such as The Metropolitan Museum of Art in New York City, The Museum of Modern Art in New York City, The New York Graphic Society, the Chicago Art Institute and The Unesco Catalogue of Colour Reproductions of Paintings are consulted.

c. Maps

Free and inexpensive maps are collected from available sources. Some others may be purchased, especially Arizona maps. Clearness of type and accuracy are essential.

d. Music (sheet music)

This collection has relied largely on gifts but may be supplemented by purchase. Demand will be considered.

e. Pictures

Pictures are gathered from discarded books and magazines, advertisements and free materials. Occasionally, pictures are purchased when a demand arises.

6. Paperbacks

The same aids used in selection of hard backs are used in selection of paperbacks.

7. Telephone Directories

Telephone directories are received as gifts from the Mountain States Telephone Company and others. The collection may be supplemented by purchase or exchange.

IV. POLICIES GUIDING EXCLUSION OF LIMITED ACQUISITION OF LIBRARY MATERIALS

A. General Statement

Books in the following categories are not selected:

1. Books which seem offensive to good taste and contrary to moral and ethical standards, unless recognized as substantial literature.

2. Books on public questions when written in a violent, sensational, inflammatory manner

3. Pornographic books

B. Areas of Limited Acquisition

1. Law

The library, recognizing the difficulty of the layman in understanding legal publications, purchases for circulation only those books written for the layman; for example, books on jury duty and taxation. In the reference collection are located such books as dictionaries of legal terms, the U.S. Code, the Tucson Code, the Arizona Revised Statutes and Martindale-Hubbell Law Directory. No attempt is made to build an inclusive collection.

2. Medicine

Books on health, hygiene and common diseases written for the layman are purchased for the circulating collection. In the reference collection are placed such books as medical dictionaries and encyclopedias. No attempt is made to build an inclusive collection.

3. Textbooks

Textbooks are not added to satisfy school demands but to provide information on subjects where there is little or no material available in any other form. Customarily, textbooks used in the local schools and colleges are not purchased, but exceptions may be made if the text is considered useful to the general reader.

4. Sex

a. Nonfiction

Books written for the medical specialist, pseudo-scientific works and sensational books are not purchased. Selection is geared to the needs of various ages and groups so that authoritative, up-to-date, scientific books on the subject are available. Materials in this area are not rejected on the basis of protest expressed by some borrowers.

b. Fiction

Judgment of fiction is made on the total book, rather than on parts that might in themselves be considered objectionable.

(1) "Although no single standard of literary quality can be established, it may be said that the library's policy is to acquire fiction, whether serious or amusing, realistic or imaginative, which is well written and based upon authentic human experience and to exclude weak, incompetent or cheap sentimental writing, as well as the intentionally sensational, morbid or erotic. If the author is seriously trying to give an honest picture and if the book meets other standards, the library may buy it even though the author has felt it necessary to include

a certain amount of vulgar language and frankness of detail in order to accomplish his purpose."*

(2) "In its consideration of modern fiction, the public library should first of all hold to the principle that censorship is not its province; selection is.

"It must select from the mass of current literature in every field. Selection may be defined as the choice of what is adjudged the best, from standards of literature and from practical standards of usefulness or timeliness or legitimate demand.

"You cannot get a contemporary literature made to order. And in dealing with contemporary literature there must be sympathy, or understanding, with acceptance of contemporary life. Our present-day leveling of former barriers, our disregard of former standards, our analyzing, experimenting, working out all kinds of theories, are all reflected in fiction.

"Selection should be representative of types and tendencies in fiction--new methods in style, new experiments in theme and treatment; and in this, the larger public library should especially be tolerant and inclusive."**

5. Religion

a. Books

The library will maintain an impartial recognition of conflicting points of view subject to the specific points listed below.

As an educational institution emphasizing goodwill and understanding among different races and religions, the library has a definite moral and social obligation to evaluate carefully sectarian propaganda material which tends to foster hatred or intolerant attitudes toward other groups.

In the book collection, an attempt is made to represent the doctrine and history of all denominations and faiths. For those faiths not represented by organizations in this city and by adequate book material, the library attempts coverage by comparative religious books.

b. Periodicals

The library is faced with a problem of limited space for display and storage of religious periodicals and for any extended collection of books dealing with sectarian problems.

---

*The Dayton Public Library Book Selection Policies.

**The Library Journal, January 1, 1967, p. 77, Vol. 92, No. 1.

The library will add religious materials under the following conditions:

(1) The library is not obligated to accept or add to its collection any unsolicited gift

(2) Gifts or subscriptions to periodicals are accepted if they meet _one_ of the following provisions:
   (a) That the periodical is indexed in the Readers' Guide
   (b) That the periodical represents denominations or faiths which have organized groups in this community

(3) The library accepts as a gift only one periodical representing a religious faith, preferably a magazine which covers the broad aspects or program of a particular denomination

(4) Periodicals are accepted with the provision that only those which are indexed in the Readers' Guide can be considered for display on the periodical racks

(5) The library keeps back files on all indexed periodicals at least one year

(6) The library is under no obligation to duplicate copies of any religious periodical, either at the Central Library or in the branches

6. Genealogy and Heraldry

The library does not purchase genealogies of individual families, except in the case of historically famous ones. In the field of heraldry, books on rules and terminology are purchased, but books containing arms of individual families are not purchased. Standard reference works, such as Burke's Peerage, are purchased, however.

7. Pseudo-Scientific Materials

Books in the borderline areas of science which are unsound scientifically or potentially harmful and are not recognized by reputable scientific authority are not added. The librarian who is not a specialist relies on the opinion of the medical profession or on expert opinion of leaders in the field of knowledge in question.

8. Synopses

Synopses and summaries are sometimes purchased for reference, as adults other than students occasionally find this material useful. Classics shortened and retold in simple language recommended for the adult who is learning to read and for those of limited reading skills are sometimes purchased.

9. Foreign Language Books

There is a demand for books in Spanish because of the large Spanish-speaking population in Tucson. Books, both classic and modern, are purchased in the areas of fiction, biography, drama and some on scientific, social and economic problems. Books in other languages may be bought as the demand arises. Books in those languages for which there is little demand are borrowed on interlibrary loan.

Books in languages other than English are not purchased for a branch library, unless the branch is located in an area that is bi-lingual. Such a collection is built only after consultation with the Coordinators.

C. Policy on Disposal of Library Materials

1. The discarding of materials is selection in reverse. Library materials are discarded for one or more of the following reasons:

   a. Unserviceability
   b. Irreparable damage
   c. Obsolescence
   d. Insufficient use or basic value

2. Materials discarded from the library are either in unusable condition or present obsolete information. Therefore, the following policy is established concerning disposal of library materials:

   Obsolete materials and materials which are so badly worn as to be unusable are destroyed. Certain materials are discarded from time to time which might be of use to another library, such as duplicates which were purchased to fill a demand that no longer exists. Any recognized social or civic organization may have these materials by request. They may be picked up at a designated location. No attempt is made by the library to notify any group that discarded materials are available, nor does the library mail discarded material to any location.

   a. Encyclopedias which are replaced by new editions are either traded in to field representatives or transferred to another agency of the library.

   b. Any reference book which is replaced by a later edition may either be added to the circulation collection or transferred to another agency of the library. It may also be given to another city department, when requested.

   c. If a patron damages library material beyond repair and pays for its replacement, he may have the damaged article if he so requests.

   d. Upon approval of their request, magazines, pamphlets and newspapers which can no longer be used by the library may be given to any recognized social or civic organizations.

   e. Gift books not added to the library collection are sold to second-hand book dealers at a fair market price or to other libraries. Such books are also given to other libraries on an exchange basis. Gift books not added to the library collection are also available to any recognized social or civic organizations at their request.

    f.   All material with library identification markings must have said markings removed or over-stamped with "Discarded" before disposal.

    g.   Regular means of disposal of library material is by city trash removal or by sale as waste paper.

D. Gifts

    1. General Policy

The library retains the right to make the most advantageous use of materials it accepts. Gifts of books and other materials are accepted but without any commitments as to final disposition and with the understanding that they are not necessarily to be added to the collection. The same criteria used for the selection of all other materials will be used in evaluating gift materials.

Gift materials will be shelved in the regular collection where they are most useful rather than on separate shelves that take them out of the logical sequence.

As a general rule, the library does not accept for deposit materials which are not outright gifts. Certain objects which might be more appropriate for a museum are not accepted.

Gifts are not added to any branch, trailer or department uncatalogued or without approval. Titles not represented in the Central Library collection are never assigned to other points of service. Gift books accepted at a branch will be processed and returned to the branch if so desired, provided copies are in the main collection.

    2. Memorial Books

The library welcomes gifts of books and other library items as memorials.

    a.   Donors wishing to present a memorial gift should contact the director's office.

    b.   Materials accepted must conform to the criteria established for selection of books and materials other than books.

    c.   In general, works of fiction and popular nonfiction are not desirable. The donor usually wishes to present material which will remain in the collection for a number of years. The donor may make a specific request for use of his contribution, or he may leave the selection to the discretion of the director. If the person honored has had a specific field of interest, books reflecting that interest often are purchased.

    d.   All memorial items will be added to the collection at the Central Library. Should a donor request their assignment to a branch, an attempt will be made to comply with his request.

e. Checks for memorials are made payable to the Tucson Public Library. The donor will be given a receipt, and the money is turned in to the Administrative Offices. A thank-you note is sent to the donor, and the family is notified.

f. Materials carry a gift plate showing name of donor and the person honored.

V. STAFF RESPONSIBILITY FOR SELECTION OF MATERIALS

All professional staff members participate in determining the selection of library materials. Each member contributes his knowledge of the community and the needs of the individuals and groups with which he has contact. Staff members are appointed to study various sections of the collection and to make recommendations for purchase, but it is the responsibility of division and section heads to develop and maintain their collections.

People in the community who are experts in various fields are consulted for advice. Requests made by the public are considered.

The ultimate responsibility for acquisition of library materials rests with the director.

BIBLIOGRAPHY

Blackshear, Orrila T. Building and Maintaining the Small Library Collection. (Library Administration Division. Small Libraries Project. No. 5). Chicago, American Library Association, 1963.

Leigh, Robert D. The Public Library in the United States. New York, Columbia University Press, 1950.

Wheeler, Joseph L. and Goldhor, Herbert. Practical Administration of Public Libraries. New York, Harper and Row, 1962.

White, Ruth M., ed. Public Library Policies: General and Specific. (The Public Library Reporter, No. 9). Chicago, American Library Association, 1960.

Book Selection Policy Statements of the following libraries:
Dayton Montgomery County Public Library
Des Moines Public Library
East Chicago Public Library
East Orange Public Library
Enoch Pratt Free Library
Knoxville Public Library

PART 2

YOUNG ADULT BOOK SELECTION POLICIES

I. OBJECTIVES OF SERVICE

Young adults of high school age who come to the library need a variety of materials for enjoyment and personal enrichment, for some school assignments, for

167

reference information and for their continuing education when they are no longer enrolled in school. The objectives of work with this group are: to help them become
lifetime readers and users of libraries, to enable them to become critical readers,
to increase their knowledge and enjoyment of reading, to awaken their curiosity about
many fields of human endeavor, to broaden their awareness and knowledge of the
world, and to guide them in the transition from children's books to adult books.

II.   GENERAL PRINCIPLES

A.   The young adult book collection is part of the adult book collection and is
governed by the same book selection policies. Approximately 80% of the
titles are adult titles which have already met the requirements for inclusion in the library's general collection. These titles must also meet the
policies guiding the selection of young adult materials.

B.   The approved list is established by the Young Adult Book Selection Committee as a result of recommendations in approved lists such as the
Standard Catalog for High School Libraries, the American Library Association Basic Book Collection for High Schools and personal analysis by
professional staff.

C.   The Young Adult sections at Central and branch libraries choose from this
list those titles best suited to the readers in the areas they serve. These
basic collections are supplemented by borrowing from the juvenile or
adult collections those titles which are approved by the Young Adult
Librarian.

D.   At stated intervals, the collection is re-evaluated by the Young Adult
Librarian and the Committee. Titles may be discarded, retained or duplicated, as justified by need.

E.   Titles in the Children's or the Adult Collections are duplicated in the
Young Adult section when they are especially suited to this group.

III. POLICIES GUIDING SELECTION OF LIBRARY MATERIALS

A.   Fiction

1.   Girls' stories, career stories, science fiction, sports stories, adventure and fictionalized biography should be adequately written,
but not judged solely on their literary merit. They serve their purpose as bridges to transfer young adults' interests from children's
stories to adult novels.

2.   The Young Adult Committee reads and evaluates new adult fiction
considered for inclusion in the collection. Books which intentionally treat undesirable social behavior in a sensational way are felt
to be unsuitable for young adults. The overall purpose of the work
is the deciding factor in considering for purchase titles in which
objectionable features appear.

B.   Nonfiction

1.   Books of information in subject categories are included for both
their factual and their recreational appeal to many young adults.

The standards applied in judging them are accuracy, readability and general interest.

   2. Books about the physical changes which take place during adolescent years are included; they are placed on open shelves, readily available to young adults. They must meet the accepted standards of good taste, be scientifically accurate and unemotionally presented.

   3. No attempt is made to have a Young Adult reference collection. The Young Adult Librarian assists the patron in the adult reference section. Frequent requests for material relative to particular subjects are brought to the attention of the Adult Book Selection Committee.

   4. Books and pamphlets on vocations are purchased for the Young Adult Collection.

C. Periodicals

   1. Periodicals of special appeal to young adults are added to the collection.

   2. An effort is made to maintain a file of the current issues of all local high school newspapers.

D. Paperbacks

   A circulating collection of paperbacks is maintained in the Young Adult Collection.

   Paperbacks must meet the same standards as other books added to the collections.

BIBLIOGRAPHY

Edwards, Margaret A. "Selection Policies for Books for Young Adults"; Appendix B to Book Selection Policies. Enoch Pratt Free Library, February, 1962.

Hanna, Geneva R., and McAllister, Mariana K. Books, Young People, and Reading Guidance. New York, Harper, 1960. pp. 103-131.

Landers, Lora. Young Adult Service in a Small Public Library. (Library Administration Division. Small Libraries Project. No. 11). Chicago, American Library Association, 1962.

Munson, Amelia H. An Ample Field. Chicago, American Library Association, 1950.

Public Library Association. Committee on Standards for Work with Young Adults in Libraries. Young Adult Services in the Public Library. Chicago, American Library Association, 1960.

PART 3

CHILDREN'S BOOK SELECTION POLICIES

I.   OBJECTIVES OF SERVICE

A. Introduction

The Children's Division is conscious of the tremendous responsibility which is involved in selecting books for children; therefore, this policy as formulated, aspires to be practical, yet to set a high standard in accordance with the accepted general philosophy of library service to children.

B. Statement of Objectives

The Children's Division of the Tucson Public Library, in its book selection for children, endeavors to create a book collection that:

1. Reflects the community served

2. Has books and materials for all ages, abilities and reading levels-- slow, average and gifted. It also provides materials for the parents and teachers working with various age children

3. Is alert to changing patterns and provides accurate up-to-date information in all fields of knowledge of interest to children

4. Provides pleasurable reading for reading's sake

5. Emphasizes the book that stimulates the imagination, provides for mental growth, develops a taste for good writing and draws attention to the beautiful and artistic

6. Shows balance by reflecting the needs of all its borrowers and contributes to their growth as intelligent citizens

II. GENERAL POLICY IN SELECTING OF LIBRARY MATERIALS

A. The library receives, through the Greenaway Plan, review copies of new juvenile publications; and, in addition, through reviews in Kirkus, The New York Times Book Review, Horn Book, Booklist and other reputable review sources, orders books which seem worthy of consideration.

B. The following criteria are used in this selection:

1. Use--Is there a need for this title, or are there enough other books on the subject? Will its use be reference, recreational or supplemental? Is this book for the discriminating reader or is its appeal general?

2. Style--Has the author produced a well written book with words, phrases and sentences combined in an interesting manner? Is the vocabulary used varied and distinguished, or is it a collection of trite words? Is the style of writing suitable to the age for which the book is intended?

3. Authenticity--Is the information as presented accurate and up to date? This is particularly important in reference and nonfiction material, although it should also be considered with fiction.

4. Author--Is the author a qualified writer, and does he have a reputation in his field? What other books has he written? What is his place in the field of juvenile literature?

5. Illustrator--Does the artist's work reflect the text, and do the illustrations serve as a kind of background in tune with the words? Are the illustrations in good taste? Is the artist qualified, and does his technique show individuality?

6. Format--Is the format appropriate to the subject? Are the illustrations well done and in keeping with the text? Are the margins wide enough to permit rebinding? Is the type good, clear and suitable in size to the age for which the book is intended?

7. Price--Is the title worth the cost of the book? Does it contribute to the collection as a whole?

III. SPECIFIC POLICIES

A. Duplication

This depends largely on size of book budget, demand for a given title and community served. On occasion, a title may be duplicated in Adult and Young Adult Collections because of interest or reading level.

B. Replacement

All books replaced are first checked with children's catalog or approved lists and consideration is given to their current place in the collection. Every effort is made to keep standard juvenile titles in the collection.

C. Textbooks

In general, textbooks as such are not added to the collection unless there is little material available from any other source. Some titles are purchased in the fields of mathematics, grammar and spelling. These are added only for giving the collection full coverage in various fields of knowledge.

D. Readers

Primers, first and second grade readers and a few third grade readers are purchased, not to answer actual school needs, but to furnish an incentive to children with limited reading ability. The library feels its responsibility lies in supplementing rather than in including readers to any great extent.

E. Books on Sex

Although the library believes this subject to be primarily the responsibility of the parents, it does provide books on sex and reproduction, written in a dignified simple manner for the use of either child or parent. These books are shelved in a controlled area and are circulated to any child on request, although intended primarily for use with parents.

F. Books on Religion

The spiritual development of a child is the responsibility of the parents, but the library does supply certain general books on religious subjects that meet the standard criteria for adding children's books. Books on specific religious teachings as such are not included. Such titles may be found in the Adult Department.

G. Books on Self-Defense

The library does not wish to provide information on judo, jujitsu, karate and other books on self-defense to children who are not old enough to understand the warnings written in all books of this type.   Although books on this subject may be found in other divisions, it is felt that these sports are not intended for users of the Children's Division.

H. Books on Guns

It is felt that books on the repair, care and handling of guns, while a necessary addition to other divisions, should not be available in the Children's Division where harm might come from them.

I. Series Books

These are purchased sparingly and with considerable evaluation as to their place in the collection. There is a marked tendency for long series to become mediocre and below standard quality in literary merit.

J. Exclusion of Material

1. Some books are not selected because their value does not justify expenditure, or the subject of a book is not presented in an accurate manner, or poor taste has been shown in either presentation or illustrative material.

2. Gift books are accepted for use in the library if they conform to the established criteria already in use.

BIBLIOGRAPHY

Enoch Pratt Free Library. Selection Policies for Children's Books. 1962.

Grosse Pointe Public Library. Statement of Policy on Book and Nonbook Materials. 1961.

[Freedom to Read]   [Library Bill of Rights]

Reprinted by Permission of Tucson Public Library, Mr. Frank Van Zanten, Director.

SCHOOLS

Greater Anchorage Area Borough School District
Anchorage, Alaska
December, 1966

MATERIALS SELECTION POLICY

I. PHILOSOPHY

    A. The school learning resource center implements classroom activity and is an integral part of the curriculum, paralleling it at all points in all departments. The center exists primarily for educational purposes. It offers enrichment for the students and resource material for the faculty. Its materials are selected from all forms of media available for interest, vocabulary, maturity, and ability levels of all students within the school served.

    B. The school resource center provides additional materials to attract students to reading, viewing and listening as sources of pleasure and recreation over and above needed subject content.

    C. It attempts to foster reading as a lifelong activity through pleasurable exposure to printed material.

II. GENERAL POLICY

    A. The legal responsibility for materials in the school center rests with the school district governing board. Responsibility for the final selection shall be delegated to professionally trained personnel who know the course of study, the methods of teaching, and the individual differences of the pupils in the schools for which the materials are provided, such selection to be in accordance with the statement of specific policy given below.

    B. The selection of school resource materials shall be in accordance with the following objectives:

        1. To enrich the curriculum.

        2. To further the development of youth intellectually, emotionally, culturally, and spiritually.

    C. The school board subscribes in principle to the statements of policy on library philosophy as expressed in the American Association of School Librarians' School Library Bill of Rights, a copy of which is appended to and made a part of this policy.

III. SELECTION

    A. Instructional Materials selection shall be a cooperative continuing process in which administrators, teachers, librarians, and students should participate. The basic factors influencing selection shall be the curriculum, the reading interests, the abilities, the backgrounds of the students using the centers and the quality and accuracy of available materials.

B. The following recommended lists shall be consulted in the selection of materials, but selection is not limited to their listings.

    1. Bibliographies (latest edition available, including supplements)

        Audio-visual Equipment Directory
        Basic Book Collection for Elementary Grades
        Basic Book Collection for High Schools
        Basic Book Collection for Junior High Schools
        Childrens' Catalog
        Educational Film Guide
        Educational Media Index
        Elementary School Library Collection
        Filmstrip Guide
        Junior High School Catalog
        National Tape Recording Catalog
        Standard Catalog for High School Libraries
        Vertical File Index

    Other special bibliographies, many of which have been prepared by educational organizations for particular subject matter areas.

    2. Current Reviewing Media:

        The Booklist and Subscription Books Bulletin
        Wilson Library Bulletin
        Library Journal
        Junior Libraries
        Horn Book
        Educational Screen and Audiovisual Guide

    Professional magazines from subject departments
    Other current periodicals

    If these are not available in the school, they may be borrowed from the Instructional Materials Center. Those most frequently used should be included in each school's collection.

C. Additional suggestions will come from exchange of materials with neighboring district school libraries, visits to book exhibits and displays, examination of bookstore stock, publishers' samples, reading lists from other school systems, texts and courses of study approved for use within the district, teachers, students, Parent-Teacher Associations, other educational organizations, and individuals of the community. These must be evaluated with special care according to the criteria set forth in paragraph 1 above.

IV. PROCEDURE FOR HANDLING OBJECTIONS

A. The suitability of particular books or other materials may be questioned. All criticism shall be presented to the Assistant Superintendent for Instructional Services on the Citizen's Request Form for Re-evaluation of

Materials. He will forward duplicate copies to the principal and librarian of the school involved.

B. The material in question shall be reviewed by a committee of five composed of:

Assistant Superintendent for Instructional Services
Building Principal
Teacher from the building involved in the subject field
    of the questioned material
PTA representative appointed by the building organization
Lay person interested in school affairs appointed by the
    Assistant Superintendent for Instructional Services

The review committee shall function at the call of the Assistant Superintendent upon receipt of a complaint. The material shall be considered with the specific objections in mind. The majority and minority report of this committee shall be completed as rapidly as possible and submitted directly to the District Superintendent who will in turn submit it for approval to the school district governing board, whose decision shall be sent to the complainant. The committee's report and the action of the board should be sent to all schools in the district.

C. No material shall be removed from use until the governing board has made a final decision.

D. The review of questioned materials shall be treated objectively and as an important matter. Every opportunity shall be afforded those persons or groups questioning school materials to meet with the committee and to present their opinions. The school librarian and any other persons involved in the selection of the questioned material shall have the same opportunity. The best interests of the students, the curriculum, the school, and the community shall be of paramount consideration.

INSTRUCTIONS TO EVALUATING COMMITTEE

"... free men and free inquiry are inseparable."
President Lyndon B. Johnson

Bear in mind the principles of the freedom to learn and to read and base your decision on these broad principles rather than on defense of individual material. Freedom of inquiry is vital to education in a democracy.

Study thoroughly all materials referred to you and read available reviews. The general acceptance of the materials should be checked by consulting standard evaluation aids and local holdings in other schools.

Passages or parts should not be pulled out of context. The values and faults should be weighed against each other, and the opinions based on the material as a whole.

Your report, presenting both majority and minority opinions, will be presented to the superintendent who will forward it to the Board for action.

[School Library Bill of Rights]

CITIZEN'S REQUEST FORM FOR RE-EVALUATION OF LEARNING RESOURCE CENTER MATERIALS

Initiated by _____

Telephone _____ Address_____

REPRESENTING

Self _____ Organization or group_____
                                              (name)
School _____

MATERIAL QUESTIONED:

BOOK: Author _____ Title_____
_____ Copyright date_____

AV MATERIAL: Kind of Media_____
                              (film, filmstrip, record, etc.)
Title_____

OTHER MATERIAL: Identify_____

Please respond to the following questions. If sufficient space is not provided, please use additional sheet of paper.

1. Have you seen or read this material in its entirety? _____
_____

2. To what do you object? Please cite specific passages, pages, etc. _____
_____

3. What do you believe is the main idea of this material? _____
_____

4. What do you feel might result from use of this material? _____
_____

5. What reviews of this material have you read? _____
_____

6. For what other age group might this be suitable? _____
_____

7. What action do you recommend that the school take on this material? _____
_____

8. In its place, what material do you recommend that would provide adequate information on the subject? _____
_____

_____   _____
Date   Signature

_____

Reprinted by Permission of Anchorage Borough School District, Joe D. Montgomery, Superintendent.

POLICY AND PROCEDURE FOR SELECTION
OF INSTRUCTIONAL MATERIALS

I.   OBJECTIVES

The primary objectives in the selection of educational materials are these:
(1) To implement, enrich, and support the educational program of the school;
(2) To consider the needs and interests of individual students;
(3) To choose materials which are carefully balanced to include various points of view on any controversial subject, while upholding American ideals and underlying principles.

II.   RESPONSIBILITY FOR SELECTION

Instructional materials are selected cooperatively by the librarian and/or the audiovisual coordinator in consultation with the administration, faculty, students, and patrons of the individual school.

Final recommendations for purchase rest with the librarian and/or audiovisual coordinator with the approval of the school principal.

III.   CRITERIA FOR SELECTION

Criteria for the selection of materials are based on the needs of the individual school, as determined from a knowledge of the curriculum and requests of administrators and teachers, the needs of the individual student as determined from a knowledge of children and youth, and the requests of parents and students.

Materials are examined for selection of those in which the presentation and the subject matter are suitable for the grade and the interest level at which they are used.

A wide range of materials is provided on all levels of difficulty, with a diversity of appeal and presentation of different points of view.

Factual accuracy, authoritativeness, balance, and integrity are required in the materials provided.

Materials of high artistic quality and superior format are chosen, with consideration given to stimulating presentation, including imagination, vision, creativeness, and style appropriate to the idea.

IV.   PROCEDURE IN SELECTION

All faculty members and students are encouraged by the librarian and the principal to offer recommendations of materials.

The librarian with a faculty library committee, representative of the various departments or grades, is responsible for selection of materials. It is desirable that the committee members serve three years, with some members to be dropped and others to be added each year.

The librarian is responsible to the principal and the faculty library committee for: (1) allocating funds to each department or grade; (2) providing definite instructions for selection procedure; (3) introducing reputable, professionally-prepared selection aids for the selection of materials; (4) acquainting the faculty with the availability of special book and audiovisual exhibits and collections.

Before recommendations for purchase are submitted to the Department of Instructional Materials Services, the librarian secures the principal's approval of the order.

A. Selection from Exhibit Bibliographies

Subject matter and grade level teacher-supervisor committees, individual teachers, and librarians regularly evaluate print and non-print materials to be considered for inclusion in individual school library-media centers and in the Audiovisual Center Library.

To help teachers and librarians with the problem of library-media selection, the Department of Instructional Materials Services arranges special exhibits during the year. These exhibits consist of recent print and non-print educational materials at all grade levels, and earlier basic materials to support courses of study as they are revised.

Materials in these exhibits may be checked against an annotated book exhibit bibliography and an audiovisual bibliography furnished each school.

Audiovisual selection at all levels must be made from the audiovisual exhibit bibliography.

In addition, the Department of Instructional Materials Services maintains in the Professional Library a basic collection of books for elementary school libraries and review copies of books at all levels. Some audiovisual items are also available for examination purposes.

V. KINDS OF MATERIALS IN SCHOOL LIBRARIES

A. Books

1. Basic collections consist of recreational books, reference books, research books, and materials for curriculum enrichment. Interests and local needs expand the collections. The book collection is well balanced between recreational and informational materials and provides for various reading levels.

2. In elementary schools, library binding is specified when available. Easy books and picture books are ordered prebound if not available in library binding.

B. Periodicals and Newspapers

    1. Secondary Schools

        a. Junior and senior high schools provide well-rounded collections of at least fifty periodicals, both informational and recreational. Indexing in <u>Readers' Guide</u> and certain special needs may influence the selection of informational periodicals.

        b. A minimum of one daily newspaper is provided and the Sunday edition of some newspaper of national importance such as <u>The New York Times</u>.

    2. Elementary Schools

        In the elementary school, ten well-selected periodicals are recommended, excluding those for teachers. Selection is made from the list found in the <u>American Library Association Basic Collection for Elementary Grades</u>.

C. Pamphlets and Clippings

    Scarcity of information and demand govern inclusion of materials in the pamphlet and clipping collection. This file is regularly weeded of information that is no longer useful.

D. Audiovisual Materials

    The audiovisual collection in the school library consists of recordings, filmstrips, 8mm film loops, viewmaster reels, slides, maps, globes, tapes, transparencies, and flat pictures. The library is the central agency within the school through which such materials and equipment are administered. Films and art prints are available from the Audiovisual Center.

VI. GIFT BOOKS

Gift materials are examined in terms of the same standards observed in the selection of materials to be purchased. Before gifts are accepted a consultation with the Director of Instructional Materials Services is in order.

VII. HANDLING QUESTIONS RAISED ABOUT MATERIALS

Any complaint to be considered is to be submitted in writing to the principal and the complainant properly identified.

Immediate steps are taken to assure that the full facts surrounding a complaint are known to the librarian and the Director of Instructional Materials Services.

Action is deferred until full consideration is given to the complaint. Materials are withheld from use pending a decision regarding the complaint.

Criticism of materials is submitted by the principal to a faculty committee composed of persons teaching in the subject matter field of the materials challenged. The materials are judged by the committee as to conformity to the aforementioned objectives. The recommendation of the committee is submitted in writing to the principal and a copy of the complaint and the recommendation is forwarded to the Department of Instructional Materials Services where it is filed for future reference.

In the event of an appeal from a decision of the principal by the complainant, the principal brings the matter to the attention of the Director of Instructional Materials Services. Further appeals may be made to the appropriate Assistant Superintendent and to the General Superintendent of Schools, with the School Board as the final arbiter.

Reprinted by Permission of Houston Independent School District, Elenora Alexander, Director of Instructional Materials Services.

Jackson School District
Jackson, New Jersey
December, 1968

LIBRARY MATERIALS SELECTION POLICY

I.   INTRODUCTION

In the education of children and youth, an abundance of printed and non-printed materials is essential if individual interests, needs, and abilities are to be met. These resources are the basic tools needed for effective teaching and learning. The school library program also contributes something more to the overall education of youth than just materials and services geared only to curricular needs. The scope of knowledge has become too vast to be covered extensively within the boundaries of classroom instruction, superior though that instruction may be. Through the school library, these boundaries can be extended immeasurably in all areas of knowledge and in all forms of creative expression, and the means provided to meet and stimulate the many interests, appreciations, and curiosities of students and teachers alike.

The Board of Education has the legal responsibility for providing instructional materials for use in the schools that make up the Jackson School District. The volume of learning materials, both printed and non-printed, currently being produced makes the wise selection of appropriate materials a problem of utmost importance to the Board. For this reason, the following materials selection policy has been developed as a summation of the philosophy, the standards, and the principles which underlie the choice of resource materials for the school libraries of the Jackson School District.

The purpose of this materials selection policy is:
(1) To provide a statement of philosophy and objectives for the guidance of those involved in the procedures for selection.
(2) To define the role of those who share in the responsibility for the selection of instructional materials.
(3) To set forth criteria for selection and evaluation of materials.
(4) To outline the techniques for the application of the criteria.
(5) To clarify for the community the philosophy and procedures used in evaluating and selecting instructional materials.
(6) To provide a procedure for the consideration of objections to the use of particular materials in the educational program.

II.   PHILOSOPHY AND OBJECTIVES

The School Library Bill of Rights sets forth the philosophy of materials selection as it is related to the educational program of the school. It is endorsed by the American Association of School Librarians (a division of the American Library Association and a department of the National Education Association) and by the Jackson School District Board of Education.

"School libraries are concerned with generating understanding of American freedoms and with the preservation of these freedoms through the development of informed and responsible citizens. To this end the American Association of School Librarians reaffirms the LIBRARY BILL OF RIGHTS of the American Library Association and asserts that the responsibility of the school library is:

To provide materials that will enrich and support the curriculum, taking into consideration the varied interests, abilities, and maturity levels of the pupils served.

To provide materials that will stimulate growth in factual knowledge, literary appreciation, aesthetic values, and ethical standards.

To provide a background of information which will enable pupils to make intelligent judgments in their daily life.

To provide materials on opposing sides of controversial issues so that young citizens may develop under guidance the practice of critical reading and thinking.

To provide materials representative of the many religious, ethnic, and cultural groups and their contributions to our American heritage.

To place principle above personal opinion and reason above prejudice in the selection of materials of the highest quality in order to assure a comprehensive collection appropriate for the users of the library."

The school library thus stands as a symbol for the truthful expression of man's knowledge and experiences. The extent to which many Jackson students of today will be creative, informed, knowledgeable, and, within their own years, wise, will be shaped by the boundaries of the content and services of the library resources available within our schools. We must educate our students for a high degree of independence and self-direction in learning: developing students who recognize that learning is a lifetime process; who have a sense of independence; who have the inner courage that enables them to make and act on decisions and the inner security that allows them to face great difficulties.

Our school libraries are the settings through which educators can bring students into immediate contact with the flow of knowledge by teaching them how to make their own way in the materials of a subject and thus maintain themselves as independent learners. Our libraries are reservoirs of all the information man has at his fingertips: past, present, future. The task of the professional faculties is defined as properly setting students loose on the surface and underground waters of the reservoir.

The following outline describes the specifics that make up the length and breadth and depth of the school libraries in Jackson. It is implied in this outline that each school adapts its material and personnel to the grade levels it serves.

A. The Library is a person.

  1. The Librarian creates a personal image that affects service in a very real way: friendly; concerned; open-minded; objective.

183

2. The Librarian is "in love" with the students and teachers: respects individuals; believes in an individual's ability to work independently; is a catalyst.

3. The Librarian functions as what he _is_ not what he _knows_: likes to explore, search for information.

B. The Library is a resource center.

1. Books
2. Magazines
3. Newspapers
4. Pamphlets
5. Films and filmstrips
6. Tapes and records
7. Pictures and slides
8. Maps and globes
9. Realia
10. Transparencies
11. Microfilm and microforms
12. Games

Hughes Mearns has written that "Good teaching is not solely the business of instructing; it is also the art of influencing another. Primarily, it is the job of un-covering and enlarging native gifts of insight, feeling, and thinking." Good li-brarying is like good teaching. The use to which pupils, teachers, and librarians put the school library is an indication of at least one influence each has on another.

The objectives of the Jackson school libraries focus upon the work with stu-dents and teachers and the schools' over-all objectives of which they are a part. In addition to this primary function, the library program contains many areas of in-struction, service, and activities. The program is designed so that students can:
(1) Derive the fullest benefit from their classroom instruction.
(2) Extend the boundaries of their knowledge and experience.
(3) Pursue self-directed learning of all kinds.
(4) Explore and satisfy their many curiosities and interests.
(5) Find enjoyment in the rich stores of the imaginative expressions of creative artists.
(6) Learn how to use libraries and to evaluate the materials of communication.
(7) Obtain materials that meet their individual needs and abilities.
(8) Establish desirable intellectual habits that last for life.

The program is also designed so that teachers and counselors can:
(1) Achieve their instructional objectives to the fullest degree.
(2) Enrich course content.
(3) Prepare assignments that provide for the needs and abilities of individual students.
(4) Motivate students to use materials for curricular and noncurricular purposes.
(5) Have the materials needed in counseling students in many aspects of guidance work.
(6) Use materials directly with students in the classroom.
(7) Teach students how to use materials and libraries.

(8) Have materials easily accessible and efficiently organized so that time is not wasted in locating materials for examination and use.

(9) Keep abreast with the best ideas and practices in education.

(10) Use materials to broaden their own knowledge and to derive personal enrichment.

III. RESPONSIBILITY FOR SELECTION

The purchase of library materials is legally vested in the Board of Education. The Board delegates to the library staff the responsibility to develop final recommendations for purchase. The actual selection of materials is the responsibility of professional trained personnel on the library staff who know the courses of study, the methods of teaching, and the individual differences of the pupils. The librarians will choose materials that are keyed to the interests and needs of the students and faculty and that will open up possibilities in cultural, social, and economic fields. In this task, the librarians will be aided by initial purchase suggestions from administrators, faculty, students, and parents. The widest participation is encouraged. The individual school librarian is responsible for the final evaluation and selection of materials for his school's library.

IV. PRINCIPLES OF EVALUATION AND SELECTION

A. Evaluative criteria used in the selection of materials

1. All materials shall have these elements of quality:

   a. Relevancy or permanent value
   b. Accuracy
   c. Authoritativeness
   d. Clear presentation and/or readability
   e. Format

2. All materials should appear in one or more of the recognized professional media or approved lists (such as professional book selection aids, basic general lists, current general lists, special bibliographies for reference materials and for subject fields, and book reviewing journals). No one publication need determine selection, and the critical opinions of reviewers should be checked against each other. (See statement on procedures for evaluation and selection).

3. When doubt arises, approval copies shall be examined by both the librarian and the subject-specialist faculty.

B. Factors influencing selection

1. Needs of the school

   a. Based on the curriculum
   b. Based on requests from administrators and faculty

2. Needs of the students

   a. Based on a knowledge of backgrounds and reading abilities of students
   b. Based on requests from parents and students
   c. Based on availability of leisure reading materials outside of school

3.   Size of budget

4.   Need to develop a balanced collection

    a.   Based on materials already in collection
    b.   Based on providing an objective view of all sides of an issue

C.   The libraries welcome gifts of books and other materials provided:

1.   They meet the same standards of selection as those applied to original purchases.

2.   They can be integrated into the general library collection and do not need special housing.

3.   The library staff may dispose of the gift at its discretion if it is out-of-date or in poor physical condition, not warranting the cost of repair.

D.   The libraries welcome commercially sponsored materials provided:

1.   They meet the same standards of selection as those applied to original purchases.

2.   They are of real value to the instructional program of the school with a purpose to educate rather than just promote sales.

3.   They are free from advertising which is excessive, obtrusive, or objectionable.

V.   PROCEDURES FOR EVALUATION AND SELECTION

The selection of library materials is the particular responsibility of the professionally trained librarian with the approval of the principal and the superintendent under authorization from the Board of Education. The procedure is cooperative, materials being recommended by the administrators, faculty, parents, and students. An order card is prepared by the person who requests purchase of materials. This card provides space for personal recommendation and/or reference to reviews. The requests, upon being presented to the librarian, are again evaluated before a requisition is made. Materials are also requisitioned by the librarian based on the principles stated above. Materials selection is a continuous process. New titles acceptable in content and suitable to the maturity level of the students are searched out of lists of new materials. The library staff is constantly seeking current materials to fill shortages of information revealed when classes and individuals use the library. Wherever possible, the librarian examines the material itself in depositories, shops, and publishers exhibits.

An annotated list of reviewing materials used in the evaluation and selection of materials for the school libraries can be found in SELECTING MATERIALS FOR CHILDREN AND YOUNG ADULTS, prepared by the American Library Association, 1967.

VI. CONSIDERATION OF OBJECTIONS

The review of questioned materials will be treated objectively, unemotionally, and as an important routine action. Every effort will be made to consider objections, keeping in mind the best interests of the students, the school, the curriculum, and the community. Since differences of opinion do exist in our society, the following procedure shall be observed to recognize those differences in an impartial and factual manner.

A. All criticism shall be presented in writing to the building principal who will forward a copy to the school librarian. The REQUEST FOR RECONSIDERATION form (approved by the American Library Association) shall be used. It should be filled out as completely as possible and shall be signed and identified so that a proper reply can be made.

B. The material in question will be withdrawn from circulation until it is read and discussed by a library committee, which will be convened by the principal and the librarian. This committee shall consist of a member of the subject-specialist faculty of the area so questioned, a member of the superintendent's staff, a member of the P.T.A. officers of the school, the school principal, the school librarian, and a member of the Board of Education.

C. The committee will review the questioned material and all critical evaluations available. General acceptance of the material shall be checked by consulting authoritative lists in light of the selection policies of the school district. A thorough review of questioned materials shall be treated objectively: passages shall not be taken out of context and the material shall be evaluated as an entity.

D. The final decision of the committee shall be implemented by the principal and the librarian.

E. The complainant shall be sent a copy of the evaluating report and decision.

F. A copy of this procedure shall be available in each school library and the front office of each school.

REQUEST FOR RECONSIDERATION

Author: Title:

Request initiated by:

Address: Telephone:

Person making request represents: ___himself; ___group/organization (give name):

School in which the material is used:

1. To what do you object? (Please be specific; cite examples)

2. What do you feel might result from the use of this material?

3. For what age group would you recommend this material?

4. Is there anything good about this material?

5. Did you read the entire book, or view entire film? _____ What parts?

6. Are you aware of the judgment of this material by experts in the field?

7. What do you believe is the theme or purpose of this material?

8. What would you like the school to do about this material?

_____

Reprinted by Permission of Jackson School District, Mr. Nicholas V. Sciarappa, Assistant Superintendent.

Minneapolis Public Secondary Schools
Special School District No. 1
Minneapolis, Minnesota
Revised June 8, 1971

GUIDELINES FOR MATERIALS SELECTION

In a democracy, public education endorses the students' freedom to learn. To this end Minneapolis secondary personnel, administrative and instructional, affirm and support the AASL's School Library Bill of Rights and NCTE's Students' Right to Read.

It is the goal of educators to provide print and non-print materials which will enrich and support the curriculum and provide students an opportunity to explore the knowledge, thinking, and imagination of mankind. The students' right to learn must be recognized and protected by a selection policy which provides materials of the highest quality available.

Print and non-print materials selected for the media center and other instructional areas should reflect the needs of the school community. They should include materials which satisfy these needs whether they be for academic or recreational purposes.

Materials which can be used to develop critical thinking, objective evaluations, and aesthetic appreciation suitable to the varied maturity levels, abilities, and interests of students should be provided.

Accurate materials which present various interpretations of controversial subjects should be readily accessible. No professional personnel shall restrict the use of materials by acting as censors.

Qualified personnel select materials by examination, from reviews, recommended lists, and standard bibliographic tools. Students and faculty should be encouraged to participate in the selection of learning materials. Gifts of material are acceptable only when they meet criteria for selection.

I. FICTION

Because fiction reflects all segments of life, it deserves a permanent place in the school curriculum as well as media centers, and thoughtful consideration must be given to its selection. The novel is an important educational tool and frequently plays a significant role as a molder of public opinion. For this reason, the author's purpose in writing the book and his success in achieving this purpose, should be carefully considered in judging fiction.

Guidelines in selection of fiction would include the following suggestions:

Fiction should reflect, in so far as possible, all sides of political, social, religious, and racial issues. The use of offensive language or frankness in dealing with sex should not preclude

189

the inclusion of titles if they contribute to the accuracy of the character portrayal and assist in expanding the reader's attitudes on certain subjects.

II. NON-FICTION

Materials in the social sciences should be selected to support areas of the curriculum, to reflect the ethnic, cultural, and socioeconomic diversity of life, and to provide information on topics of current interest. An effort should be made to include local historical materials. Selection is made on the basis of accuracy, reasoned opinion, or representative viewpoint.

Science materials should include all branches of pure and applied science, their history, philosophy, and sociology. Pseudo-scientific topics should be included in order to show these phenomena in their true perspective.

Since many controversial issues center on questions of political, economic, or social values, care must be taken to represent the many sides of public opinion. Examples of propaganda and extremist viewpoints should be provided to enable students to assess conflicting value judgments. The inclusion of controversial material does not imply endorsement of the ideas by Minneapolis school personnel.

To foster interest in the fine arts and literature, both classical and contemporary, students should be provided with media that enrich their thought and expression. Quality should not be compromised to protect or shield young people. A broad spectrum of creative works can be used to help students develop a sense of discrimination and acquire habits of critical thinking.

As of September 1971, the Guidelines for Materials Selection in Minneapolis Public Secondary Schools, Special School District No. 1 have not been adopted by the Minneapolis Board of Education, but have been declared a guideline under which secondary schools will operate until review and adoption by the Minneapolis Board of Education.

Reprinted by Permission of Minneapolis Public Schools, Jane D. Strebel, Consultant in Library Services.

Oakland Public Schools
Oakland, California
Revised October, 1968

BOOK AND AUDIO-VISUAL MATERIALS SELECTION

I.   GUIDELINES FOR MATERIALS SELECTION

It is the policy of the Oakland Unified School District to establish procedures for the selection and approval of books and audio-visual materials that will

(1) Support and enrich all subjects of the curriculum, taking into consideration the varied interests, abilities, and maturity levels of the pupils served.

(2) Present the many racial, ethnic, religious, and cultural groups and portray the role of their contribution in the development of America.

(3) Give an extensive background of information and factual knowledge which will enable pupils to make intelligent judgments in their daily lives.

(4) Support and be consistent with the objectives and goals of specific courses of study approved by the Board of Education.

(5) Stimulate growth in knowledge, literary appreciation, aesthetic values, and ethical standards.

(6) Present all aspects of social, economic and political systems and issues so that students have practice, under guidance, in the processes of critical reading, thinking and evaluating--processes that undergird an informed citizen's part in the preservation of American institutions and ideals.

(7) Offer the student an opportunity to develop an awareness of a social order which values freedom and allows for the fullest development of the individual.

(8) Develop the life-long habit of wide reading which fosters freedom in the exchange of ideas, a basic principle in the operation of democracy.

Principal and reason (rather than personal opinion and bias) shall be used in the selection of materials of the highest quality in order to assure a comprehensive collection for the public schools. In no case should any instructional material be excluded because of race or nationality, or the political or religious views of the writer.   (Adapted from the School Library Bill of Rights of the American Association of School Librarians.)

If adequate materials are not available in the areas described above, it will be the duty of the division of instructional media, Oakland Unified School District, to inform publishers and/or producers of the district's needs.

The division of instructional media routinely sends copies of this administrative bulletin to publishers and producers to keep them informed of the guidelines and procedures for materials selection in the district.

The director of instructional media involves representatives of appropriate community groups in the materials selection procedure of the district.

II. PROCEDURES

The Oakland Unified School District has adopted the following selection procedures to implement the guidelines for materials selection noted above.

A. Library Books--Elementary

1. An Elementary Library Book Evaluation Committee is appointed by the Superintendent for a three-year term. The committee includes librarians, teachers, supervisors, visiting children's librarians from the public library, the PTA 28th district reading chairman, the director of elementary education, and the director of instructional media, who serves as chairman.

2. The committee develops criteria for the selection of elementary library books consistent with the guidelines for materials selection noted above.

3. Publishers submit samples of books for evaluation by the committee.

4. The committee reviews the books submitted and annually compiles a list of approved titles.

5. Selections are also made from national lists published by the American Library Association, National Council of Teachers of English, Association for Childhood Education, H. W. Wilson Company, R. R. Bowker Company, and other selective lists appearing in library and education journals.

B. Library Books--Secondary

1. A Junior High School Library Book Evaluation Committee and a Senior High School Library Book Evaluation Committee are appointed by the Superintendent. The two committees include all junior high and senior high librarians respectively, plus teacher representatives of subject fields. The director of instructional media serves as chairman of the committees.

2. The committees develop criteria for the selection of secondary library books consistent with the guidelines for materials selection noted above.

3. Publishers submit samples of books for evaluation by the committees.

4. Annotated lists of approved books are published at intervals.

5. Selections are also made from national lists published by the American Library Association, National Council of Teachers of English, Association for Childhood Education, H. W. Wilson Company, R. R. Bowker Company, and other selective lists appearing in library and education journals.

C. Textbooks--Elementary

1. An Elementary Supplementary Textbook Evaluation Committee is appointed by the Superintendent for a three-year term. The committee includes teachers, principals, and supervisors, and is co-chaired

by the director of elementary school education and a member elected by the committee.

2. The committee develops criteria for the selection of supplementary elementary school textbooks consistent with the guidelines noted above.

3. Textbook publishers submit samples of textbooks for evaluation by the committee.

4. The committee reviews the textbooks submitted and annually compiles a list of approved titles.

5. This list of supplementary textbooks is next submitted to the assistant superintendent of elementary schools and the Superintendent for Board of Education approval.

6. Following approval, the list is used by individual schools as an order list for supplementary textbooks for the following year.

Seventh and eighth grade textbooks are of two kinds: supplementary textbooks purchased by the Oakland Unified School District and those provided by the State of California.

State textbooks are ordered on requisition forms supplied by the state. Allotments are based upon enrollment data.

D. Textbooks--Secondary

1. Subject matter committees or department chairmen and the supervisor of the respective subject matter area request new adoptions of secondary textbooks in needed fields. Areas for the next year's adoptions are determined each September.

2. Textbook committees are appointed by the Superintendent at the time that textbook adoption areas are determined.

3. Criteria for books are developed by teacher committees, consistent with the guidelines for materials selection noted above. Announcements and criteria are sent to publishers and committee members.

4. Sample copies of textbooks are submitted by publishers. Copies are sent to the chairman of the committee and to committee members. Additional copies are displayed in the Teachers' Professional Library.

5. A list of committee members with their available time for conferences is sent to the publishers, whose representatives are permitted to call upon committee members at the school site by appointment.

6. The committee, taking into consideration the finding of teachers throughout the district, draws up final reports which are submitted to the assistant superintendent through the director of secondary education.

7. All titles recommended for adoption are then forwarded to the Superintendent for Board review and approval.

8. Books are adopted by the Board of Education for a period of not less

than four years in accordance with sections of the <u>Education Code</u>.

9. The superintendent officially notifies the publisher whose book is adopted. All other publishers who submit books are notified of the adoption.

10. A supplementary textbook list is revised each year through teacher-committee suggestions.

E. Audio-Visual Materials--Elementary

1. Elementary audio-visual materials for the district audio-visual library are selected by the Elementary Audio-Visual Materials Selection Committee, the members of which are appointed by the Superintendent for a three-year term. The committee consists of teachers, librarians, elementary assistants, supervisors, principals, the supervisor of the audio-visual department, the director of elementary school education, and the director of instructional media. The supervisor of the audio-visual department and the director of instructional media serve as co-chairmen.

2. The audio-visual department sends for materials that have been requested by teachers and supervisors for previewing.

3. Materials are previewed and evaluated by the members of the elementary audio-visual committee according to criteria that are consistent with the guidelines for materials selection noted above.

4. Approved selections that are purchased for district audio-visual library are added to the subject catalogs published regularly.

5. Audio-visual materials for school library collections are previewed and evaluated by teachers and librarians at their schools according to criteria that are consistent with the guidelines for materials selection noted above.

6. Selections are submitted to the supervisor of the audio-visual department and to the director of instructional media for approval.

7. Approved selections that have been purchased for school library collections are described in school library card catalogs.

F. Audio-Visual Materials--Secondary

1. The audio-visual department sends for materials that have been requested by teachers and/or supervisors for previewing.

2. Materials are previewed and evaluated by teachers at their schools with the cooperation of students and secondary subject supervisors. Several evaluations are submitted for each item.

3. Materials are approved by the supervisor of the audio-visual department and the director of instructional media on the basis of the evaluations and recommendations submitted to the audio-visual department.

4. Approved materials which have been purchased for the district audio-visual department library are added to the catalogs published regularly

194

by the audio-visual department. Approved materials which have been purchased for school library collections are described in school library card catalogs.

G. Television

Educational television programs are previewed and evaluated by teachers, supervisors, and administrators according to criteria that are consistent with the guidelines for materials selection noted above. Evaluations are submitted to the supervisor of the audio-visual department and to the director of instructional media for each series or individual program under consideration. Approved programs are listed by the audio-visual department for recommendation to the schools.

H. Special Projects

Experimental courses, e.g. Negro Culture--History, Mexican-American History, and special projects may obtain certain books and audio-visual materials that suit the immediate needs of the course or project and that are consistent with the guidelines for materials selection noted above. In these cases, the materials are recommended jointly by teachers, administrators, supervisors or directors to the appropriate assistant superintendent. Lists of all such appropriate materials shall be forwarded to the director of instructional media.

I. Request for Re-evaluation of Materials

Since opinions concerning the usefulness and merits of books and audio-visual materials which have been selected may differ, the following procedures are observed in recognizing those differences in an impartial and factual manner.

1. The Superintendent shall establish review committees broadly representative of (1) teachers competent in, and teaching in the area of, the content covered by the book or audio-visual material and (2) administrators, directors, and supervisors appropriate to the level and/or subject for which the book or audio-visual material is used; and (3) the director of instructional media, who shall serve as chairman.

2. Objections to books and audio-visual materials and requests for re-evaluation must be presented in writing on Form 13-0083-01, Request for Reevaluation of a Book or Audio-Visual Material, obtainable in the principal's office or the office of the Superintendent.

3. Initial action on a written request on the proper form shall be taken no later than ten school days after receipt of the request.

4. A written report from the review committee shall be submitted to the Superintendent for transmittal to the person who has requested the reevaluation.

5. Textbooks approved by the Board of Education shall not be subject to reevaluation for a period of one year following their adoption and use.

6. Once instructional material has been adopted and reevaluated the

material cannot be subject to further review without special approval by the Board of Education.

7. The Board of Education may request that instructional material be evaluated by a committee of recognized scholars from the staffs of Bay Area colleges and universities in the discipline covered by the material. Such a committee shall be selected by the Superintendent in consultation with representatives of the institutions concerned.

8. Questioned materials shall remain in use in the schools pending final decision.

OAKLAND PUBLIC SCHOOLS
Office of the Superintendent

It is the policy of the Oakland Unified School District to accept written requests for reevaluation of books and audio-visual materials used in our schools. Please use this form if initiating a request. There are established procedures for the review of questioned materials. Copies of the procedures and additional forms are available in the office of the Superintendent of Schools. Completed forms should be addressed to: Dr. Marcus A. Foster, Superintendent of Schools, 1025 Second Avenue, Oakland, California, 94606.

REQUEST FOR REEVALUATION OF A BOOK OR AUDIO-VISUAL MATERIAL

Book:

Author _____ Hardcover_____ Paperback_____

Title_____

Publisher (if known)_____ Date of Publication_____

Audio-Visual Material:

Title_____

Producer_____

Type of Material (filmstrip, motion picture, etc.)_____

Request initiated by_____

Telephone_____ Address_____

City_____ Zone_____

School(s) in which book (or audio-visual material) is used_____

Person making the request represents

_____
(Individual)

_____
(Group or Organization

1. To what in the book (or audio-visual material) do you object? (Please be specific; cite pages, or frames, etc.) _____

   _____

2. In your opinion what harmful effects upon pupils might result from use of this book (or audio-visual material)? _____

   _____

3. Do you perceive any instructional value in the use of this book (or audio-visual material)? _____

   _____

4. Did you review the entire book (or examine all the audio-visual material)? ____
   If not, what sections? _____

5. Should the opinion of any additional experts in the field be considered?
   _____ Yes. Please list: _____

   _____

   _____ No.

6. In the place of this book (or audio-visual material) would you care to recommend other material which you consider to be of superior quality? _____

   _____

   _____

7. Do you wish to make an oral presentation of 15 minutes or less to the Review Committee?

   _____ Yes. (a) Please call the office of the Superintendent   836-2622,
                   Ext. 600, for an appointment.

              (b) Be prepared at this time to indicate the approximate
                  length of time your presentation will require.

   _____ No.

_____   _____
(Date)   (Signature)

_____

Reprinted by Permission of Oakland Public Schools, Mrs. Helen W. Cyr, Consultant, Instructional Media.

Pittsburgh Public Schools
Pittsburgh, Pennsylvania
no date

BOOK SELECTION POLICIES

I. FOREWORD

The Board of Public Education, Pittsburgh, Pennsylvania, delegates authority for the selection of library materials through the Superintendent of Schools to committees of school librarians under the guidance of the Director of School Libraries and the School Library Supervisors. What follows is a description of practices and policies. These are always somewhat flexible and in a state of evolution. In arriving at a statement of a school's book selection policies, it is logical to introduce each policy with a function of the library in a school.

II. POLICY I

The main function of a school library is to give service to teachers and pupils in reference and supplementary materials. Policy I is to select first from available funds those materials which will meet the demands of the curriculum, and by "curriculum" is meant not just the course of study but all experiences provided by the school for children. Those materials include nonfiction and fiction. Novels for book reports for English class and for enrichment in other fields such as history, home economics, science, and vocational guidance are essential curriculum aids. All criteria for nonfiction, such as accuracy, authority of author, interest, and importance of the subject, balance, etc., and similarly appropriate criteria for fiction are, of course, applied. Specialists in the field are consulted frequently; science books are sent to science teachers, art books to art teachers, etc., for review.

Within this general policy, many specific decisions must be reached:

A. Citizenship

There is always a pressing obligation to supply materials which will develop in children an appreciation of their nation's heritage, of their own responsibilities as citizens in a democracy, and of their country's contribution to the United Nations.

B. Human Relations

In the field of intercultural relations, books are selected which have the positive values of respect for human dignity and of insight into many cultural patterns. Those which produce negative attitudes through stereotypes, caricatures, epithets, and dialect (except in a historical or local setting) are avoided.

C. Growth and Development of the Individual

Since in our society adolescence is not considered a state of complete maturity, it is necessary to exercise some discretion in the selection of

198

books for school libraries. All books should enlighten, rather than confuse, young people. Realism is important to emotional maturity, but books must be completely defensible in such aspects as literary quality, general moral tone, truth, and beauty of spirit. Books are not rejected because of isolated passages if the book as a whole has undeniable merit.

A special effort is made to have strong collections in hygiene, etiquette, personal appearance and development, and other such aspects of self-improvement as are of natural and absorbing interest to adolescents.

Spiritual tenets such as human dignity, man's yearning for good, his belief in a Supreme Being, and his striving toward better relations with his fellow man are reflected throughout the collections. Biographies of religious men like Roger Williams, Albert Schweitzer, and Father Flanagan, and compilations of the world's great religious literature are available. No books or magazines setting forth purely sectarian views are purchased.

D. Controversial Issues

Regarding controversial subjects, the school library feels under no obligation to present material giving extreme points of view on social, political, and economic matters. Ideas are not censored, but selection is made of objective, factual materials on both sides of an issue. Propaganda in school books and pamphlets is useful only if it is to be studied and discussed as such. The School Library Bill of Rights of the American Association of School Librarians serves as our conscience, and its principles are applied with judgment and discretion.

E. Purchases Contrary to the Educational Principles of Other Departments

Drawing books which use either circles and triangles or patterns to be copied are not purchased. Science fiction is rejected if the science basic to the story is not sound.

F. Preferred Forms for Informative Material

Preference is given to factual information presented in informational rather than narrative form. Science or travel books which are sugarcoated and complicated by fictional characters are avoided. Vocational novels are bought only if the story and its treatment are good enough to justify purchase apart from the vocational slant.

G. Special Considerations

Material may fit the subject in the curriculum and yet not be recommended for purchase. Some of the reasons are:

1. There may be more information on the subject than is needed, or the treatment may be too detailed, special, or technical.

2. The book may assume background information or skills students do not yet have.

3. The Board's relations with Carnegie Library of Pittsburgh make it possible to borrow from the School's Department collection or Central Lending books that would be used only occasionally.

4. Better material is perhaps available; there may be no new material in the book under consideration or the book may be expensive for what is offered.

5. The subject or treatment may be of doubtful appropriateness for the students.

III. POLICY II

A second function of the school library is to give reading guidance. Unlike the public library, the school libraries reach all the children and all the young people going to public schools and must meet their needs. They are scheduled to the library in the elementary grades whether they are readers or not. In junior high school they are brought in by classes, and increasingly so in some senior highs. Therefore, policies cannot be made independently of the borrowers; standards cannot be set at any arbitrary level, perhaps an ideal or purely literary level, consistent with some-one's notion of what children at any given grade level should be able to achieve. Children are compelled by law to be in school. Their ability to achieve should be considered realistically and their needs provided for.

Policy II is that materials be selected so as to make it possible for students to grow, beginning where they are today. This is not the same as acceding to demand; it does not mean supplying comic books for the comic book readers. Comic book readers who really read the text are capable of reading and are encouraged and expected to read something else in school libraries. Others may look at pictures in the better publications. It does mean that if books with a third-grade vocabulary are needed in junior high schools, the attempt will be made to find some that are suitable for that age or if the right psychological climate has been built up, even reading textbooks will be supplied. We prefer to omit many mediocre but popular books in favor of others with no literary quality at all if those without literary quality have the necessary requisites for improving reading ability; i.e., mature enough interest, simple vocabulary, simple sentences. Conversely, it means supplying materials both in subject matter and in treatment which will challenge our best and most mature readers, such as the classics, books about the great figures and important ideas of the ages, and those about the burning issues of today.

As part of reading guidance also the school library, like all libraries, has an educational function in and of itself, and so we buy books to create interest in the world about us, to widen horizons, to quicken the imagination, and to develop character. The school librarian has the incomparable privilege of reaching at least thirty students period after period, and she is not doing her job unless she is stimulating children and young people to read books they might easily pass by otherwise.

IV. POLICY III

A third function of the school library is to provide for individual differences. Again, because the school library has all of the children of all of the people, we have the greatest possible diversity of interest as well as of ability.

Materials are selected so as to make it possible for students to find something which will interest them, be it hobbies, personal appearance or behavior, future careers, special skills (cooking, dancing, music), sports, games, parties, or many other things which may be unrelated to their present school subjects.

A. We keep in mind always the developing age interests such as fairy tales or adventure or romance.

B. There are, however, some subjects for which interest exists which we do not attempt to buy, among them murder mysteries, judo, and card games.

C. We provide a wide range of materials in kind also: pamphlets, magazines, books, and pictures. In the Pittsburgh Public Schools, although visual materials are purchased and supplied by the Section on Audio-Visual Aids, we are beginning to buy some filmstrips, records, and tapes for our libraries.

V. POLICY IV

A fourth function of the school library is to contribute to the in-service program. We supply some professional books and magazines; we do not buy recreational reading for the teachers, magazines which come with membership in professional organizations, nor books teachers need for university courses.

VI. OTHER CONSIDERATIONS

In addition to these functions, a few other considerations affect our buying policies:

A. Format

Books with spiral bindings or margins too narrow for rebinding are usually rejected outright. Those that are too easily pocketed and those that are hard on the eyes are avoided.

B. Textbooks

Pittsburgh basic texts are never added to the school libraries. Supplementary texts are used somewhat more extensively than in the public library and more in the high school than in elementary school libraries.

C. Editions

Worn-out editions are replaced with new ones, but no attempt is made to supplant usable old editions unless the amount of new material justifies it. Classics are supplied in the attractive editions, but extremely popular titles are usually purchased inexpensively. Paperbacks are bought to provide duplicates and to attract pupils who are reluctant to read.

D. Discarding

Because judicious discarding is as important as book selection in assuring accuracy of information, continuous and systematic weeding of obsolete material is encouraged in all Pittsburgh school libraries. Librarians are urged especially to discard instead of to rebind unless they deem the potential use of the book to be at least equal to past use.

Reprinted by Permission of Pittsburgh Public Schools, Mary L. Molyneaux, Assistant Superintendent Curriculum and Instruction.

SCHOOL LIBRARY POLICIES AND PROCEDURES:
CRITERIA FOR SELECTION OF MATERIALS

SECTION ONE--PHILOSOPHY, AIMS AND OBJECTIVES

I.   PHILOSOPHY, AIMS AND OBJECTIVES

The school library strives to provide the books, periodicals, audio-visual and other resource materials necessary to the fulfillment of the curriculum and for the independent study or recreational reading of the students.

The selection of books and materials shall be guided by the following high principles expressed in the American Association of School Librarians' School Library Bill of Rights.[1]

"School libraries are concerned with generating understanding of American freedoms and with the preservation of these freedoms through the development of informed and responsible citizens. To this end the responsibility of the school library is:

A.   To provide materials that will enrich and support the curriculum, taking into consideration the varied interests, abilities, and maturity levels of the pupils served.

B.   To provide materials that will stimulate growth in factual knowledge, literary appreciation, aesthetic values, and ethical standards.

C.   To provide a background of information which will enable pupils to make intelligent judgments in their daily life.

D.   To provide materials on opposing sides of controversial issues so that young citizens may develop under guidance the practice of critical reading and thinking.

E.   To provide materials representative of the many religious, ethnic, and cultural groups and their contributions to our American heritage.

F.   To place principle above personal opinion and reason above prejudice in the selection of materials of the highest quality in order to assure a comprehensive collection appropriate for the users of the library."

---

[1]Endorsed by Council of American Library Association, July, 1955.

I. **GENERAL STATEMENT**

The success of the school library in meeting the needs of the pupils and teachers depends to a great extent upon the size, range and quality of the book and other resource material available in the library. The foremost consideration of any material for a school library is whether it contributes to the fulfillment of the curriculum and meets the individual needs of the pupils and teachers of that particular school. These criteria may be applied in the selection of books or any other materials for purchase, for acceptance as gifts, or for determining whether the materials now on the shelves should be removed. This judgment shall be made by the certified librarian in consultation with the teachers and administrators.

II. **SELECTION AND EVALUATION OF MATERIALS**

A. The word, materials, as used in this policy statement, includes: books, periodicals, pamphlets, pictures, maps, films, recordings and all other materials which are used by the pupils and faculty in fulfilling the curriculum requirements of the school in which the library is located.

B. The selection of materials is a continuous process because of the changing curriculum content and the publishing of new materials. The selection process is as follows:

1. Materials are selected by qualified representative personnel consisting of librarians, teachers, coordinators and administrators through individual and committee study and recommendations.

2. The librarians, teachers and administrators shall be aided in their selections by the various standard lists and book catalogs approved by the American Library Association and the State Department of Public Instruction.

C. The following evaluative criteria are used as they apply:

1. The materials meet high standards of quality in factual content and presentation and are appropriate to the ability and needs of the pupils in the various subject areas.

2. The materials are selected because of the content and the value of the work as a whole.

3. The materials contribute to literary appreciation or have aesthetic value.

4. The authors are competent and qualified in the field.

5. The materials are objectively and impartially selected to provide a balanced collection for the library.

6. The materials present information for which the student is socially and emotionally prepared. For this reason an otherwise good book may be omitted from a school library.

SECTION THREE--CONTROVERSIAL MATERIALS, CRITICISM AND CENSORSHIP

I.   GENERAL STATEMENT

The library stands for the freedom of communication, for the freedom of intellectual activity, and for the freedom of thought. It strives to provide an opportunity for the students and teachers to gain information and the various points of view on controversial issues.

II.   CRITERIA FOR SELECTION OF CONTROVERSIAL MATERIALS

The major areas of controversial materials are race, sex, politics, religion, literature and economics. In selecting material on any of the above areas the following criteria are given consideration:

A.   The materials on controversial issues should be representative of a particular point of view and a sincere effort made to select equally representative materials covering contrasting points of view.

B.   The material does not unfairly, inaccurately or viciously disparage a particular race or religion. A writer's expression of a certain viewpoint is not to be considered a disparagement when it represents the historical or contemporary views held by some persons or groups.

C.   The materials on religion are chosen to explain rather than convince and are selected to represent the field as widely as necessary for the school purposes.

D.   The selection of materials on political theories and ideologies, or on public issues is directed toward maintaining a balanced collection representing various views.

E.   In a literary work of established quality, the use of profanity or the treatment of sex is not an adequate reason for eliminating the material from the school library.

F.   Materials on physiology, physical maturation or personal hygiene should be accurate and in good taste.

G.   Materials should be selected for their strengths rather than rejected for their weaknesses.

SECTION FOUR-- METHODS OF JUDGING CRITICISMS AND CENSORSHIP

I.   METHODS OF JUDGING CRITICISMS AND CENSORSHIP

A.   Citizens of the community may register their criticism of library materials with the school authorities or with the Board of Directors.

B.   The criticism presented to the Board of Directors must be in writing.

1.   The statement must include specific information as to the author, title, publisher and page number of each item to which objection is being made.

2. The statement must be signed and identification given to permit a reply to be made after the criticism has been investigated.

3. The Board of Education, through the Superintendent, will appoint a committee of school personnel to re-evaluate the materials being questioned and make recommendations concerning them.

4. The committee shall consist of one teacher representative from junior and senior high schools and college, one teacher representative from the school in question, one certificated librarian and one school administrator.

5. The committee may call in representative citizens from the community for consultation when desired.

6. The findings and recommendations of the committee will be submitted to the Superintendent for presentation and recommendation to the Board of Directors.

SECTION FIVE--GIFTS AND BEQUESTS OF MATERIALS

I. GIFTS

The library welcomes books and other resource materials from individuals and organizations but reserves the right to refuse unsuitable materials. The materials, to be acceptable, must meet the same high standards and criteria established for the selection of all library materials. A special book plate will be placed in the front of the material to recognize the giver.

II. MEMORIALS AND BEQUESTS

Citizens and organizations often consider memorials or bequests to libraries, in the form of funds, for the enrichment of the lives of the youth in general or in specified areas of knowledge. The Board of Directors and school officials would gladly work with any individuals or organizations in the formation of policies regarding such memorials or bequests.

SECTION SIX--READING LISTS FOR STUDENTS

I. READING LISTS FOR CLASSWORK

The library policies and procedures are applicable to the supplementary reading lists prepared by teachers for use by the pupils.

Reprinted by Permission of Port Angeles Public Schools, Mr. George J. Ellis, Superintendent.

APPENDICES

FREEDOM TO READ STATEMENT

Adopted June 25, 1953
by the ALA COUNCIL

The freedom to read is essential to our democracy. It is under attack. Private groups and public authorities in various parts of the country are working to remove books from sale, to censor textbooks, to label "controversial" books, to distribute lists of "objectionable" books or authors, and to purge libraries. These actions apparently rise from a view that our national tradition of free expression is no longer valid; that censorship and suppression are needed to avoid the subversion of politics and the corruption of morals. We, as citizens devoted to the use of books and as librarians and publishers responsible for disseminating them, wish to assert the public interest in the preservation of the freedom to read.

We are deeply concerned about these attempts at suppression. Most such attempts rest on a denial of the fundamental premise of democracy: that the ordinary citizen, by exercising his critical judgment, will accept the good and reject the bad. The censors, public and private, assume that they should determine what is good and what is bad for their fellow-citizens.

We trust Americans to recognize propaganda, and to reject obscenity. We do not believe they need the help of censors to assist them in this task. We do not believe they are prepared to sacrifice their heritage of a free press in order to be "protected" against what others think may be bad for them. We believe they still favor free enterprise in ideas and expression.

We are aware, of course, that books are not alone in being subjected to efforts of suppression. We are aware that these efforts are related to a larger pattern of pressures being brought against education, the press, films, radio and television. The problem is not only one of actual censorship. The shadow of fear cast by these pressures leads, we suspect, to an even larger voluntary curtailment of expression by those who seek to avoid controversy.

Such pressure toward conformity is perhaps natural to a time of uneasy change and pervading fear. Especially when so many of our apprehensions are directed against an ideology, the expression of a dissident idea becomes a thing feared in itself, and we tend to move against it as against a hostile deed, with suppression.

And yet suppression is never more dangerous than in such a time of social tension. Freedom has given the United States the elasticity to endure strain. Freedom keeps open the path of novel and creative solutions, and enables change to come by choice. Every silencing of a heresy, every enforcement of an orthodoxy, diminishes the toughness and resilience of our society and leaves it the less able to deal with stress.

Now as always in our history, books are among our greatest instruments of freedom. They are almost the only means for making generally available ideas or manners of expression that can initially command only a small audience. They are the natural medium for the new idea and the untried voice from which come the original contributions to social growth. They are essential to the extended discussion which serious thought requires, and to the accumulation of knowledge and ideas into organized collections.

We believe that free communication is essential to the preservation of a free society and a creative culture. We believe that these pressures toward conformity present the danger of limiting the range and variety of inquiry and expression on which our democracy and our culture depend. We believe that every American community must jealously guard the freedom to publish and to circulate, in order to preserve its own freedom to read. We believe that publishers and librarians have a profound responsibility to give validity to that freedom to read by making it possible for the readers to choose freely from a variety of offerings.

The freedom to read is guaranteed by the Constitution. Those with faith in free men will stand firm on these constitutional guarantees of essential rights and will exercise the responsibilities that accompany these rights.

We therefore affirm these propositions:

1. It is in the public interest for publishers and librarians to make available the widest diversity of views and expressions, including those which are unorthodox or unpopular with the majority.

Creative thought is by definition new, and what is new is different. The bearer of every new thought is a rebel until his idea is refined and tested. Totalitarian systems attempt to maintain themselves in power by the ruthless suppression of any concept which challenges the established orthodoxy. The power of a democratic system to adapt to change is vastly strengthened by the freedom of its citizens to choose widely from among conflicting opinions offered freely to them. To stifle every nonconformist idea at birth would mark the end of the democratic process. Furthermore, only through the constant activity of weighing and selecting can the democratic mind attain the strength demanded by times like these. We need to know not only what we believe but why we believe it.

2. Publishers and librarians do not need to endorse every idea or presentation contained in the books they make available. It would conflict with the public interest for them to establish their own political, moral or aesthetic views as the sole standard for determining what books should be published or circulated.

Publishers and librarians serve the educational process by helping to make available knowledge and ideas required for the growth of the mind and the increase of learning. They do not foster education by imposing as mentors the patterns of their own thought. The people should have the freedom to read and consider a broader range of ideas than those that may be held by any single librarian or publisher or government or church. It is wrong that what one man can read should be confined to what another thinks proper.

209

3. It is contrary to the public interest for publishers or librarians to determine the acceptability of a book solely on the basis of the personal history or political affiliations of the author.

A book should be judged as a book. No art or literature can flourish if it is to be measured by the political views or private lives of its creators. No society of free men can flourish which draws up lists of writers to whom it will not listen, whatever they may have to say.

4. The present laws dealing with obscenity should be vigorously enforced. Beyond that, there is no place in our society for extra-legal efforts to coerce the tastes of others, to confine adults to the reading matter deemed suitable for adolescents, or to inhibit the efforts of writers to achieve artistic expression.

To some, much of modern literature is shocking. But is not much of life itself shocking? We cut off literature at the source if we prevent serious artists from dealing with the stuff of life. Parents and teachers have a responsibility to prepare the young to meet the diversity of experiences in life to which they will be exposed, as they have a responsibility to help them learn to think critically for themselves. These are affirmative responsibilities, not to be discharged simply by preventing them from reading works for which they are not yet prepared. In these matters taste differs, and taste cannot be legislated; nor can machinery be devised which will suit the demands of one group without limiting the freedom of others. We deplore the catering to the immature, the retarded or the maladjusted taste. But those concerned with freedom have the responsibility of seeing to it that each individual book or publication, whatever its contents, price or method of distribution, is dealt with in accordance with due process of law.

5. It is not in the public interest to force a reader to accept with any book the prejudgment of a label characterizing the book or author as subversive or dangerous.

The ideal of labeling presupposes the existence of individuals or groups with wisdom to determine by authority what is good or bad for the citizen. It presupposes that each individual must be directed in making up his mind about the ideas he examines. But Americans do not need others to do their thinking for them.

6. It is the responsibility of publishers and librarians, as guardians of the people's freedom to read, to contest encroachments upon that freedom by individuals or groups seeking to impose their own standards or tastes upon the community at large.

It is inevitable in the give and take of the democratic process that the political, the moral, or the aesthetic concepts of an individual or group will occasionally collide with those of another individual or group. In a free society each individual is free to determine for himself what he wishes to read, and each group is free to determine what it will recommend to its freely associated members. But no group has the right to take the law into its own hands, and to impose its own concept of politics or morality upon other members of a democratic society. Freedom is no freedom if it is accorded only to the accepted and the inoffensive.

7. It is the responsibility of publishers and librarians to give full meaning to the freedom to read by providing books that enrich the quality of thought and expression. By the exercise of this affirmative responsibility, bookmen can demonstrate that the answer to a bad book is a good one, the answer to a bad idea is a good one.

The freedom to read is of little consequence when expended on the trivial; it is frustrated when the reader cannot obtain matter fit for his purpose. What is needed is not only the absence of restraint, but the positive provision of opportunity for the people to read the best that has been thought and said. Books are the major channel by which the intellectual inheritance is handed down, and the principal means of its testing and growth. The defense of their freedom and integrity, and the enlargement of their service to society, requires of all bookmen the utmost of their faculties, and deserves of all citizens the fullest of their support.

We state these propositions neither lightly nor as easy generalizations. We here stake out a lofty claim for the value of books. We do so because we believe that they are good, possessed of enormous variety and usefulness, worthy of cherishing and keeping free. We realize that the application of these propositions may mean the dissemination of ideas and manners of expression that are repugnant to many persons. We do not state these propositions in the comfortable belief that what people read is unimportant. We believe rather that what people read is deeply important; that ideas can be dangerous; but that the suppression of ideas is fatal to a democratic society. Freedom itself is a dangerous way of life, but it is ours.

Endorsed by:

AMERICAN LIBRARY ASSOCIATION
Council, June 25, 1953

AMERICAN BOOK PUBLISHERS COUNCIL
Board of Directors, June 18, 1953

Subsequently Endorsed by:

AMERICAN BOOKSELLERS ASSOCIATION
Board of Directors

BOOK MANUFACTURERS' INSTITUTE
Board of Directors

NATIONAL EDUCATION ASSOCIATION
Commission for the Defense of
Democracy through Education

Library Bill of Rights

The Council of the American Library Association reaffirms its belief in the following basic policies which should govern the services of all libraries.

1. As a responsibility of library service, books and other library materials selected should be chosen for values of interest, information and enlightenment of all the people of the community. In no case should library materials be excluded because of the race or nationality or the social, political, or religious views of the authors.

2. Libraries should provide books and other materials presenting all points of view concerning the problems and issues of our times; no library materials should be proscribed or removed from libraries because of partisan or doctrinal disapproval.

3. Censorship should be challenged by libraries in the maintenance of their responsibility to provide public information and enlightenment.

4. Libraries should cooperate with all persons and groups concerned with resisting abridgment of free expression and free access to ideas.

5. The rights of an individual to the use of a library should not be denied or abridged because of his age, race, religion, national origins or social or political views.

6. As an institution of education for democratic living, the library should welcome the use of its meeting rooms for socially useful and cultural activities and discussion of current public questions. Such meeting places should be available on equal terms to all groups in the community regardless of the beliefs and affiliations of their members, provided that the meetings be open to the public.

Adopted June 18, 1948.
Amended February 2, 1961, and June 27, 1967, by the ALA Council.

INTELLECTUAL FREEDOM STATEMENT

An Interpretation of the Library Bill of Rights

The heritage of free men is ours. In the Bill of Rights to the United States Constitution, the founders of our nation proclaimed certain fundamental freedoms to be essential to our form of government. Primary among these is the freedom of expression, specifically the right to publish diverse opinions and the right to unrestricted access to those opinions. As citizens committed to the full and free use of all communications media and as professional persons responsible for making the content of those media accessible to all without prejudice, we, the undersigned, wish to assert the public interest in the preservation of freedom of expression.

Through continuing judicial interpretations of the First Amendment to the United States Constitution, full freedom of expression has been guaranteed. Every American who aspires to the success of our experiment in democracy--who has faith in the political and social integrity of free men--must stand firm on those Constitutional guarantees of essential rights. Such Americans can be expected to fulfill the responsibilities implicit in those rights.

We, therefore, affirm these propositions:

1. We will make available to everyone who needs or desires them the widest possible diversity of views and modes of expression, including those which are strange, unorthodox or unpopular.

   Creative thought is, by its nature, new. New ideas are always different and, to some people, distressing and even threatening. The creator of every new idea is likely to be regarded as unconventional--occasionally heretical--until his idea is first examined, then refined, then tested in its political, social, or moral applications. The characteristic ability of our governmental system to adapt to necessary change is vastly strengthened by the option of the people to choose freely from among conflicting opinions. To stifle nonconformist ideas at their inception would be to end the democratic process. Only through continuous weighing and selection from among opposing views can free individuals obtain the strength needed for intelligent, constructive decisions and actions. In short, we need to understand not only what we believe, but why we believe as we do.

2. We need not endorse every idea contained in the materials we produce and make available.

   We serve the educational process by disseminating the knowledge and wisdom required for the growth of the mind and the expansion of learning. For us to employ our own political, moral, or esthetic views as standards for determining what materials are published or circulated conflicts with the public interest. We cannot foster true education by imposing on others the structure and content of our own opinions. We must preserve and enhance the people's right to a broader range of ideas than those held by any librarian or publisher or church or government. We hold that it is wrong to limit any person to those ideas and that information another believes to be true, good, and proper.

3. We regard as irrelevant to the acceptance and distribution of any creative work the personal history or political affiliations of the author or others responsible for it or its publication.

    A work of art must be judged solely on its own merits. Creativity cannot flourish if its appraisal and acceptance by the community is influenced by the political views or private lives of the artists or the creators. A society that allows blacklists to be compiled and used to silence writers and artists cannot exist as a free society.

4. With every available legal means, we will challenge laws or governmental action restricting or prohibiting the publication of certain materials or limiting free access to such materials.

    Our society has no place for legislative efforts to coerce the taste of its members, to restrict adults to reading matter deemed suitable only for children, or to inhibit the efforts of creative persons in their attempts to achieve artistic perfection. When we prevent serious artists from dealing with truth as they see it, we stifle creative endeavor at its source. Those who direct and control the intellectual development of our children--parents, teachers, religious leaders, scientists, philosophers, statesmen--must assume the responsibility for preparing young people to cope with life as it is and to face the diversity of experience to which they will be exposed as they mature. This is an affirmative responsibility that cannot be discharged easily, certainly not with the added burden of curtailing one's access to art, literature, and opinion. Tastes differ. Taste, like morality, cannot be controlled by government, for governmental action, devised to suit the demands of one group, thereby limits the freedom of all others.

5. We oppose labeling any work of literature or art, or any persons responsible for its creation, as subversive, dangerous, or otherwise undesirable.

    Labeling attempts to predispose users of the various media of communication, and to ultimately close off a path to knowledge. Labeling rests on the assumption that persons exist who have a special wisdom, and who, therefore, can be permitted to determine what will have good and bad effects on other people. But freedom of expression rests on the premise of ideas vying in the open marketplace for acceptance, change, or rejection by individuals. Free men choose this path.

6. We, as guardians of intellectual freedom, oppose and will resist, every encroachment upon that freedom by individuals or groups, private or official.

    It is inevitable in the give-and-take of the democratic process that the political, moral and esthetic preferences of a person or group will conflict occasionally with those of others. A fundamental premise of our free society is that each citizen is privileged to decide those opinions to which he will adhere or which he will recommend to the members of a privately organized group or association. But no private group may usurp the law and impose its own political or moral concepts upon the general public. Freedom cannot be accorded only to selected groups for it is then transmuted into privilege and unwarranted license.

7. Both as citizens and professionals, we will strive by all legitimate means open to us to be relieved of the threat of personal, economic, and legal reprisals resulting from our support and defense of the principles of intellectual freedom.

Those who refuse to compromise their ideals in support of intellectual freedom have often suffered dismissals from employment, forced resignations, boycotts or products and establishments, and other invidious forms of punishment. We perceive the admirable, often lonely, refusal to succumb to threats of punitive action as the highest form of true professionalism: dedication to the cause of intellectual freedom and the preservation of vital human and civil liberties.

In our various capacities, we will actively resist incursions against the full exercise of our professional responsibility for creating and maintaining an intellectual environment which fosters unrestrained creative endeavor and true freedom of choice and access for all members of the community.

We state these propositions with conviction, not as easy generalizations. We advance a noble claim for the value of ideas, freely expressed, as embodied in books and other kinds of communications. We do this in our belief that a free intellectual climate fosters creative endeavors capable of enormous variety, beauty, and usefulness, and thus worthy of support and preservation. We recognize that application of these propositions may encourage the dissemination of ideas and forms of expression that will be frightening or abhorrent to some. We believe that what people read, view, and hear is a critically important issue. We recognize, too, that ideas can be dangerous. It may be, however, that they are effectually dangerous only when opposing ideas are suppressed. Freedom, in its many facets, is a precarious course. We espouse it heartily.

Adopted by the ALA Council, June 25, 1971
Endorsed by the Freedom to Read Foundation, Board of Trustees, June 18, 1971

RESOLUTION ON CHALLENGED MATERIALS

An Interpretation of the LIBRARY BILL OF RIGHTS

WHEREAS, The LIBRARY BILL OF RIGHTS states that no library materials should be proscribed or removed because of partisan or doctrinal disapproval, and

WHEREAS, Constitutionally protected expression is often separated from un-protected expression only by a dim and uncertain line, and

WHEREAS, Any attempt, be it legal or extra-legal, to regulate or suppress material must be closely scrutinized to the end that protected expression is not abridged in the process, and

WHEREAS, The Constitution requires a procedure designed to focus search-ingly on the question before speech can be suppressed, and

WHEREAS, The dissemination of a particular work which is alleged to be un-protected should be completely undisturbed until an independent determina-tion has been made by a judicial officer, including an adversary hearing,

THEREFORE, THE PREMISES CONSIDERED, BE IT RESOLVED, That the American Library Association declares as a matter of firm principle that no challenged library material should be removed from any library under any legal or extra-legal pressure, save after an independent determination by a judicial officer in a court of competent jurisdiction and only after an adversary hearing, in accordance with well-established principles of law.

Adopted by the ALA Council, June 25, 1971.

STATEMENT ON LABELING
An Interpretation of the LIBRARY BILL OF RIGHTS

Because labeling violates the spirit of the LIBRARY BILL OF RIGHTS, the American Library Association opposes the technique of labeling as a means of predisposing readers against library materials for the following reasons:

1. Labeling[1] is an attempt to prejudice the reader, and as such it is a censor's tool.

2. Although some find it easy and even proper, according to their ethics, to establish criteria for judging publications as objectionable, injustice and ignorance rather than justice and enlightenment result from such practices, and the American Library Association must oppose the establishment of such criteria.

3. Libraries do not advocate the ideas found in their collections. The presence of a magazine or book in a library does not indicate an endorsement of its contents by the library.

4. No one person should take the responsibility of labeling publications. No sizable group of persons would be likely to agree either on the types of material which should be labeled or the sources of information which should be regarded with suspicion. As a practical consideration, a librarian who labels a book or magazine might be sued for libel.

5. If materials are labeled to pacify one group, there is no excuse for refusing to label any item in the library's collection. Because authoritarians tend to suppress ideas and attempt to coerce individuals to conform to a specific ideology, the American Library Association opposes such efforts which aim at closing any path to knowledge.

Adopted July 13, 1951.
Amended June 25, 1971, by the ALA Council.

---

[1]"Labeling," as it is referred to in the STATEMENT ON LABELING, is the practice of describing or designating certain library materials, by affixing a prejudicial label to them or segregating them by a prejudicial system, so as to pre-dispose readers against the materials.

SCHOOL LIBRARY BILL
OF RIGHTS
for School Library Media
Center Programs

Approved by American Association of School Librarians Board of Directors, Atlantic City, 1969.

The American Association of School Librarians reaffirms its belief in the Library Bill of Rights of the American Library Association. Media personnel are concerned with generating understanding of American freedoms through the development of informed and responsible citizens. To this end the American Association of School Librarians asserts that the responsibility of the school library media center is:

To provide a comprehensive collection of instructional materials selected in compliance with basic written selection principles, and to provide maximum accessibility to these materials.

To provide materials that will support the curriculum, taking into consideration the individual's needs, and the varied interests, abilities, socio-economic backgrounds, and maturity levels of the students served.

To provide materials for teachers and students that will encourage growth in knowledge, and that will develop literary, cultural and aesthetic appreciation, and ethical standards.

To provide materials which reflect the ideas and beliefs of religious, social, political, historical, and ethnic groups and their contribution to the American and world heritage and culture, thereby enabling students to develop an intellectual integrity in forming judgments.

To provide a written statement, approved by the local Boards of Education, of the procedures for meeting the challenge of censorship of materials in school library media centers.

To provide qualified professional personnel to serve teachers and students.

How libraries and schools can resist censorship

Adopted
February 1, 1962
by the
ALA Council

Libraries of all sizes and types have been under increasing pressures from persons who wish to use the library as an instrument of their own tastes and views. Such individuals and groups are demanding the exclusion or removal of books to which they object or the inclusion of a higher proportion of books that support their views. Similar attacks have been made on schools in connection with books used in their programs. In view of this fact, it seems desirable to set forth a few basic principles that may help librarians, trustees, and school administrators in preserving the freedom and professional integrity of their institutions.

The problem differs somewhat between the public library, with a responsibility to the public to present as wide a spectrum of significant reading matter as its budget can afford, and the school library, whose collections are designed to support the educational objectives of the school. In both, however, there is involved the freedom of the school or the library to meet its professional responsibilities to the whole community.

Every library or school should take certain measures to clarify its policies and establish its community relations. These steps should be taken without regard to any attack or prospect of attack. They will put the institution in a firm and clearly defined position if its book policies are ever called into question.

As a normal operating procedure, every library, and the administration responsible for it, should establish certain principles.

1. There should be a definite book selection policy. This should be in written form and approved by the board of trustees, the school board, or other administrative authority. It should be stated clearly and should be understood by members of the staff. This policy should apply to other materials equally, i.e., films, records, magazines, and pamphlets.

2. A file recording the basis for decision should be kept for titles likely to be questioned or apt to be considered controversial.

3. There should be a clearly defined method for handling complaints. Any complaint should be required to be in writing, and the complainant should be identified properly before the complaint is considered. Action should be deferred until full consideration by appropriate administrative authority.

4. There should be continuing efforts to establish lines of communication to assure mutual understanding with civic, religious, educational, and political bodies.

5. Newspapers of the community should be informed of policies governing book selection and use. Purposes and services of the library should be interpreted through a continuing public relations program, as should the use of books in the school.

6. Participation in local civic organizations and in community affairs is desirable. The library and the school are key centers of the community; the librarian and school administrator should be known publicly as community leaders.

If an attack does come, remember the following:

1. Remain calm. Don't confuse noise with substance. Most attacks come from small groups of people who have little community backing. Time after time the American people have shown that, given the facts, they will back solidly the responsible exercise of professional freedom by teachers and librarians and that they will insist on protecting their own freedom to read. Insist on the deliberate handling of the complaint under previously established rules. Treat complainants with dignity, courtesy, and good humor.

2. Take immediate steps to assure that the full facts surrounding a complaint are known to the administration. The school librarian should go through the principal to the superintendent and the school board; the public librarian, to the board of trustees or to the appropriate community administration official; the college or university librarian, to the president and through him to the board of trustees. Full, written information should be presented, giving the nature of the problem or complaint and identifying the source.

3. Seek the support of the local press immediately. The freedom to read and the freedom of the press go hand in hand.

4. Inform local civic organizations of the facts and enlist their support where possible.

5. Defend the principles of the freedom to read and the professional responsibility of teachers and librarians rather than the individual book. The laws governing obscenity, subversive material, and other questionable matter are subject to interpretation by the courts. The responsibility for removal of any book from public access should rest with this established process. The responsibility for the use of books in the schools must rest with those responsible for the educational objectives being served.

6. The ALA Intellectual Freedom Committee and other appropriate national and state committees concerned with intellectual freedom should be informed of the nature of the problem. Even though each effort at censorship must be met at the local level, there is often value in the support and assistance of agencies outside the area which have no personal involvement. They often can cite parallel cases and suggest methods of meeting an attack. Similar aid in cases affecting the use of books in the schools can be obtained from the Commission on Professional Rights and Responsibilities of the National Education Association.

Every librarian should be familiar with certain basic documents which have been prepared by the American Library Association and represent the position of this national organization of more than 26,000 librarians. Copies of each of these may be obtained by writing the American Library Association, 50 East Huron Street, Chicago 11, Illinois.

Library Bill of Rights (Adopted June 18, 1948, and amended February 1, 1961, by the ALA Council)

Statement on Labeling (Adopted July 13, 1951, by the ALA Council)

School Library Bill of Rights (Adopted July 8, 1955, by the ALA Council)

Freedom to Read Statement (Prepared by the Westchester Conference of ALA and the American Book Publishers Council, May 2-3, 1953)

Policies and Procedures for Selection of School Library Materials (Approved by the AASL, February 3, 1961)

Endorsed by:

The Adult Education Association of the USA, Executive Committee

The American Book Publishers Council

The American Civil Liberties Union

The National Book Committee

The National Council of Teachers of English

The National Education Association Commission on Professional Rights and Responsibilities

The National Education Association Department of Classroom Teachers

BIBLIOGRAPHY

American Library Association. Intellectual Freedom Committee. "How Libraries and Schools Can Resist Censorship," ALA Bulletin, LVI (March, 1962), pp. 228-229.

Asheim, Lester. "Not Censorship but Selection," Wilson Library Bulletin, XXVIII (September, 1953), 63-67.

Bendix, Dorothy. Some Problems in Book Selection Policies and Practices in Medium-Sized Public Libraries. Urbana: University of Illinois, Library School, 1955.

Broderick, Dorothy. "I May, I Might, I Must," Library Journal, LXXXVIII (February 1, 1963), 507-510.

California Association of School Librarians. Instructional Materials: Selection Policies and Procedures. Daly City, 1965.

Carter, Mary Duncan, and Bonk, Wallace John. Building Library Collections. 3d ed. Metuchen, N.J.: Scarecrow Press, 1969.

Castagna, Edwin. "Courage and Cowardice: The Influence of Pressure Groups on Library Collections," Library Journal, LXXXVIII (February 1, 1963), 501-506.

Danton, J. Periam. Book Selection and Collections: A Comparison of German and American University Libraries. New York: Columbia University Press, 1963.

Danton, J. Periam, (ed.). The Climate of Book Selection. Berkeley: University of California, School of Librarianship, 1959.

Drury, Francis Keese Wynkoop. Book Selection. Chicago: American Library Association, 1930.

Fiske, Marjorie. Book Selection and Censorship. Berkeley: University of California Press, 1959.

Gaver, Mary Virginia, (comp.). Background Readings in Building Library Collections. Metuchen, N.J.: Scarecrow Press, 1969. 2v.

Gregory, Ruth. "Principles Behind a Book Selection Policy Statement," <u>I.L.A. Record</u>, X (October, 1956), 23-26.

Haines, Helen E. <u>Living with Books: The Art of Book Selection</u>. 2d ed. New York: Columbia University Press, 1950.

Hart, Evelyn, et al., (eds.). <u>How Baltimore Chooses: Selection Policies of the Enoch Pratt Free Library</u>. 4th ed. Baltimore, 1968.

Kujoth, Jean Spealman, (comp.). <u>Libraries, Readers, and Book Selection</u>. Metuchen, N.J.: Scarecrow Press, 1969.

Merritt, LeRoy Charles. <u>Book Selection and Intellectual Freedom</u>. New York: H. W. Wilson Company, 1970.

Moon, Eric, (ed.). <u>Book Selection and Censorship in the Sixties</u>. New York: R. R. Bowker Company, 1969.

Sinclair, Dorothy. <u>Administration of the Small Public Library</u>. Chicago: American Library Association, 1965. pp. 90-109.

Wilson, Louis Round. <u>The Practice of Book Selection</u>. Chicago: University of Chicago Press, 1940.

Wofford, Azile. <u>Book Selection for School Libraries</u>. New York: H. W. Wilson Company, 1962.